Race Relations in the United States, 1920–1940

Race Relations in the United States
Ronald H. Bayor, General Editor

Race Relations in the United States, 1920–1940

LESLIE V. TISCHAUSER

Race Relations in the United States
Ronald H. Bayor, General Editor

GREENWOOD PRESS
Westport, Connecticut • London

Library of Congress Cataloging-in-Publication Data

Tischauser, Leslie Vincent, 1942–
    Race relations in the United States, 1920–1940 / Leslie V. Tischauser.
        p. cm. — (Race relations in the United States)
    Includes bibliographical references and index.
    ISBN 978–0–313–33848–9—
    ISBN 978–0–313–33717–8 (set)
    1. United States—Race relations—History—20th century.
I. Title.
    E184.A1T585   2008
    305.800973—dc22   2007047970

British Library Cataloguing in Publication Data is available.

Library of Congress Catalog Card Number: 2007047970
ISBN: 978–0–313–33848–9 (vol.)
        978–0–313–33717–8 (set)

First published in 2008

Greenwood Press, 88 Post Road West, Westport, CT 06881
An imprint of Greenwood Publishing Group, Inc.
www.greenwood.com

Printed in the United States of America

The paper used in this book complies with the
Permanent Paper Standard issued by the National
Information Standards Organization (Z39.48–1984).

10   9   8   7   6   5   4   3   2   1

Contents

Series Foreword

W.E.B. Du Bois, an influential African American civil rights activist, educator, and scholar, wrote in 1903 that "the problem of the twentieth century is the problem of the color line." Although Du Bois spoke only of the situation affecting African Americans, we now know that the twentieth century brought issues to the fore that affected all of America's racial and ethnic groups. It was a century that started with vicious attacks on Blacks and other minority Americans, as evident in the 1906 Atlanta race riot and included within its years substantial civil rights gains in legislation and public attitudes as revealed by the Civil Rights Act of 1964 and the Voting Rights Act of 1965. Everything that occurred took place during the time of two world wars, the Great Depression, the Cold War, the turbulent 1960s, the Civil Rights and Women's movements, the rise of the Conservative movement, and the Persian Gulf and Iraqi wars.

The first volumes in the *Race Relations in the United States* series include coverage of significant events, influential voices, race relations history, legislation, media influences, culture, and theories of inter-group interactions that have been evident in the twentieth century and related to race. Each volume covers two decades and encapsulates the state of race relations by decade. A standard format is followed per decade, allowing comparison of topics through the century. Historians have written the topical essays in an encyclopedic style to give students and general readers a concise yet authoritative overview of race relations for the decade studied.

Coverage per decade includes a Timeline, Overview, Key Events, Voices of the Decade, Race Relations by Group, Law and Government, Media and Mass Communications, Cultural Scene, Influential Theories and Views on Race, and a Resource Guide. Furthermore, each volume contains an introduction for the two decades and a selected bibliography and index. Historical photos complement the set.

The volumes not only deal with African Americans, Native Americans, Latinos, and Asian Americans but also with religious entities such as Jewish Americans. The history is a fascinating story that deals with such personalities as Henry Ford,

Marcus Garvey, Martin Luther King Jr., Cesar Chavez and Dolores Huerta, Russell Means, and George Wallace; defining events such as the imprisonment of Japanese Americans during World War II, the 1943 Zoot suit riots in California against Mexican Americans, the Selma to Montgomery Civil Rights march in 1965, and the American Indian Movement's occupation of Wounded Knee, South Dakota in 1973; and legislation and court cases deciding who could enter the country and who could become a citizen. The 1960s as a decade of new civil rights acts, immigration laws and cultural changes are covered along with the increase in new immigration that marked the 1980s and 90s. The volumes will familiarize readers with the role of the Ku Klux Klan, the fear of a "Yellow Peril," and the stereotypes that impeded the attainment of equality for many minorities.

The books' focus will enable readers to understand the progress that has been made in the face of relentless persecution and oppression. As the year 2000 approached and passed, the United States was a different country than it had been in 1900. Many problems remained in relation to immigration and civil rights, but the days of lynching, racially discriminatory laws, and culturally negative stereotypes have largely faded. The story is a positive one of growth and change, but one that provides lessons on the present and future role of race relations.

One of the enduring changes that can be seen is on TV where the human landscape has evolved from ugly images of racial and ethnic groups to more multicultural and accepting views. When television first appeared, African Americans, Native Americans, Asian Americans, and Hispanic Americans were portrayed in negative ways. Blacks were often portrayed as ignorant servants and Native Americans as savages. "Stepin Fetchit," Charlie Chan, wild Indians, and the "Frito Bandito" are gone. These negative images evident in the 1950s would not find a place in today's media. By itself, that represents a significant change in attitudes and indicates the progress that has been made in inter-group relations. How this happened is what students and general readers will find in these volumes.

Ronald H. Bayor
Series Editor

Acknowledgments

Along with other authors in this series I would like to thank Ronald Bayor of Georgia Tech and Wendi Schnaufer of Greenwood Press for their help and patience in producing this book. I would also like to thank Connie, my wife, and Jeffrey and Mike, my kids, for everything else.

Introduction

Violence played a major role in American race relations between 1920 and 1940. The period began with a series of bloody race riots in places like Tulsa, Oklahoma, and Rosewood, Florida. Lynchings in the South continued to mar the landscape through most of the 1920s but showed a major decline in the numbers of African Americans victimized by the end of the 1930s, although filibusters in Congress prevented passage of any bill making lynching a federal crime. Law enforcement remained in the hands of local officials, which meant that very few lynchers were ever arrested for their brutal crimes. The Ku Klux Klan emerged as a powerful political force across the nation after 1920 but quickly faded in influence (and membership) after scandals rocked the organization in mid-decade.

Asians in the United States faced prejudice and discrimination in both decades facing anti-Asian land ownership laws in California and other western states. These ordinances prevented them from owning farms and relegated all Asians to segregated "Chinatowns" in cities and towns throughout the region. Most Asians worked in agriculture at this time but as field hands and migrant workers, not as farmers and growers. The Filipino population grew rapidly, as residents of those American-owned islands were not subject to Asian exclusion laws. Yet as the number of Filipinos increased, so did the hostility and discrimination they faced. Filipino homes in segregated migrant labor camps were filthy, airless, and overcrowded. As the American economy declined by the end of the 1920s, conditions grew even worse as wages fell and anti-Filipino prejudice grew, leading to riots and murders.

Indians remained relegated to reservations in the 1920s where they faced innumerable problems of hunger, ill health, and inadequate housing during a period in which the American economy performed well. Improvements began by the end of the decade after a series of government reports depicted the terrible economic and social conditions Native Americans faced during this period of overall prosperity in other areas of American life. Then in 1934, Congress passed a bill that granted more freedom and self-government to the tribes than they had enjoyed for much of the previous century. They could speak their own languages, practice their traditional religions, dance their traditional dances, and choose their own governments. Unless their reservations were on land with lots of oil or coal, however, most Native Americans remained at the bottom of the American economic ladder, the poorest of the poor. And they continued to be prevented from voting in local and state elections in states with large Indian population despite having become American citizens in 1924.

Other "people of color" faced other kinds of mistreatment. Latinos, including those born in the United States, were rounded up and deported by the Immigration and Naturalization Service beginning in 1929 to "save jobs" for Americans who were unemployed as a result of the Great Depression. This "Mexican Removal" program, as the deportees called it, resulted in more than 500,000 Spanish-speaking people being driven out of the United States before the campaign ended in 1933.

Even white Europeans felt the sting of discrimination. In 1924, Congress passed a far-reaching immigration restriction bill that severely limited immigration from Europe for the next 30 years. The legislators based the law on bad science (that is, eugenics—which taught that "better" populations of people could be bred by following the right principles of genetic inheritance just like one could breed better horses, chickens, or laboratory rats). More "productive races," such as Germans and Swedes, received higher quotas of legal immigrants than did lesser admired groups such as Italians and Poles. In the 1930s, Adolf Hitler's scientists followed these same principles to build the master race.

This volume overviews the decades' events, highlights the key events and voices of each decade, and describes the race relations for each major ethnic group. The major laws, court decisions, and government actions during each decade that affected the lives of American racial and ethnic groups are discussed as well. Most of the time, lawmakers, judges, and government agencies at both the state and national level took actions and made decisions that made life more difficult for American minority groups. How the mass media depicted minority groups with images that usually reinforced popular (and mostly negative) stereotypes is also given consideration. In advertising, Aunt Jemima, Rastus (on Cream of Wheat boxes), and Uncle Ben all did their best to reinforce condescending views of African Americans while selling their goods. On the radio *Amos 'n' Andy* showed that most blacks were scheming, blundering, and usually very loud and very happy citizens of America. In the movies, Stepin Fetchit and his many imitators reminded whites that African Americans were dull-witted, harmless, and lazy. Hollywood also made sure that Americans remembered that Asians such as Fu Manchu, Ming the Magnificent (in Flash Gordon serials), and numerous Dragon Ladies were a menace to society and completely diabolical in their plans to destroy Western civilization. Indians, of course, were savages in war paint out to kill white pioneers doggedly moving across the plains bringing democracy and law-and-order to the untamed West (after shooting all the bad guys).

The contributions of minority group artists, poets, musicians, novelists, and playwrights to American literature and culture are considered and described. The

Harlem Renaissance saw the creation of a true African American culture for the first time in American history. Native American, Asian American, and Latino writers made contributions to American literature that opened new understandings of who Americans were and how they got that way. The ideas of major social scientists, anthropologists, and sociologists concerning the meaning of race changed significantly during these decades. Proposals for reducing prejudice varied widely among the experts, and a major split developed between geneticists, who believed that chacteristics such as intelligence, attitudes (toward work, for example), criminal potential, and morality were largely determined by the genes inherited from a person's ancestors. On the other side were social scientists—led by Franz Boas—who believed that human traits were acquired through education, life experiences, and environmental influences. Some social scientists even began to question whether race had any biological significance at all for human beings.

Racial conflict appeared to play a more prominent role in minority/majority relations in the 1920s and 1930s than did racial harmony. But there was some movement toward improving relations between the races and providing equal rights for all. After 1934, for example, control of Indian reservations was returned to the Native Americans. And by the end of the decade, the Supreme Court had taken some small steps toward opening public schools, at least at the college level, to all people. Perhaps even more important, ideas supporting white supremacy, social Darwinism ("victory belongs to the strongest"), and who could become an American were beginning to be challenged in the courts, schools, universities, literature, art, music, and the media, although true acceptance of diversity and equality remained a distant dream.

1920s

TIMELINE

1920

W.E.B. Du Bois publishes *Darkwater*, a collection of essays.

African American writer Claude McKay publishes *Spring in New Hampshire*, a poetry collection.

A total of 61 lynchings take place in the United States.

January 19   California voters approve amendments to Alien Land Act of 1913, making it more difficult for Asians and other immigrants to buy property.

February 2   The National Negro Baseball League is founded.

June 7   In *Kwock Jan Fat v. White*, the Supreme Court rules that aliens seeking to immigrate to the United States have the right to a fair hearing.

August 1   Marcus Garvey's Universal Negro Improvement Association holds its International Convention in New York City.

November 2   Ocoee, Florida "Election Day" Ku Klux Klan riot, which starts after a black war veteran tries to vote, leaves more than 50 African Americans dead.

November 11   Author James Weldon Johnson becomes first African American president of the National Association for the Advancement of Colored People (NAACP).

1921

A total of 64 Americans are lynched; all but five are African American.

May 19	President Warren G. Harding signs the Emergency Quota Act, severely limiting immigration to the United States
July 7	Comrade Society is organized by Syngman Rhee to promote freeing Korea from Japanese control.

1922

A total of 57 lynchings occur.

January 26	The Dyer Anti-lynching Bill passes the House of Representatives. Shortly thereafter, it is defeated in the Senate.
September 22	Congress passes the Cable Act revoking citizenship of any American woman married to an alien ineligible for U.S. citizenship.
November 13	*Takao v. United States* upholds the 1790 Naturalization Act prohibiting anyone not white from becoming a citizen. Asians and other "colored" races cannot become naturalized citizens.
November 15	Controversy in Congress over Bursum Bill, which sought to strip Pueblo Indians in New Mexico and Arizona of their lands.

1923

The Committee of One Hundred is appointed by Secretary of the Interior to report on conditions on reservations. It recommends better health care, improved education, and a scientific investigation of the effects of peyote on Indian health.

U.S. Commission of Education survey reports that only 14 percent of Indian children in Oklahoma are in school.

In *Terrence v. Thompson*, the Supreme Court upholds the constitutionality of Washington State's alien land law, and in *Porterfield v. Webb* it upholds a similar California law.

A total of 33 African Americans are lynched.

February 3	The Supreme Court upholds the right of parents to "bring up children . . . without interference from the state," including teaching them in German, if they choose.
February 19	*United States v. Bhagat Singh Thi* rules that Asian Indians cannot become citizens because they are not white.
	In *Moore v. Dempsey*, the Supreme Court rules that "mob-dominated" trials are invalid.
May	The American Indian Defense Association is organized by John Collier, a future Indian Commissioner, to fight for better treatment of Indians.

May 25	In *Chang Chan et al. v. John D. Nagle*, the Supreme Court rules that Chinese wives of American citizens cannot enter the United States.

1924

U.S. Border Patrol is established to control immigration from Canada and Mexico.

A total of 16 African Americans are lynched.

May 26	President Calvin Coolidge signs the National Origins Act into law. It establishes a quota system for immigration and severely reduces the number of immigrants allowed to enter the United States every year.
June 2	The General Citizenship Act gives citizenship to all Native Americans, although it allows states to prohibit Indians from voting.

1925

A total of 17 African Americas are lynched.

May 25	In *Chang Chan et al. v. John D. Nagle*, the Supreme Court rules that Chinese wives of American citizens are prohibited from entering the United States under the 1924 Immigration Act.
October 15	*The Vanishing American*, a movie based on a series of stories published in *Ladies Home Journal* by famous western author Zane Grey, appears. It criticizes mistreatment and neglect of Indians on reservations.

1926

A riot in Harlem leads to the wounding of several Puerto Ricans by New York City police.

Langston Hughes, African American poet, novelist, and essayist, publishes *The Weary Blues*, his first book of poetry.

The China Institute in America is founded to promote cultural understanding between China and United States.

Crashing Thunder: Autobiography of an American Indian, the life of Winnebago Sam Blowsnake as told to anthropologist Paul Radin, is published.

Indian Defense League is organized to promote the right of free travel between American and Canadian reservations.

Zitkala-Sa, also known as Gertrude Bonnin, establishes the National Council of American Indians after the Society of American Indians goes out of existence.

A total of 30 African Americans are lynched.

May 24   In *Corrigan v. Buckley*, the Supreme Court upholds "restrictive covenants," passed by cities to prevent white property owners from selling their homes to African Americans.

1927

Filipino Federation of Labor is founded in Los Angeles to organize migrant workers into a union.

In *Weedin v. Chin Bow*, the Supreme Court rules that a person born abroad of an American parent or parents who had never lived in the United States cannot be a citizen.

Mourning Dove (Humishuma) publishes *Co-Ge-we-a, the Half-Blood*, a novel about the life of a mixed-blood Indian woman.

A total of 16 African Americans are lynched.

March 3   Congress passes the Indian Oil Leasing Act recognizing Indian rights to the proceeds from oil leases.

March 7   In *Nixon v. Herndon*, the Supreme Court rules that whites-only primary elections are unconstitutional.

1928

The Meriam Report, *The Problem of Indian Administration*, is published. It describes the terrible economic and social conditions found on reservations and recommends drastic changes in federal Indian policy.

Daniel Venegas publishes *The Adventures of Don Chipote: Or, When Parakeets May Suckle Their Young*, the story of a young Mexican immigrant in the United States.

Dhan Gopal Mukerji, an Asian Indian, wins the Newbery Award for children's literature for *Gay-Neck: The Story of a Pigeon*.

Luther Standing Bear, an Oglala Sioux, publishes *My People the Sioux*, a series of essays describing the history and culture of the Oglala people and criticisms the government's treatment of Native Americans.

A total of 11 lynchings occur, the lowest total since records began being kept in 1882.

January 1   *The Japanese American Courier* begins publication in Seattle, Washington.

May 18   A bill is introduced in Congress to prohibit Filipino immigration, but it does not pass.

November 4	Charles Curtis, a Kaw Indian, and a U.S. Senator from Kansas, is elected Vice President of the United States.

1929

	The League of United Latin American Citizens (LULAC) is founded in Texas to promote equal rights for Latinos.
	The Urban League sponsors "Jobs for Negroes" in St. Louis and "Don't Buy Where You Can't Work" boycotts in Chicago.
	Wallace Thurman publishes *The Blacker the Berry,* a novel about color prejudice among blacks.
	Walter White publishes *Rope and Faggot: A Biography of Judge Lynch,* a history of lynching in the United States.
	Ten lynchings are recorded.
February	The Negro Experimental Theater is founded in Harlem.
April 1	Atlanta University is formed out of five historically black colleges in Georgia.
June	The National Colored Players is founded by black actors in New York City.

OVERVIEW

The 1920s began with a period of violent race relations best illustrated by the Tulsa riot in 1921 where more than 300 people died, perhaps the bloodiest episode of racial violence in American history. Lynchings remained a national curse for the first half of the decade, with more than 250 lynchings, all but 23 of whom were African Americans, from 1920 to 1925. Despite this appalling number, Congress could not pass an anti-lynching law. The intensity of racial violence discouraged many blacks who turned to the black nationalism of Marcus Garvey as a way of finding racial pride and security. In the arts, the Harlem Renaissance produced major works of poetry, music, literature, and dance, but except for some white critics, this rebirth of African American culture had little impact on segregation, discrimination, and the employment chances of blacks.

For European Americans, the decade also had a limited impact on their acceptance into the mainstream of society. Beginning with the anti-immigrant hostility displayed by judges, politicians, and Anglo Americans during the Sacco-Vanzetti trial in Massachusetts through the walls thrown up by the successes of the Immigration Restriction movement in Congress, immigrants, especially recent immigrants from Italy, Poland, and Eastern Europe, faced increasing hostility from mainstream white Americans. The 1920s were a decade of closing borders and reducing movement into the nation. This came during a time of growing national prosperity when immigrants could not really be accused of taking away American jobs. Instead, the drive for restriction was based on so-called scientific evidence produced by eugenicists and their special brand of biased science.

For Native Americans the 1920s finally meant citizenship for all. But Congress handed them this dubious prize (for many reservation Indians this meant only the right to pay taxes) amid a series of reports finding little but illness, poverty, and despair in Indian towns and villages. Since 1882, Asians had already been excluded from entering America legally, and in the 1920s, the U.S. Supreme Court added another insult to this biased legal system by ruling that Asians—even if they came legally—could not become citizens of the United States because they were not part of the "white race." Latino Americans did not escape discrimination even though a quota system did not exist for migrants from South America. Congress allowed them to cross freely into the Southwest, but only to maintain a continuous supply of cheap labor for American growers and farmers. Once here they faced little more than poverty and degradation in the fields of plenty.

In sum, the Jazz Age produced free forms of art and music but little in the way of equal rights and freedom from prejudice for America's racial and ethnic minorities. The Supreme Court used its power only one time, in *Nixon v. Herndon* (1927), to expand political rights and in this case only outlawed primary elections that excluded African Americans from voting. The Republican-controlled Congress did nothing to protect or expand minority rights. No president spoke out against lynching or other racially motivated crimes. Instead, prejudice and fear of losing a white-dominated society ruled the nation. It is no wonder that the Ku Klux Klan, professing "100% Americanism," had more than 5 million members nationwide by mid-decade. The Klansmen seemed to speak for a majority of Americans, not just 5 million.

KEY EVENTS

THE SACCO AND VANZETTI TRIAL

On April 15, 1920, two men held up a truck carrying a payroll for a shoe factory in South Braintree, Massachusetts. They killed two guards and escaped in a car containing four or five other men, according to witnesses. These same witnesses told police that the robbers looked Italian. Three weeks later, after questioning dozens of men, police arrested Nicola Sacco and Bartolomeo Vanzetti and charged them with the crime. Their motivation: they needed the money (around $15,000) to finance their political activities.

Bartolomeo Vanzetti (left) and Nicola Sacco, manacled together and surrounded by heavy guard and onlookers, about to enter the courthouse at Dedham, Massachusetts, where they will receive the death sentence for murder. Courtesy of the Library of Congress, LC-USZ62-124547.

Sacco and Vanzetti were anarchists and they published a newspaper promoting their cause. They had no money of their own, so fellow anarchists from around the United States set up a Sacco and Vanzetti Defense Committee headed by Carlos Tresca, the most famous anarchist in the country. Anarchists were the most feared political group in American society. They promoted assassinations, bombings, and other acts of terrorism. Despite their small numbers—probably no more than a few hundred took an active role in their direct action campaign—the ideas associated with anarchists created fear in the minds of the American public. This image, however, frequently had little to do with reality. Many anarchists, including Sacco and Vanzetti, believed that their philosophy of society without government would lead to a world without war based on peace and goodwill.[1]

Sacco and Vanzetti came to the United States from relatively prosperous peasant families in Italy in 1908. Sacco came for a sense of adventure, and Vanzetti left his home in sorrow after the death of his mother. Neither man had been involved with anarchism in Italy. They became politically involved only after working in the United States for several years. The terrible conditions experienced by workingmen in New England factories convinced them that capitalism had to be destroyed before a world of beauty and love emerged. As Sacco wrote to his daughter, his political radicalism came from witnessing "the nightmare of the lower class."[2]

The trial for first-degree murder began on May 31, 1921 in Dedham, Massachusetts. Police surrounded the courthouse and searched everyone who entered. Judge Webster Thayer, the trial judge, had a reputation for harboring a deep bias toward "aliens," especially Italians, and he did not hide that attitude during the trial. "There is no better word in the English language than 'loyalty,'" he said in his charge to the jury.[3] In addition, loyalty, even more than direct evidence, became a primary theme in the prosecution's case. Both of the accused had opposed American participation in World War I and both had left the country to avoid the draft. The war had ended less than two years before and "war fever," as one observer commented, still gripped the jurors. Shortly after the war ended, the federal government, under the leadership of Attorney General R. Mitchell Palmer, had launched a campaign to find and remove aliens and "agitators" from the United States. This drive against communists, socialists, anarchists, and other political radicals was called the Red Scare.[4] (Red was the color of the revolutionary flag in Europe, where the Communist Party had taken control of Russia in 1918.)

The Sacco and Vanzetti Defense Committee hired Fred H. Moore, a well-known attorney from California and a long-time defender of radical causes, to take charge of the case. The prosecution presented seven eyewitnesses who identified Sacco as one of the men they saw at the robbery, but none could place Vanzetti at the scene of the crime. Other evidence included a gray cap found at the scene. A medical expert told jurors that hairs in the cap lining matched Sacco's hair. A gun found in Sacco's possession was the same make as a revolver stolen from one of the murdered guards. He explained that he had bought the revolver for $18 but could not explain when or where. A ballistics expert testified that one of the bullets from the Colt automatic matched a bullet taken from the body of one of the victims. Two defense experts disputed this finding, but the jury was not convinced. In interviews after the trial, jurors related that the prosecution's ballistic expert presented the most convincing evidence in the case against the accused. (In 1961, more sophisticated tests conducted by the police seemed to prove that the bullet had really come from Sacco's gun.)[5]

When the defense began its case, both men presented their alibis. Vanzetti said that at the time of the robbery he was in Plymouth, Massachusetts selling fish—that was his job, fishmonger. Sacco told the jury that he had taken the day off from his job in a shoe factory. He and his wife went to have their pictures taken for a passport at the Italian consulate in Boston. Seven witnesses testified that they had seen the couple in a restaurant at the time of the crime. Six others said they had observed Vanzetti in Plymouth, about 25 miles from the scene of the robbery, selling fish. All of the witnesses were Italian and all were friends of the accused. The district attorney suggested to the jury that this friendship made their testimony very unreliable.[6] (In 1952, one of the witnesses admitted that he had lied about seeing Sacco because they had similar anarchist political views.)

At one point, Sacco tried on the cap and it did not fit. Much of the rest of their testimony concerned their political beliefs. Defense attorney Moore believed that if they openly admitted their anarchist principles, he could convince the jury that their arrest had been politically motivated and had nothing to do with the real crime. His clients had been arrested only because they were radical, Italian, and poor.

The prosecutor reminded the jury that Sacco and his friend Vanzetti had run away to Mexico in 1917 to avoid the draft. This cowardly act demonstrated the basic character, or more precisely lack of character of the accused. They were "agitators" who had supported and even led strikes before the war. Since returning from Mexico, they had continued their radical actions. Sacco had been arrested for unlawful picketing and Vanzetti had led a strike at a rope factory. One example of the district attorney's tactics came in the first questions he asked Vanzetti:

Question by District Attorney Frederick Katzmann: So you left Plymouth, Mr. Vanzetti in May 1917, to dodge the draft, did you?
Answer, Yes, sir.
Q. When this country was at war, you ran away, so you would not have to fight as a soldier?
A. Yes.

The next day Sacco took the stand.

Q. (By Mr. Katzmann) Did you say yesterday you love a free country?
A. Yes.
Q. Did you love this country in the month of May 1917? (One month after the U.S. entered the war against Germany.)
A. I did not say,—I don't want to say I did not love this country.

After several follow-up questions concerning loyalty, Sacco finally admitted that "Yes," he did love the United States. To which the district attorney responded, "And in order to show your love for this United States of America when she was about to call upon you to become a soldier you ran away to Mexico." The prosecutor went on for the rest of the afternoon attacking the patriotism of the accused. He barely asked one question concerning the robbery and the murder. Why had Sacco run away rather than join the fight for "freedom?"[7]

Sacco said he had gone to Mexico because he did not want to kill fellow workers in Europe or anywhere else. As he explained in his broken English, "The war is not like Abraham Lincoln and Abe Jefferson's (*sic*), to fight for a free country, for better education, to give a chance to any other peoples. . . . They are war for business, millions of dollars come on the side. I want to destroy those guns. . . . That is why I like people who want education and living, building, who is good, just as much as they could. That is all."[8]

Judge Thayer stressed two themes in his charge to the jury—first the accused were aliens and second they were draft-dodgers. Little that he said had anything to do with the evidence or lack of it presented during the trial. "The Commonwealth of Massachusetts called upon you," he told the jurors, "to render a most important service. Although you knew that such service would be arduous, painful and tiresome, yet you like the true soldier, responded to that call in the spirit of supreme American loyalty. There is no better word in the English language than "loyalty." He concluded with an impassioned appeal for the jury to do its patriotic duty, "I call upon you to render this service here that you have been summoned to perform, with the same spirit of patriotism, courage and devotion to duty as was exhibited by our soldier boy across the seas."[9] The two Italian anarchists who had left the United States rather than face the draft, he implied, were neither loyal Americans nor brave soldiers and therefore probably guilty of the charges against them.

The jury took five-and-a-half hours to make up its mind. "Guilty," the foreman announced. Sacco cried, "Sono innocente!" ("I am innocent.") Judge Thayer sentenced the men to death. A few days after the jury announced its verdict, protest demonstrations in major cities in Europe, the United States, and South America were held to denounce the verdict. Thousands of demonstrators filled the streets of Paris, Rome, Moscow, New York City, Chicago, and San Francisco. Someone threw a bomb at the American embassy in Paris.[10]

Fred Moore, the defense attorney, filed a series of motions asking for a new trial. He argued that the prosecution's ballistics expert had deliberately misled the jury when he said that one of the bullets came from Sacco's gun. Moore presented evidence that the expert's first test had shown just the opposite, but Judge Thayer rejected the motion and all others. The defense's appeals were also rejected. In 1926, when the Supreme Judicial Court of Massachusetts finally heard the appeal of Thayer's dismissal, it ruled that there had been no misconduct on the part of the police or the judge and ordered the executions to proceed.

While awaiting the verdict on the various appeals on death row, Sacco attempted to commit suicide. After Sacco was diagnosed as a paranoid psychotic, Moore arranged for his transfer to the Bridgewater State Hospital for the Criminally Insane. Sacco then fired his attorney calling him my "implacable enemy now and forever." After five months, authorities released Sacco from the asylum and returned him to death row.[11]

In another round of appeals, the new counsel for the defense, William Thompson, produced a "confession" from another anarchist prisoner. He said that he had been one of the men involved in the robbery and that neither Sacco nor Vanzetti had been involved. Judge Thayer rejected the confession; it was "unreliable," he said. As the appeals continued, the worldwide protests grew larger and more violent. Future U.S. Supreme Court Justice Felix Frankfurter, then a professor at Harvard Law School, took up the cause in a book and a lengthy magazine article. Had it not been for the intense hostility showed by Judge Thayer and the prosecution toward "aliens" and radicals, he doubted whether the two men would have been convicted. In this view, Frankfurter received the support of many prominent American educators, legal experts, and liberal political leaders. Sacco and Vanzetti received support from John Dewey, the famous educational philosopher; Walter Lippman, the political journalist; the poet Edna St. Vincent Millay; Senator Robert La Follette from Wisconsin, who ran for president in 1924 on the Progressive Party ticket; Socialist Party leader Norman Thomas; and the entire membership of the American Communist Party.

After receiving petitions from around the world with more than a half-million names, Massachusetts Governor Alvan T. Fuller appointed a blue-ribbon commission, headed by Harvard President A. Lawrence Lowell, to review the trial and the verdict. After a three-month investigation, the Lowell Commission reported that Sacco was guilty "beyond a reasonable doubt." The evidence against Vanzetti, on the other hand, was not quite as clear, although "on the whole," he appeared guilty. Fuller did not feel that the commission's report warranted reducing the death penalty to life imprisonment.[12]

After the governor's failure to act, the Sacco and Vanzetti Defense Committee called for all supporters to "come by train and boat, come on foot or in your car! Come to Boston: Let all the roads of the nation converge on Beacon Hill."[13] People's positions on the case came down to politics—supporters of the guilty verdict saw themselves as defenders of America, protecting the nation from alien ideas (anarchism and communism). Sacco and Vanzetti were terrorists who robbed banks to support their campaign against capitalism, American civilization, and "law and order."

The protestors tended to be radicals from the American Communist Party, labor organizers, immigrants, and Italians. Among European immigrant groups in the United States, Italians ranked very low in the minds of white, English-speaking Protestants. They had several marks against them, including the relatively dark color of their skin and their Catholic faith. Thirty-nine Italians had been lynched in the South between 1891 and 1920 because of the color of their skin. In northern cities, they already were being associated with "the Mafia" and other criminal gangs. An Italian anarchist had tried to assassinate the attorney general of the United States in 1919, but the bomb he delivered to his house exploded early, killing the assassin and the attorney general's butler. Being Catholic added to the burden of being Italian in the early 1920s in a nation where "papists" still were considered more ready to follow the pope than the president of the United States. Attitudes such as these created an atmosphere of fear and prejudice, which made the conviction of Sacco and Vanzetti a certainty no matter what kind of evidence was presented against them.

In late July 1927, Governor Fuller interviewed Vanzetti who pleaded for clemency. The governor's mind did not change, however, and he refused to stop the executions scheduled for August 23. The U.S. Supreme Court rejected a stay of execution three times in the last week, saying it had no role in intervening in a state court's ruling. President Calvin Coolidge refused to take any action and at midnight on the scheduled date, the electrocutions took place. Sacco shouted "Long live anarchy!" Then as the executioner pulled the switch on the electric chair, Sacco said his last word, "Mama!" Vanzetti went next still proclaiming his innocence. His last words were "I now wish to forgive some people for what they are doing to me."[14]

In Boston, Paris, Rome, London, Moscow, and other cities around the world, thousands of protestors filled the streets. In Berlin, six people died in a demonstration that turned bloody.

Were they guilty? Francis Russell, an investigative journalist, made the most detailed examination of the case in a book published in 1986. Russell started out thinking that both men were innocent. After reviewing the evidence, including doing a more sophisticated test of the gun used in the robbery and talking to surviving friends of the two anarchists, however, he concluded that Sacco was guilty. Vanzetti, on the other hand, was surely innocent. The evidence against him was very weak. More than likely he had told the truth when he said he was selling fish in Plymouth on the day of the crime.[15]

THE TULSA RACE RIOT OF 1921

By 1921, Tulsa, Oklahoma billed itself as the oil capital of the world. In 1910, barely more than 18,000 people lived in the city. Ten years later it had 90,000 residents; 12 percent were African American. The chamber of commerce claimed that Tulsa had the highest per capita income of any city in the United States. Oil made the city rich and World War I set off a boom that made many oilmen fabulously wealthy. Even Tulsa's black population shared in the prosperity. The black neighborhood known as Greenwood had its share of beautiful homes and gardens. Black-owned stores, restaurants, and banks lined a commercial district that residents proudly referred to as the "Black Wall Street." (Whites called the area "Little Africa.")[16]

Tulsa also had its darker side. A black sociologist called it the most segregated city in the United States, and behind "Wall Street" stood a district "a mile square of shacks, huts, and hovels." Only the business district had paved streets; in the rest of Greenwood, badly rutted dirt roads turned into mud in the rain and into dust in the heat of the long summers. Many homes had cardboard walls and no windows and lacked running water and electricity. Public services barely existed anywhere in Tulsa and were even less visible in Greenwood. The city had no public hospital, only a few parks all in the richer white neighborhoods, and a badly financed public school system. No one collected the garbage in Greenwood, streetlights did not exist, and Greenwood had only a small volunteer fire department. Tulsa's 45-man police force had exactly two black officers, and it had a reputation for corruption and racism.

The city had a violent past. Its most recent lynching took place in July 1920. A mob lynched a white man accused of killing a taxicab driver. Witnesses reported that police officers directed traffic in and around the scene of the lynching so that everyone could get a good view. They did not arrest any of the participants in the murder.

Tulsa had experienced several lynchings before that event but no race riot. That history ended on May 30, 1921 when the city exploded into the deadliest race riot in American history. Tulsans still dispute the number of people killed. Estimates vary from an officially certified 36 deaths (26 blacks and 10 whites) to what some African American survivors believe to have been more than 150 people, all black, killed and hundreds more wounded.

The riot began on Memorial Day Monday, May 30, 1921. Dick Rowland, a 19-year-old African American who worked in a shoeshine shop, entered an elevator in a downtown office building. He wanted to ride to the fourth floor to use the "Colored" bathroom. As he entered the elevator, he accidentally stepped on the foot of its white operator, 17-year-old Mrs. Sarah Page. She staggered and Rowland grabbed her hand to keep her from falling. When Rowland touched her, she screamed and he ran from the building. Page called the police and told them that a black man had tried to rape her and that she could identify her attacker.

The police arrested Rowland the next day. The afternoon headlines in the *Tulsa Tribune* screamed that a "negro" had attacked a white girl in a downtown elevator in broad daylight. Richard Lloyd Jones, the editor, demanded that the good white men of his city "avenge the purity of a white woman," although he did not suggest how. Many observers believe Jones shared much of the blame for the coming reign of terror because of his loud and openly racist editorials demanding action.[17]

The police interviewed Page once more but she did not press charges (and never would). That evening, however, a mob of more than 300 whites gathered outside the city jail and demanded that the sheriff hand over "the boy." In Greenwood, word spread that whites were about to lynch Rowland. To prevent this, a group of 30 blacks, many of them—just like their white foes—veterans of World War I, marched to the jail, rifles in hand. They shouted at the whites but the sheriff persuaded both groups to go home. A few hours later armed blacks and whites returned to the jail and this time neither side retreated. Shots rang out when a white man tried to take a gun away from a black. Fighting continued throughout the night as the whites steadily drove the blacks back toward Greenwood. As they swept into the black neighborhood, they set fires to houses and stores and shot randomly at anyone in the streets.

By Tuesday afternoon, the white mob numbered more than 10,000 men, women, and their children. Mayor T. D. Evans finally wired the governor's office and requested National Guard troops be sent to help end the "negro uprising." In Greenwood, white war veterans in their army uniforms carried cans of oil into Little Africa setting houses, factories, and businesses on fire but only after looting them. In one particularly ugly incident, whites broke through the front door of house and shot an elderly couple in the back of their heads while they prayed. Another mob attacked the home of A. C. Jackson, a black surgeon. Jackson fought to protect his wife and children. One of the mob leaders assured the doctor that if he put down his rifle, he and his family could safely leave their home. Jackson put down his gun. Shortly thereafter a member of the mob shot and killed him, although his wife and children survived.

Oklahoma's governor eventually responded to the mayor's plea for help, and several hundred troops entered the burning city early Wednesday morning. Their commander told the governor that thousands of whites, many of them drunk and "armed to the teeth," had taken over the city, looting and burning without restraint. He then ordered his troops to sit down and have breakfast.

Shortly before noon, the all-white Guard units marched into Greenwood with fixed bayonets and began arresting men, women, and children (mostly black) by the thousands. Airplanes dropped "turpentine balls," wooden balls soaked in oil and set afire, and dynamite into the streets, while trucks with machine guns mounted on their backs strafed porches and doorways of those houses still standing. Whites cheered as the Guardsmen and police drove Greenwood's residents—with their hands over their heads—to "detention camps" hastily set up at the city's convention center. Other Guard troops and police entered black-owned businesses and houses in groups of four or five smashing furniture and stealing valuables before setting them on fire. White women and children joined in the looting and destruction, having, as one participant reported, "a rollicking good time."[18]

Not all whites took part in the riot; a few even opened their doors to help the victims. Holy Family Catholic Church provided 400 refugees with food and shelter. The First Presbyterian and First Baptist churches turned their basements into medical clinics and temporary hospitals. So many wounded sought help that they had to lie on the floor. The Young Women's Christian Association opened a Hostess house. The Red Cross provided much of the relief. Its doctors and nurses treated hundreds of the victims and fed thousands more in several shelters. The Oklahoma Red Cross spent so much money on these relief efforts that it took more than 10 years to repay the debts accumulated during the riot.

By the end of the fourth day, "everything had been destroyed," according to one witness, "except the earth on which the town was built. I guess that if there had been any way to set fire to the soil, it would be gone too," he concluded.[19] Greenwood disappeared. Those blacks not detained in the detention centers fled the city and took refuge in several all-black towns that dotted northeastern Oklahoma. Most would not return to their ruined community for more than a year. None of them received any compensation—ever—for any of their losses. Officially, the mobs burned 1,256 homes, worth more than $4 million, to the ground. At least 2,000 people suffered broken bones and other wounds from beatings, machine gun fire, and bombs. Mayor Evans refused to allow funerals, so the true number of victims remains unknown. Churches could not hold funerals because mourners might plan more riots, the mayor reasoned. Greenwood survivors claimed that at least 150 people died during the four days of destruction, with many of the bodies dumped into a nearby river. An all-white grand jury created to investigate the riot put the number at only 56; all but 10 of the victims were African American.[20]

That same jury placed the entire blame for the riot on Tulsa's black community. "The arrival of armed Negroes" at the county jail had ignited the violence in this view. Continuing "agitation" for social equality on the part of the city's "colored" race played a major role in inspiring the African American mob to carry out its massive destruction. The jurors indicted Dick Rowland for "attempting to ravish, rape and carnally know Sarah Page." A judge dismissed the charge, however, because Sarah Page never appeared in court.[21]

The sheriff and chief of police faced charges of failing to "take proper precautions for the protection of life and property during the rioting." At their trial, however, the state's attorney asked the jury to go easy on the officers. They had not violated any laws and had not caused the violence; neither had the white mob. The white citizens of Tulsa had merely come to the defense of a police force too small to put down the black uprising and had to take "matters into their own hands."

What caused the riot? Fear and hate among the participants? But where did such feelings come from? Some students of the riot trace the hostility to segregation, the total separation of people by skin color that made Tulsans complete strangers. Neither community knew anything about the other except what they thought they "knew" from images they picked up from newspapers, movies, and other sources of racist stereotypes (churches, families, schools, etc.). Whites saw an uprising by "black savages, " the "bad negroes," as the Tulsa *World* called them, who were trying to take over their city. Racist thinking was so pervasive in white culture—with a few exceptions found in those churches that provided assistance for the victims—that when authority broke down, white citizens felt free to unleash their bitter resentment and hatred, especially toward those blacks who had achieved more success than they had achieved.

The rioters hated and feared all blacks, every black—rich, poor, young, or elderly, men, women, or children, but especially successful African Americans. Black success directly challenged their belief in white supremacy. Black success told rioting whites that something must be wrong with them, or else how could a black person achieve more than they had accomplished. Whites preferred childlike, or ignorant, or drunken, drug-addicted, violent, murderous "n——s." At least, they fit the stereotype and reinforced the vision of white supremacy that infected American society. The riot showed that given the opportunity and a feeling that they could get away with it because law and order had disappeared, many whites would kill blacks, destroy their property, burn their homes, smash their bones, and be very happy about it.[22]

In the aftermath of the bloodiest race riot in American history, little in Tulsa changed. The city never rebuilt Greenwood as it had promised. Richard Lloyd Jones, whose newspaper had done much to fuel the riot by spreading rumors and inflaming the mob with a series of racist editorials and calls for action, found some "blessings" in the destruction. Blacks confined at detention centers discovered that many whites cared about their welfare and safety. Out of the ashes of Greenwood, Tulsans could come together to build a new neighborhood with decent housing to replace the shacks the fires had destroyed. Two years after the riot, the citizens of Oklahoma elected a Ku Klux Klansman governor.

In 1997, the Oklahoma Commission to Study the Tulsa Race Riot of 1921 offered a radically different conclusion. It found the white mob directly responsible for the death and destruction. It called on the state legislature to provide reparations to the few remaining elderly survivors, mostly in their eighties and nineties, of the riot. The state legislature rejected that idea, however. It was too costly, they said, and the legislators did not want to set a precedent for paying money to victims of past wrongs. Once that practice got started who knew where it would end? Many people had suffered wrongs in the past. Reparations for all past wrongs could run into the billions of dollars. The governor and the legislature offered an apology but no more than that.

CONGRESS CONSIDERS ANTI-LYNCHING LEGISLATION

Between 1882 and 1930, lynch mobs killed at least 4,730 people: 3,437 African Americans and 1,293 whites, of the latter at least 597 were Mexican. In all, 95 percent of the lynchings took place in the Southern states of (in order of frequency) Mississippi, Georgia, Texas, Florida, Louisiana, and Alabama. Most of the Mexican lynchings took place in Texas, Arizona, California, and New Mexico. The law defined lynching as putting someone to death by mob action without due process of law or legal authority. The crime of lynching was murder and therefore, unless committed on federal government property, a violation of state law. Not a single person, however, had gone to jail in any of these states for taking part in a lynching. As most lynchings took place in front of screaming mobs, and the participants usually did not wear masks or hoods or try to hide their faces, it seemed obvious that local authorities, sheriffs, police chiefs, and governors could have arrested hundreds of people. That they did not showed how little they cared about the killing of African Americans or Mexicans.[23]

The failure of local authorities to enforce anti-lynching laws (and most of the states involved in lynching had laws forbidding it) led to a move in Congress to make lynching a federal crime. Congressman George H. White of North Carolina, the only black member of the House of Representatives, introduced such a bill in 1901, but it failed to gain much support. Ten years later Representative Leonidas C. Dyer, a Missouri Republican from a largely African American district in St. Louis, tried again but with no success. After a terribly vicious lynching in Duluth, Minnesota in 1920, Dyer reintroduced his legislation. This time the bill attracted more support. Duluth was not in the South. Nevertheless, the bloodthirstiness of the white mob that burned, tortured, and mutilated the bodies of three black workers for a traveling circus caught the attention of members of Congress from northern cities. The Duluth killings showed to them that as more and more blacks moved north—as had happened during the "Great Migration" years, 1915–1919—lynching moved north, too.[24]

The June 1920 lynchings in Duluth followed a pattern similar to many other events in the South. A white girl (later admitting that she lied) claimed that "circus niggers" had raped her. A doctor who examined the victim reported that no rape had taken place. That news went unreported but a rumor that she had died (false, of course) spread quickly through the white community. The police arrested three black men and took them to jail. That night a violent mob gathered, rushed the jail, took the victims out, and burned them alive. Entrepreneurs sold postcard photographs of the victims as souvenirs.[25]

The Duluth lynchings shocked the nation. In a message to Congress, delivered shortly after his election to the White House, President Warren G. Harding asked for action "to wipe out the stain of barbaric lynching from the banners of a free, and orderly, representative democracy."[26] The Dyer Bill, had it passed, would have made it a federal crime for any law officer to allow a lynching to take place. If a state did not prosecute participants in a lynching, the U.S. Department of Justice would. A county government would have to pay $10,000 to the survivors of any lynching that took place within its boundaries.[27]

These three provisions raised constitutional problems concerning state versus federal power. Do we really want a national police force interfering with local officials, opponents asked? Such "states' rights" issues provided a convenient cover for the racist hostility that fueled the enemies of the anti-lynching legislation. "Who acts if states will not act?" a supporter asked. If the federal government could prohibit the sale of alcohol, as it had done after ratification of the Nineteenth Amendment, the Prohibition Amendment, why could it not act to prohibit murder?

After a brief discussion of constitutional matters, the debate switched to the problem of race. Lynching was an act of justice whereby white men defended the purity of white women. "You do not know where the beast is among them," a representative from Texas shouted in reference to African Americans in his district.[28] Passage of the Dyer Bill would encourage more rapes, warned another member of the House. In reality, fewer than 20 percent of the victims had been accused of rape and according to a study of lynchings by Arthur Raper, a white sociologist at the University of North Carolina, about one-third of the accused had done nothing at all except, perhaps, be in the wrong place at the wrong time.[29]

The arguments focused on black/white lynchings, with little mention of anti-Mexican killings largely because few in Congress seemed aware of such great hostility toward Spanish-speaking citizens. The bill passed the House 231–119. A few weeks later, the Senate took up the measure but not before 12 lynchings had taken place in the single month of May. The most horrible of these lynchings took place in the small town of Kirvin, Texas. The brutality of the mob, made up of men, women, and even children, shocked even some of the most steadfast critics of the Dyer Bill. Three young black men were arrested and charged with killing a white woman. That evening a mob gathered at the courthouse. The sheriff made no effort to stop them from breaking into the jail and removing the prisoners. The mob tortured and mutilated the victims before covering their bodies with oil and setting them on fire. They burned for six hours before the three innocent men mercifully died. The next day two white brothers confessed to the murder, although a few days later the sheriff released them without filing charges. The case was never reopened. As debate continued in the Senate, lynch mobs killed nine other victims that month. Still, the Senate failed to act on the legislation.

The National Association for the Advancement of Colored People (NAACP) started a nationwide petition drive in support of a new crusade to get an anti-lynching law. It gathered hundred of thousands of signatures calling on the Senate to end its filibuster and pass the bill. The NAACP, the nation's largest civil rights group founded in 1909, had made passage of a federal anti-lynching law one of the first items on its agenda. It had published *Thirty Years of Lynching in the United States, 1889–1918* in 1919, a study of the causes of hundreds of lynchings during that time hoping to arouse the conscience of America into supporting its cause. In 1922, a group of black women, all members of the NAACP, started a group called the Anti-Lynching Crusaders, led by Mary B. Talbert, president of the National Association of Colored Women (NACW). They adopted a slogan, "A Million Women United to Stop Lynching." The women would donate $1 each to pay for newspaper ads and a new petition drive. The group's most famous ad asked Americans, "Do you know that the United States is the only land on earth where human beings are burned at the stake?"[30]

Along with raising money for ads and petitioning Congress, the crusaders also hoped to use the power of prayer to change the hearts and minds of enemies of the Dyer Bill. A million crusaders would unite in a special prayer calling on Congress to pass an anti-lynching law. Talbert encouraged white women to join the campaign and a few thousand did, many of them affiliated with the Young Women's Christian Association (YWCA), but the vast majority of members were African American.[31]

Another new group, the Commission on Interracial Cooperation (CIC), founded by two white southern ministers in 1919, Will Alexander and Willis D. Weatherford, tried a different approach to end lynchings. Shortly after its founding, the CIC invited five prominent black leaders to join its board of directors, including John Hope, the president of Morehouse College in Atlanta, Georgia. If the "best people" of both races in the South could come together, Alexander believed, and talk about the race question, they could begin resolving the problem. Southerners needed discussion and dialogue, not political action. In 1921, the commission created a Women's Committee, also interracial, to promote racial understanding, especially among southern Christians.

Alexander and Weatherford chose not to challenge Jim Crow laws that segregated whites and blacks in the South. That would be too dangerous and had little chance of success. Segregation would fall, Alexander wrote, but only "by the wisdom and justice of oncoming generations."[32] For now, however, the best that could be expected from southern legislatures would be appropriating money to equalize spending for black and white school districts and other segregated facilities. Thus the CIC chose not to support the Dyer Bill, arguing that what needed changing before the horrible violence ended were the minds of white southerners. A law would have little effect on that. Instead, the CIC offered a medal of honor to any white sheriff who prevented a lynching. A sheriff in Kentucky received the first award for preventing a lynching in Lexington.[33]

The Senate took up the debate again in late 1922 with the usual result, a southern filibuster that prevented any action. An attempt to end debate and have a vote failed; Senate rules at that time required a two-thirds majority for that to happen, and the votes were not there even though four more lynchings occurred in the South during the two weeks the Senate considered the legislation.

Lynchings did decline in the United States after 1923 from an average of 62 per year from 1910 to 1919 to 10 per year in the decade after. Why this happened is still a mystery. Perhaps the reasons included a growing opposition to the violence of the mob among white church leaders in the South and a feeling on the part of more moderate governors in a number of states that lynching was an embarrassment. Several newspapers took up the campaign including the Columbus, Georgia *Enquirer-Sun*. In 1926, its editor Julian Harris (son of Joel Chandler Harris, author of the "Uncle Remus" stories) won a Pulitzer Prize for a series of anti-lynching editorials. The problem, however, did not totally go away. Several extremely brutal lynchings shocked the nation in the 1930s. The NAACP reported 277 lynchings between 1922 and 1934, the next time Congress debated the issue.[34]

After another particularly horrible lynching that year, during which a Florida mob dragged its victim, Claude Neal, across the state line into Alabama before torturing him, mutilating his body, and only then killing him, Congress took up new legislation making lynching a federal crime, the Costigan-Wagner Act. Edward F. Costigan, Democrat of Colorado, successfully sponsored the bill in the House, with Senator Robert F. Wagner, Democrat of New York, leading the Senate effort. Debate in that body, however, ended with the same outcome as in 1922—no bill was passed. The NAACP called on President Franklin Roosevelt to offer his support; however, for political reasons, he decided not to. He needed southern senators' support for his economics program and did not want to lose their votes by defending any kind of "civil rights" or "pro-Negro" legislation, as many white southerners called the anti-lynching act. Therefore southern senators again blocked a vote with a lengthy filibuster defending the honor of white women and attacking the evils of government interference in local affairs. A senator from Louisiana argued that only the fear of lynching kept "savages" from raping white women. The minority opposed to Costigan-Wagner once again prevented its passage. Congress had made a number of crimes federal offenses by this time, including auto theft, bank robbery, kidnapping, and telephone extortion, but not lynching.[35]

Three years later, the anti-lynching forces made one more try. This time Representative Joseph A. Gavagan, Democrat from New York, led the effort. Once more, a gruesome killing, a death by blowtorch in Alabama, inspired the effort. One more time the House passed the bill and one more time it was hung up in the Senate. The filibuster tied up the upper house for 30 days and then ended with no action on the proposal. Congress never passed a bill making lynching a federal crime. A Gallup Poll revealed that more than 60 percent of Americans favored passage of the Gavagan Bill.[36]

Mob violence and lynching left a lasting legacy in the South. It increased racial hatred and division and helped keep African Americans second-class citizens. It psychologically damaged blacks everywhere and fostered a culture of violence among white southerners. As Richard Wright, the famous black novelist observed, whites did not have to kill many blacks to keep them "in their place," just one lynching sent the black community a message: cross the line, be in the wrong place at the wrong time, or simply "look the wrong way" at a white woman and you faced torture and death.[37] Lynching was a form of terrorism; it was the consistent use of fear (of a horrible death) to coerce a population into submission. For too many years it worked.

IMMIGRATION RESTRICTION: 1921–1924

Congress passed the first law restricting immigration in 1882. It prohibited Chinese laborers from entering the United States. Twenty-five years later, President Theodore Roosevelt signed a "gentleman's agreement" with Japan adding immigrants from that country to the excluded list. Anti-immigrant organizations soon began a campaign to add Europeans to that list. The anti-Asian laws reflected intense hostility to people from the Far East. Later, the anti-immigrant lobbyists cited "scientific evidence," also based on racism and prejudice, to support their view that people from certain European countries lacked the intelligence and character to become good Americans.

At first, supporters of expanded restriction belonged to groups such as the American Protective Association and the Immigration Restriction League. They lobbied Congress to require a literacy test for prospective newcomers. Three times, between 1895 and 1917, Congress passed a bill authorizing such a test, but three times three different presidents—Grover Cleveland, William Howard Taft, and Woodrow Wilson—vetoed it. Economic interests, mainly those who benefited from cheap labor, supported open borders. Opponents of restriction included corporations and farmers. Unrestricted immigration benefited these sections of the American economy by providing a constant supply of labor and these workers kept wages low. World War I began in Europe in 1914, cutting off the supply of European workers coming to the United States until it ended five years later. Immigration fell to its lowest level since the Civil War.

In a burst of patriotic, anti-immigrant fervor, Congress passed a literacy bill in 1917 and this time managed to override President Woodrow Wilson's veto. The new law required that adults prove they could read. The language did not matter, any language, including Yiddish and Hebrew, counted. The act also created a "barred zone." No one from this area of the world, including virtually all of Asia except for the Philippine Islands, which at this time belonged to the United States, could legally enter American territory.

The literacy test did not live up to the hopes of its supporters. Of the more than 800,000 immigrants entering the United States between July 1920 and July 1921, fewer than 1,500 failed the test. Expanding access to public education in Europe had greatly increased literacy. The ability to read and write no longer proved to be a barrier for those wanting to enter the United States. After the devastation of World War I and its aftermath of hunger and homelessness, those numbers seemed large indeed. To keep many of these people out, the anti-immigration lobby in the United States turned to science to achieve its goal and Congress proved willing to listen.[38]

In the 1920 presidential election, Republican nominee Warren G. Harding called for legislation that would keep out people with racial characteristics that would prohibit them from adopting American values and principles. After winning the election, Harding did just that, signing into law the Emergency Quota Act of 1921. The law established a limit of 358,000 legal immigrants per year. Each nation received a quota equal to 3 percent of that country's population in the United States based on the 1910 census. Exceptions included the "barred zone" of Asia. The quota for this region stayed at zero. The law placed no limit, however, on immigration from nations in the Western Hemisphere. Farmers in Texas, California, and many other states relied heavily on migrant workers from Mexico and other Latin American countries to pick their crops and tend their fields.

The U.S. House of Representatives Committee on Immigration and Naturalization listened to many witnesses while considering the legislation. The science of eugenics, or "scientific racism" as critics called it, played a major role in legislation the committee produced. Eugenicists believed that just as better proper breeding produced stronger chickens and horses, a stronger, healthier human race could emerge by eliminating "hereditary defectives" and weaker members of the species. As an example of how eugenicists worked, Harry Laughlin, superintendent of the Eugenics Record Office, provided the committee with the results of a survey he had conducted of American prisons and jails. The high number of foreign-born prisoners from Italy and the nations of Eastern Europe demonstrated the low level of intellectual and moral development found in these areas of the world. In another study of mental hospitals, Laughlin claimed to have discovered that the highest percentage of patients in these institutions came from these same places. Actually, his data showed nothing of the kind. Instead, his tables clearly showed that the highest percentage of patients in mental hospitals were German and Irish. No committee member questioned Laughlin's data, however. They just accepted whatever information confirmed their racist view of reality.[39]

To keep the American population from further "pollution" by "socially inadequate" and "mentally or physically defective" members of the human race, Congress needed to control and severely limit the numbers of immigrants from morally and biologically inferior ethnic and racial groups. Chairman Albert Johnson, very impressed by this "science," appointed Laughlin the "expert eugenics agent" for his committee, a post he filled until 1931. The committee's bill eventually passed the House by a wide margin. Senate approval came a few weeks later and President Harding signed it into law.

Still, this legislation did not satisfy the anti-immigration forces. Their movement for even more restrictive legislation gained force after Harding died from heart failure in 1923. Calvin Coolidge, the new president, proved himself an even greater friend of restriction than his predecessor. He also believed more steadfastly in eugenic principles. In a 1921 magazine article, the then vice president wrote that "biological laws" proved that "Nordics," a popular term for immigrants from northern and western European countries, deteriorated physically, intellectually, and morally, when allowed to intermarry with other races. The country needed strict laws controlling immigration to save the white race, the president concluded. The House Immigration Committee held new hearings on the issue of restriction and accumulated vast amounts of statistical information on the hereditary traits of Americans. In 1923, Chairman Johnson became head of the Eugenics Research Association of America.[40]

In 1924, President Coolidge urged Congress to take immediate action on the immigration issue. The number of legal immigrants "should be limited to our capacity to absorb them into the ranks of good citizenship. America must be kept American."[41] Harry Laughlin returned to Washington and informed the Immigration Committee that new research showed conclusively that Italians, Poles, Jews, and Slavs carried genetic traits that made them extremely susceptible to crime, insanity, and moral degeneracy. He advocated a simple solution to this problem. Most immigrants from these countries had come after 1890, he noted. His solution: change the census base for establishing the quotas from 1910 to 1890. By using this earlier date, the law automatically cut the percentage of people coming from southern and Eastern Europe. Under the new base, Italian immigration would fall from 41,000 to 4,000 immigrants per year.

First, Congress dealt with the problem of immigration along the Mexican and Canadian borders. Border state governors, local officials, and members of Congress became alarmed at the vast number of legal and illegal migrants crossing the Rio Grande every year. Paying an $18.00 visa fee made one legal. More than 100,000 Mexicans per year came legally, but many thousands more avoided or could not afford the fee (because Mexican agricultural laborers made about 12 cents every 12 hours they worked) and entered the United States illegally. Americans farmers did not mind how their workforce got here; the more people who came, the less they had to pay. Unions, on the other hand, argued that uncontrolled access to the United States kept wages down for everyone.

Racial prejudice entered the picture, too. Representative John Box, Democrat of Texas, voiced the view of many Americans in his speeches attacking immigration policy with Mexico. Mexicans posed a threat to the United States because of their "racial and cultural inferiority." Large majorities of Mexicans were of "mixed-race" and, under the laws of many American states, were counted as Indians. Also, they were mostly Catholic and spoke an alien tongue.

They could never become good citizens, Box argued. Farmers might need their labor but that did not mean they needed to be accepted as equals or to become citizens.

Congress established the United States Border Patrol to guard America's southern and northern borders. Entry to the United States became more difficult than ever before. Border Patrol agents could arrest and deport people now called "illegal aliens." Workers who entered without paying the visa fee faced felony charges and imprisonment for two years. Most often, however, Border Patrol agents rounded them up, took them back to the border, and let them go. Many times the agents acted without checking for the right papers. They just assumed that anyone who looked Hispanic had come here illegally.[42]

In 1924, immigration restrictionists had new statistical evidence to support their cause. During World War I, the U.S. Army had given intelligence tests to every draftee. The results of these IQ tests clearly showed the effects of "race" and ethnicity on the human mind, at least in the eyes of eugenicists. The "mental age" (one of the things measured by the test) of officers, for example, differed widely depending on the racial and ethnic background of the test taker. According to Laughlin's studies, white officers' mental age averaged 17.26 years but that of Italian descent stood at only 11.8 years; German-Americans scored a little higher at 12.83 years. African Americans from southern states had the lowest mental age of all, 10.3 years, (although southern whites were not far behind). The committee ignored one significant statistic: northern blacks scored higher than southern whites. No one raised the issue of cultural bias in testing during this debate. Based on these findings and the other evidence proving the "criminality" and tendency to insanity among southern and eastern European groups, the House voted to move the census base back to 1890.[43]

The Senate balked at this change and questioned the whole method of establishing immigrant quotas based on past censuses. The results of this process had no relationship to the current population of the United States. According to the 1920 census, only 12 percent of Americans listed as their nationality a southern or eastern European country. Yet under the quota system established in 1921 using the 1910 census, they received 44 percent of the available slots. Senator Henry Cabot Lodge, Republican of Massachusetts and a leader of the anti-immigrant bloc in the Senate, called this system "biased" and demanded that it be replaced. Senator David Reed proposed the "national origins" system. According to this system, the government would take a new census that required all citizens to list the homeland of the first generation of their ancestors who had come to America. Both the Senate and the House accepted Reed's idea and passed the Johnson-Reed Bill also known as the Immigration Restriction Act of 1924.[44]

The old system remained in effect for two years, although in the new act Congress cut in half the total number of immigrants allowed to enter the United States every year. It also reduced the quota from 3 percent to 2 percent of that nation's population in the United States as of 1890. Any nations without a presence in America, except for the Asian states, could send no more than 150 people per year to the United States. Since European imperial powers controlled all but two African nations, Ethiopia and Liberia, immigrants from these colonial outposts were counted as part of their colonial ruler's total, although very few Africans came into the United States during this time. Ethiopia and Liberia received a quota of 150.

The quota system became complicated after adoption of the "national origins" idea. Determining the national origins of all Americans proved impossible. People whose ancestors had come to America before 1820 had no way of proving their heritage; records of the homeland of immigrants coming into the country before that year no longer existed or had never been recorded. Immigration authorities did not list the country of origin for people entering the United States until 1850. The Census Bureau did not ask about the country of origin of foreign-born citizens until 1890. In an attempt to overcome these deficiencies, the Census Bureau created The Committee on Linguistic and National Stocks in the Population of the United States.

The social scientists and statisticians on this committee analyzed records beginning with the 1790 census. They determined national origins of persons by counting surnames. The investigators decided that all people named "Smith" came from England, although the name might once have been the German "Schmidt," or even more likely the last name of an African American. This method undoubtedly increased the quota for Great Britain. When using the 1890 census, 21 percent of the immigrant population came from England. That percentage more than doubled under the new system, leading to a much higher quota for Great Britain than it should have been granted. Whatever numbers used by immigration officials, ethnic groups from southern and Eastern Europe got a far lower quota than the preferred groups from England, Germany, Ireland, and the Scandinavian states. Italian, Greek, Serb, Polish, and Russian immigrants accounted for only 9 percent of the yearly quota, whereas northern and western Europeans got 86 percent. The rest of the world received the remaining 5 percent. These proportions remained part of American immigration law until 1965.

The immigration laws of 1921 and 1924 accomplished their goal. The number of immigrants coming from anywhere fell rapidly. Only a few countries ever filled their yearly quota, no matter how small. "Scientific racism" helped keep people out of the country, sometimes at their own peril. The law did not distinguish "refugees" from immigrants, so victims of terrorism and mass murder had no recourse. If their countries' quota had been filled, they died. Only a few members of Congress objected to the new policy. One, Adolph Sabath, a Jewish American born in Europe and a Democrat from Chicago, spoke out against the "pseudoscientific proposition" that race and ethnicity determined a person's character, intelligence, and prospect for becoming an American. The whole glorification of the "Nordic race," however, threatened the American ideal of the equality of all people.[45]

INDIAN CITIZENSHIP, 1924

On June 2, 1924, Congress passed the Indian Citizenship Act, making all Indians in the United States American citizens. This was largely a symbolic act finalizing a process that had begun many years earlier. By 1924, many Native Americans had already acquired citizenship. Thousands became citizens by special acts of Congress as happened in 1901, when a bill made all Indians in Oklahoma, not yet a state and still officially Indian Territory, American citizens. Citizenship, in this case, did not automatically lead to the right to vote; under the American Constitution states established qualifications for voting and no state with a large Native American population gave them the right to vote. (They did have to pay taxes, however.) Some Indians married white men or women who were citizens, thus becoming citizens; others received citizenship after serving in the American military. Others fulfilled the requirements for citizenship laid out in the General Allotment Act of 1887. These actions were necessary because the American Constitution declared that Indians were not citizens and that they could not become citizens under various naturalization acts passed by Congress unless they renounced membership in their tribe.

Government policy toward Indians had changed many times over the decades, but the goal remained the same, assimilating Indians into American culture. Congress confined Indians to reservations in 1871 where they became "wards" of the U.S. government. This meant that they would receive food and shelter ("rations") from the Indian Service every month. Indians could not leave reservations without permission of the agent in charge. In the beginning, Indians were not required to work for their supplies. After a few years, Congress reversed this policy and required that any Indian receiving government assistance had to work. Because most reservations were far away from any major city, jobs were scarce and reservation agents reported many cases of extreme hunger. Indians faced another problem; if they left the reservations without permission, the U.S. Army would hunt them down and return them to their "homes." Many Indian wars resulted from this policy. No wonder Indians referred to the reservations as "prisons on the Plains."

Indians experienced terrible times on reservations, including starvation and disease. Congress consistently appropriated far less money for the Bureau of Indian Affairs (the BIA—sometimes called the Indian Service) needed to fulfill its responsibilities. Officials in the all white BIA expected (and hoped) that given enough time—a hundred years or so—the reservations would be gone because the Indians would be gone. They felt this was possible because Indian civilization was too backward and primitive to succeed in the modern world. Others promoted "assimilation," hoping that their wards would accept reality and become Americans just like everybody else. The BIA never attracted the highest quality federal workers. A study of government agencies conducted by the private, non-partisan Brookings Institution concluded that the Indian Service had the "lowest quality" employees of any government agency. A small number of Indians worked for the BIA, but they did not fill any important policymaking positions. Even on the reservations, the top administrators were all white. Under this system, conditions on reservations grew increasingly worse.

The BIA had responsibility for administering Indian policy. The General Allotment Act of 1887, commonly called the Dawes Act (after its chief sponsor Senator Henry Dawes, Republican of Massachusetts), sought to abolish reservations, thereby forcing Indians to assimilate. They deserved to be treated like other Americans, no better and no worse. The law provided a way for Indians to become full American citizens, responsible for their own lives, property, and advancement. Indians now had a chance to become regular citizens rather than live on government handouts. This would take time and much effort, but the prospect of complete assimilation into the white world made the project worthwhile. According to the new policy, any Indian head-of-household (male or female) would get 160 acres of reservation land on which they could grow their own food and become self-sufficient property owners and taxpayers. All single Indians over 18 would receive 80 acres. If they lived on this land for 25 years, improved it, and gave up membership in their tribe, the BIA would grant them American citizenship. In addition, Indians would then get title to the land they had been living on; in the meantime it would be held in trust by the Bureau. The bill's supporters believed that land ownership was the key to "civilizing" American Indians; once they experienced the power and pride of ownership, they would be ready to become good Americans. A key provision of the legislation said that the BIA could sell any land not allotted to Indians to the highest bidder, Indian or not. By this method, reservations in the United States would eventually disappear.[46]

Things did not work out the way the bill had intended. Instead, reservations became more miserable places than before, filled with hunger, disease, and social problems. By the 1920s, Indian reservations had the highest rates of alcoholism, suicide, and crime in the nation. Indians had an average life span less than half that of white Americans, and Indian children under five died at twice the rate of white children.

By time the allotment program ended in 1934, non-Indians had purchased more than 90 million acres of land, whereas Indians retained about 54 million acres. Indians lost, leased, or sold more than two-thirds of their allotments; yet most Indians remained poor, malnourished, and unassimilated. A Brookings Institution study revealed that only 2 percent of Indian families had incomes of more than $500 per year, and most of this income came from renting their allotment or leasing their mineral rights to white farmers, cattle ranchers, and oil companies. In all, 96 percent of Indian families survived on less than $200 per year. (White families averaged $2,400 per year.) These economic problems did not seem to trouble the BIA or many members of Congress. If nothing else, these statistics reinforced the view that Indians were an inferior people and their civilization was just naturally wasting away.[47]

Only competent Indians could become citizens. Thousands of Indians became citizens by proving their "competency" to a BIA Board of Examiners. A competent Indian had to show an ability to take care of his or her allotment by farming the land or by leasing the mineral rights under it to someone outside the tribe, in other words, to a white. Many Indians chose this latter option because most reservation land proved unsuitable for agriculture. By 1920, the BIA had declared almost two-thirds of Indians "competent" and they became citizens, many reluctantly, because now they had to pay state and local property taxes. Most Indians could not pay these taxes because they were so poor, so they had to sell their land to pay delinquent tax bills. If they did not, jail awaited and their property would be sold at auction, with the proceeds going to pay the delinquent taxes.

During World War I, 21,000 Indians were drafted and served in the military. Unlike African Americans, however, Indians served along side whites rather than in segregated units. For their patriotic contributions to the war effort, Congress granted the veterans citizenship in 1921, although only a few actually filled out the correct forms. Therefore, by 1924, only a few Indian veterans had gained citizenship.

Assimilationists, or Americanizers, aimed their policies at making Indians citizens, whether by competency hearings, or by turning Indians into small farmers, or through military training did not really matter. No organized group fought against citizenship, but many Indians only reluctantly accepted becoming fully American. For them it meant little more than the right to pay taxes and the right to vote, though that would be restricted to federal elections. States retained the right to prohibit reservation Indians from voting in state and local elections. This meant that in states such as Arizona, Montana, New Mexico, and South Dakota, Indians could not vote in state elections until the 1950s. Citizenship did not give Indians the same rights as other Americans. It may have been an honor for some, but for most native peoples life remained harsh and difficult. Citizenship did not end their lives of poverty, despair, and desperation.

VOICES OF THE DECADE

MARCUS GARVEY

Marcus Mosiah Garvey (1887–1940) was born in Jamaica and came to the United States in 1916. He founded the Universal Negro Improvement Association (UNIA) and *The Negro World*, a successful black newspaper. He also launched several businesses from his headquarters in Harlem, including the Black Star Shipping Line. He became a leader of the black nationalist movement and advocated a spiritual return to Africa for African Americans. He was arrested for mail fraud in 1927 and sentenced to seven years in prison. While in Atlanta Federal Prison, he wrote a short essay, "The History of the Negro," from which the following reflections on history are taken.

Marcus Garvey delivering constitution for Negro rights at a convention, New York, 1920. Courtesy of the Library of Congress, LC-USZ62-109628.

History is written with prejudices, likes and dislikes, and there never has been a white historian who ever wrote with any true love or feeling for the Negro. . . .

White historians and writers have tried to rob the black man of his proud past in history, and when anything new is discovered to support the race's claim and attest to the truthfulness of our greatness in other ages, then it is skillfully rearranged and credited to some other unknown race or people.

Negroes, teach your children that they are the direct descendants of the greatest and proudest race who ever peopled the earth; and it is because of the fear of our return to power, in a civilization of our own, that may outshine others, why we are hated and kept down by a jealous and prejudiced contemporary world. . . .

The 400,000,000 Negroes of the world have a beautiful history of their own, and no one of any other race can truly write it but themselves. . . . The white man's history is his inspiration, and he would be untrue to himself and negligent of the rights of his posterity to others, and so1 also the Negro. Our history is as good as that of any other race of people, and nothing on this side of Heaven or Hell will make us deny it, the false treaties, essays, speculations and philosophies of others notwithstanding.

From *The Philosophy and Opinions of Marcus Garvey* (New York: Universal Publishing House, 1926).

ALAIN LOCKE

Editor, philosopher, and essayist Alain Locke (1886–1954) was one of the most important leaders of the Harlem Renaissance. In 1925, he edited the March edition of the magazine *Survey Graphic*. Titled *Harlem, Mecca of the New Negro*, it included works of poetry, fiction, nonfiction, and philosophy. It became the defining text of the Harlem Renaissance. In the essay, "Enter the New Negro," Locke tried to define that term. Here he tried to identify the place of African Americans in American society and history.

The Negro mind reaches out as yet to nothing but American wants, American ideas. But this forced attempt to build his Americanism on race values is a unique social experiment, and its ultimate success is impossible except through the fullest sharing of American culture and institutions. There should be no delusion about this. American nerves in sections unstrung with race hysteria are often fed the opiate that the trend of Negro advance is wholly separatist, and that the effect of its operation will be to encyst the Negro as a benign foreign body in the body politic. This cannot be—even if it were desirable. The racialism of the Negro is no limitation or reservation with respect to American life; it is only a constructive effort to build the obstructions in the stream of his progress into an efficient dam of social energy and power. Democracy itself is obstructed and stagnated to the extent that any of its channels are closed. Indeed they cannot be selectively closed. So the choice is not between one way for the Negro and another way for the rest, but between American institutions frustrated on the one hand and American ideals progressively fulfilled and realized on the other. . . .

More and more, however, an intelligent realization of the great discrepancy between the American social creed and the American social practice forces upon the Negro the taking of the moral advantage that is his. Only the steadying and sobering effect of a truly characteristic gentleness of spirit prevents the rapid rise of a definite cynicism and counter-hate and a defiant superiority feeling. Human as this reaction would be, the majority still deprecate its advent, and would gladly see it forestalled by the speedy amelioration of its causes. We wish our race pride to be a healthier, more positive achievement than a feeling based upon a realization of the shortcomings of others. But all paths toward the attainment of a sound social attitude have been difficult; only a relatively few enlightened minds have been able as the phrase puts it "to rise above" prejudice. The ordinary man has had until recently only a hard choice between the alternatives of supine and humiliating submission and stimulating but hurtful counter-prejudice. Fortunately from some inner, desperate resourcefulness has recently sprung up the simple expedient of fighting prejudice by mental passive resistance, in other words by trying to ignore it. For the few, this manna may perhaps be effective, but the masses cannot thrive on it.

From *Survey Graphic*, March 1925, 4–7.

ZITKALA-SA

Zitkala-Sa (Gertrude Bonnin), a Yankton Nakota, published *American Indian Stories* in 1921. Many of the stories and essays describe her education and brief tenure as a teacher at the Carlisle Indian Industrial School in Carlisle, Pennsylvania. The section of the essay reprinted here, "My Mother's Curse Upon White Settlers," reveals her mother's rejection of assimilation into white society and her growing anger at the injustices done to Native Americans by Americans. In 1921, she helped organize the Indian Welfare Committee and later worked for the American Indian Defense Association. She worked for justice and political power for Native Americans until her death in 1938.

One black night mother and I sat alone in the dim starlight, in front of our wigwam. We were facing the river, as we talked about the shrinking limits of the village. She told me about the poverty-stricken white settlers, who lived in caves dug in the long ravines of the high hills across the river. A whole tribe of broad-footed white beggars had rushed hither to make claims on those wild lands. Even as she was telling this I spied a small glimmering light in the bluffs.

"That is a white man's lodge where you see the burning fire," she said. Then, a short distance from it, only a little lower than the first, was another light. As I became accustomed to the night, I saw more and more twinkling lights, here and there, scattered all along the wide black margin of the river.

Still looking toward the distant firelight, my mother continued: "My daughter, beware of the paleface. It was the cruel paleface who caused the death of your sister and your uncle, my brave brother. It is this same paleface who offers in one palm the holy papers, and with the other gives a holy baptism of firewater. He is the hypocrite who reads with one eye, 'Thou shalt not kill,' and with the other gloats upon the sufferings of the Indian race." Then suddenly discovering a new fire in the bluffs, she exclaimed, "Well, well, my daughter, there is the light of another white rascal!"

She sprang to her feet, and, standing firm beside her wigwam, she sent a curse upon those who sat around the hated white man's light. Raising her right arm forcibly into line with her eye, she threw her whole might into her doubled fist as she shot it vehemently at the strangers. Long she held

Zitkala-Sa (Gertrude Bonnin), 1921. Courtesy of the
Library of Congress, LC-USZ62-119349.

her outstretched fingers toward the settler's lodge, as if an invisible power
passed from them to the evil at which she aimed.

From *American Indian Stories* (Lincoln: Center for Great Plains Studies, University of
Nebraska-Lincoln, 1980), 93–98.

LANGSTON HUGHES

In this excerpt from the essay "The Negro Artist and the Racial Mountain,"
Langston Hughes discusses the problems of being an African American artist
in the United States. Hughes became one of the most famous and critically acclaimed writers of the Harlem Renaissance and, as he explains here, was greatly
influenced by jazz. This is also an early statement of Black Power in the arts and
a call for truthfulness in describing African American life.

Most of my own poems are racial in theme and treatment, derived from the
life I know. In many of them I try to grasp and hold some of the meanings
and rhythms of jazz. I am sincere as I know how to be in these poems and yet
after every reading I answer questions like these from my own people: Do

you think Negroes should always write about Negroes? I wish you wouldn't read some of your poems to white folks. How do you find any thing interesting in a place like a cabaret? Why do you write about black people? You aren't black. What makes you do so many jazz poems?

But jazz to me is one of the inherent expressions of Negro life in America: the eternal tom-tom beating in the Negro soul—the tom-tom of revolt against weariness in a white world, a world of subway trains, and work, work, work; the tom-tom of joy and laughter, and pain swallowed in a smile. Yet the Philadelphia clubwoman is ashamed to say that her race created it and she does not like me to write about it. The old subconscious "white is best" runs through her mind. Years of study under white teachers, a lifetime of white books, pictures, and papers, and white manners, morals, and Puritan standards made her dislike the spirituals. And now she turns up her nose at jazz and all its manifestations—likewise almost everything else distinctly racial. She doesn't care for [certain] portraits of Negroes because they are "too Negro." She does not want a true picture of herself from anybody. She wants the artist to flatter her, to make the white world believe that all Negroes are as smug and as near white in soul as she wants to be. But, to my mind, it is the duty of the younger Negro artist, if he accepts any duties at all from outsiders, to change through the force of his art that old whispering "I want to be white," hidden in the aspirations of his people, to "Why should I want to be white? I am a Negro—and beautiful!"

So I am ashamed for the black poet who says, "I want to be a poet, not a Negro poet," as though his own racial world were not as interesting as any other world. I am ashamed, too, for the colored artist who runs from the painting of Negro faces to the painting of sunsets after the manner of the academicians because he fears the strange un-whiteness of his own features. An artist must be free to choose what he does, certainly, but he must also never be afraid to do what he might choose.

. . . We build our temples for tomorrow, strong as we know how, and we stand on top of the mountain, free within ourselves.

From "The Negro Artist and the Racial Mountain." *The Nation*, June 23, 1926.

RACE RELATIONS BY GROUP

AFRICAN AMERICANS

In the 10 years between 1920 and 1930, more than 900,000 African Americans left their homes in the South and crowded into northern cities. The black populations of Chicago, Cleveland, Detroit, and other industrial cities nearly tripled during that decade. This "Great Migration" had begun before World War I around

1914 and continued into the 1920s. Southern blacks came north to escape the segregated schools, racial intimidation, and violence, along with the lack of basic civil rights they found in their old homeland. They came north to find wartime jobs, more political and economic opportunity, and general freedom that many believed existed in the North for them. Early migrants wrote back to their families expressing awe at the amount of freedom they enjoyed in cities such as Chicago compared with life in the segregated Jim Crow South. In the North, black people could actually vote without fearing for their jobs or their lives. Compared with life in the Cotton Belt, the North looked like the promised land of joy and equality.

Economic conditions in the South favored the white race. Only 20 percent of black farmers owned their own land, while the rest worked as field hands, sharecroppers, and tenant farmers. Sharecroppers and tenants lived at the mercy of white property owners. They signed contracts every year that spelled out exactly what they had to grow (usually cotton) that committed them to give at least half of everything they grew to the landowner. They seldom came out ahead as the owners subtracted money for the two-room shacks the impoverished farmers rented, the food they bought at the plantation store, and the tools they used to grow the crops. Farmers could not leave the land they worked on until they had paid all their debts. In many parts of Alabama, Georgia, Mississippi, and other states of the Old South, whipping of tenants who argued with their bosses was common.

In one extreme case in rural Georgia, a plantation owner with the assistance of one of his black tenants murdered 11 African Americans who worked as virtual slaves on the plantation. Clyde Manning, the black assistant, killed the workers because John S. Williams, the property owner, told him to kill these "peons." The Bureau of Investigation of the Justice Department in Washington (later the FBI) had been investigating Williams for violation of the Thirteenth Amendment forbidding slavery, and he wanted to get rid of the evidence. Manning carried out his orders—without protest—disposed of the bodies of his victims, all killed within a few days of each other, by burying eight in shallow graves and dumping the three others in the Alcovy River. Williams was tried first, convicted by a jury, and sentenced to prison—perhaps the first white person imprisoned for his involvement in the killing of African Americans in Georgia history. Another first, the guilty verdict was based on the testimony of a black man.

Manning confessed to the horrible crimes but claimed he had no choice because Williams would have killed him if he did not obey. During the entire process, he showed no remorse or emotion. He talked about the killings as if they had no impact on him at all. He might as well have been swatting flies. Several other blacks working on the plantation testified that Williams—father of 12 children—was a brutal, violent man who would have no trouble killing anyone. The judge dismissed this testimony, however, because in his view black people could never tell the truth, even under oath. After three days of testimony, the all-white jury reached its decision in 40 minutes: "Guilty" of murder but then they surprised everyone in the courtroom by recommending a life sentence rather than death by hanging. For a black man in Georgia convicted of murder, this seemed like an act of mercy. Manning had killed black men, 11 of them. Had they been white no such mercy would have ever been possible.[48]

Lynch mobs continued to take the lives of black men in the South. During the 1920s, lynchings averaged more than 30 per year. Congress debated legislation that made lynching a federal crime. The bill passed the House but a southern-led filibuster in the Senate prevented its passage. Six southern states passed "racial integrity" laws that made it a crime for blacks and whites to marry. Because of literacy tests and poll taxes, less than 5 percent of eligible African Americans in Alabama, Georgia, Louisiana, and Mississippi could vote.

Race riots in Chicago and other cities in the North in 1919 demonstrated that the region was not the promised land many migrants hoped to find. The Ku Klux Klan—proclaiming itself as "One Hundred Percent American"—emerged as a major political force in states as diverse as Illinois, Indiana, Maine, Oregon, and Wisconsin. Klansmen in those states were elected to city councils, state legislatures, and city halls. Scandals and corruption led to the quick decline of the Klan by the mid-1920s, but in its prime, it exerted great influence all the way to Congress. In 1924, more than 40,000 Klansmen marched in their masks and robes down Constitution Avenue in support of the Immigration Restriction Bill. That same year at the Democratic Party Convention, delegates failed to pass a platform plank condemning the Klan for its secrecy, violent activities, and support for white supremacy.

On the positive side, the 1920s witnessed the emergence of the "New Negro" movement and the Harlem Renaissance. "New" Negroes, many of them veterans of the Great War, challenged white supremacy and stood solidly in support of political and social equality. The term implied that African Americans no longer accepted bad schools, discriminatory laws, unfair treatment by the police and by courts, and second-class status anywhere in the United States. They would fight for full and equal acceptance, be proud of their heritage, and demonstrate their intellectual and artistic genius as a people. The philosopher Alain Locke captured the New Negro spirit when he denounced the "Uncle Toms," "aunties," "mammies," and "Sambos,"—the "old Negroes"—who accepted inferiority and segregation. New Negroes bore the responsibility of "rehabilitating the race in world esteem from that loss of prestige for which the fate and conditions of slavery have so largely been responsible." African Americans could begin this rebirth by creating great art, great music, great literature, and other cultural achievements that would win the respect of all peoples.[49]

The NAACP and the National Urban League led the fight for racial and economic justice in this decade, as they continued to do long into the future. The NAACP launched an anti-lynching campaign in 1922. In a series of newspaper advertisements, it called on Americans to support the Dyer Bill being considered by Congress. This legislation made lynching a federal crime—rather than a state crime—taking prosecution out of the hands of local authorities, many of whom supported lynching. The bill was bottled up in the Senate, however, and failed to pass. Therefore, for the remainder of the decade, the number of lynchings averaged about 30 per year.

The NAACP also challenged voting discrimination in the South, where in some states as few as 5 percent of eligible voters actually registered to vote. In a major victory, NAACP lawyers convinced the U.S. Supreme Court that a Texas law excluding African American participation in primary elections violated their rights (*Nixon v. Herndon*, 1927). The Texas legislature responded to this ruling by making primaries "private" political party elections and gave the parties the power to declare who could or could not vote. The primaries remained all white.

Black voters in the North had more success. In 1928, blacks in Chicago sent the first African American to sit in the House of Representatives since 1901 and the first black congressional representative ever from the North. Oscar DePriest (1871–1951), a Republican, served two terms before losing to Arthur Mitchell, an African American Democrat in 1934. Before his election to the House, DePriest had been a successful real estate developer in Chicago after leaving Florence, Alabama, his place of birth. In Congress DePriest sponsored legislation calling for a monthly pension for ex-slaves and another bill to make Lincoln's birthday a national holiday. Neither bill passed. After his defeat, he retuned to Chicago and was elected to the city council until 1947, four years before he died.

DePriest's election provided a ray of hope for African Americans; at least they now had a voice, however small, in Washington, D.C. African Americans were treated to another sort of victory when a jury in Detroit found Ossian Sweet, a black physician, not guilty of killing a white man. The case drew national attention because Clarence Darrow, the most famous lawyer in the nation, agreed to defend the doctor. Sweet had bought a house in an all-white neighborhood and while he and his wife began moving furniture into their new home, an angry mob gathered on their sidewalk. The Sweets were not deterred despite being hit by several rocks. That evening Sweet and several friends and relatives stayed in the half-empty bungalow to protect it from vandals.

The next day the mob became angrier and more hostile and the police seemed nowhere in sight. Shots rang out from the house killing one man in the crowd and injuring another. When the police arrived, they arrested Sweet and his 10 companions and charged them with murder. At the trial, Darrow argued that Sweet had acted in self-defense. In his testimony, the doctor told the story of his childhood in Florida where a constant fear of lynching pervaded the black community. He explained how the mob he faced in front of his home was "the same mob that hounded my people throughout its entire history."[50] Darrow's witnesses included members of the Urban League in Detroit and Walter White, future president of the NAACP. White described the history of lynching in the United States for the jury. After an impassioned summation by Darrow, the jury deliberated for almost two days before informing the judge that they were hopelessly divided. The judge declared a mistrial. At the second trial, Darrow presented the same defense that ended with an eight-hour summation retracing the history of racial violence in the United States. This time the jury agreed that Sweet had fired in self-defense and he was acquitted.

Sweet's victory was unusual, even in the North, where a black killing a white person usually meant life imprisonment or death. Perhaps progress was being made in race relations. After the death of his wife from tuberculosis, Sweet spent most of the rest of his life living alone in a small apartment above a drugstore he owned. He became increasingly bitter and angry, finally taking his own life in 1960 by putting a pistol to his head and pulling the trigger.[51]

By the end of the decade, life for African Americans, especially in the North, improved somewhat. Sharecroppers and tenant farmers in the South continued to exist at the mercy of their landlords. All African Americans—no matter what their wealth, income, or expertise—however, faced daily threats of violence, prejudice, and open discrimination as the Sweet case illustrated. The promised land of the North fell short of expectations on the issue of race relations; however, for many African Americans, it was still better than anything the segregated South had to offer.

EUROPEAN AMERICANS

The Sacco and Vanzetti trial in Massachusetts demonstrated the anti-immigrant not just the anti-Italian hostility of the Jazz Age. The alleged Italian inclination to criminal behavior became more apparent with the emergence of Al Capone and other Italian gangsters when Prohibition became the law of the land, but many people seemed to forget that Irish, Jewish, and German gangs fought with Capone for control of illegal liquor. Immigration restriction became the most important issue of the day for European Americans. The war had aroused a spirit of patriotic fervor that carried over into the 1920s: "One Hundred Percent Americans" kept on the lookout for communists, anarchists, socialists, and other European ideas that might infect the American character with the deadly disease of radicalism. Newly elected President Warren G. Harding called for a "return to normalcy" after the uncertainty of the war years. For many Americans that meant a return to white supremacy and keeping out trouble-making aliens like Sacco and Vanzetti. The 1920s became a decade of closing America's borders to immigrants and creating a truly white American race.

German Americans emerged from the hysteria of the war years battered, shaken, and disorganized. The hostility faced by the community had not unified the group but had created severe divisions. Some Germans faced the anti-German crusade by turning superpatriotic or by changing their names to more American-sounding ones, such as Schmidt to Smith. Some of these new "100% Americans" celebrated the collapse of militarism in the old homeland and welcomed the birth of a new democracy. Others turned away from the world and became more religiously isolated, and still others began to search for a German identity that might mark them as different from the Anglo-Saxon majority whom they hated so fervently. If German Americans really loved America, one of their leaders asserted, "They must see to it that German culture does not die here."[52] Many others, however, turned as far away as possible from identification with the humiliated German homeland and tried to forget what had happened altogether. Those memories could not be so quickly abandoned, they soon found out.

The extraordinarily chaotic conditions in their old homeland kept the memories alive. "Hate against militarism and autocracy does not have to be direct against children," one visitor to Berlin reported.[53] Stories of mass starvation, of homeless and abandoned children roaming the streets, of hundreds of elderly men and women eating rats and dead horses, and of the constant threat of a "Bolshevik Revolution" such as the one that destroyed the old Russia in 1917, filled the newspapers. On top of this misfortune came the catastrophe of the Versailles Treaty that officially ended the Great War. A "brutal injustice aimed at a helpless and starving country," a German American newspaper declared. The "brutal rape of right and good faith," said another.[54]

Then in August 1920 came the news of "the Black Terror" on the Rhine. French African soldiers from the colony of Somalia had been stationed in the Rhineland at the end of the war to maintain order. Now they were raping German women and molesting German children. Action had to be taken immediately by all civilized governments to pressure France into an immediate removal of this "black horror." German Americans everywhere had to come together to save the old homeland from an even worse degradation than losing the war. What were "uncivilized savages" doing in Germany?

German American organizations rallied in Chicago, St. Louis, Milwaukee, New York, and other major cities to demand that President Woodrow Wilson, still bedridden from a stroke he had suffered the previous year, pressure the French to get those "animal-like Senegalese" out of the old country. The pressure worked. The French government removed the African troops within a year. It took appeals to racism to provoke a unified response by German Americans and as soon as the French removed the Somalis, the unity ended.[55]

For European Americans immigration restriction was the biggest issue in the 1920s. The restriction campaign had a direct impact on every European ethnic group in the United States, and it symbolized for them the intense hostility still expressed by so-called real Americans, or as the Ku Klux Klan labeled itself "100% Americans." Anti-immigrant hostility entered the presidential campaign in 1920 as Republican candidate Warren G. Harding called for strict limits on the number of people coming into the country from war-torn Europe. Congress moved quickly to restrict immigration after the Republican victory in 1920. It passed a law restricting the number of immigrants to 350,000 per year, less than half the average reached before World War I without much debate, and Harding quickly signed The Emergency Quota Act of 1921 into law.

Anti-immigrant prejudice grew with the release of a series of reports by eugenic scientists issued by Congress in 1922–1923. Based on studies of prison populations, mental health hospital patients, and "intelligence tests," the statistics indicated that Italians were criminally inclined (because a higher proportion were in jail than any other group); Serbs and Russians had a high potential for insanity (because they had high rates of incarceration in "insane asylums"); and Poles,

H. W. Evans, Imperial Wizard of the Ku Klux Klan, leading his Knights of the Klan in a parade held in Washington, D.C., 1926. Courtesy of the Library of Congress, LC-USZ62-61303.

Greeks, and Hungarians scored very low on IQ tests, suggesting they were less intelligent than other ethnic groups. If the United States wanted to become a truly powerful, intelligent, and morally upright nation, people from these "unfit" ethnic groups needed to be kept out of the country.

Congress achieved that goal in the 1924 Immigration Restriction Act, a bill that received heavy support from the Ku Klux Klan and other white racist organizations. The new law created a quota system based on ethnicity. It cut Italian immigration from an average of 41,000 per year before World War I to 4,000. The numbers for Poles declined from 31,000 to 6,000, and Greece saw a decrease from 3,000 to only 100 of its citizens legally allowed into the United States in any year. Most members of Congress favored these reductions; the only criticism came from Representative Adolph Sabath, a Democrat from Chicago, and a few of his colleagues. Sabath rightly insisted that the new quotas promoted disunity (not "racial integrity," as supporters argued) among Americans by pitting immigrants from Western Europe (Ireland, Germany, Great Britain) against the peoples of southern and eastern Europe. Congress passed the bill anyway by a wide margin in the House and Senate. Germany, Sabath reminded his opponents, had only recently fought a savage war against America but now could send a greater number of immigrants here than could any other country in Europe.

Despite the restrictions imposed in 1924, anti-immigrant forces remained unsatisfied. To construct a perfect race of Americans, the nation needed even tighter control of its borders. And that required an end to the quota system census and the adoption of a "national origins" method of selecting eligible migrants. This required a survey of the American population that identified every citizen's ethnic or racial ancestry. The Census Bureau created the Committee on Linguistic and National Stocks in the Population of the United States to gather the data. Beginning in 1927, the annual quota for any nationality (except Asian) would be proportional to that people's representation in the census of national origins. Congress capped the total number of immigrants at 150,000 per year. Each nationality would get the number of slots equal to its percentage in the population. If the Census Bureau identified 10 percent of Americans as Germans in origin, Germany's yearly quota would be 15,000 immigrants per year.

The "national origins" system had the effect desired by the anti-immigration lobby. Immigration from Europe almost stopped and never reached 150,000 per year. Because if a country did not reach its quota—say Italy had a quota of 10,000 but only 5,000 Italians actually came to the United States, the remaining 5,000 slots would remain unfilled for that year, another country could not take the open slots. Ethnic leaders protested the new system but to no avail; the new quotas remained in effect until 1953.

The 1924 immigration act harshly affected the Jewish community. The Ku Klux Klan denounced Jews as the chief architects of the Communist Revolution in Russia. Detroit industrialist Henry Ford's notoriously anti-Jewish newspaper the, *Dearborn Independent,* reported that Jewish bankers already controlled European banks and were now working to take over the American banking industry. The *Independent* published the complete text of *The Protocols of the Elders of Zion.* It allegedly contained the complete text of a secret Jewish plan to take over the world economy and establish a Jewish dictatorship. Actually, the Russian Czar's secret police wrote the text and it bore no resemblance to reality. The State Department reported to Congress that Jews coming to the United States were "of the usual ghetto type . . . filthy, un-American, and often dangerous in their habits . . . abnormally twisted, their dullness and stultification resulting from past years of oppression and abuse."[56]

Anti-Semitic prejudice existed almost everywhere, even in America's leading educational institutions. Most colleges and universities had quota systems limiting the number of Jewish students to 1 percent of the freshman class in any year. Harvard and Yale had that quota and so did most other elite institutions and public universities. Medical and law schools had extremely limited quotas. Northwestern University Law School had never had a Jewish student and in 1925 rejected future Supreme Court Justice Abe Fortas, primarily, he thought, because he was Jewish. Only after World War II did such professional schools open their doors a bit wider.

NATIVE AMERICANS

All Indians in the United States became American citizens in 1924, but citizenship did little to improve their economic and social position. Government policy toward Indians in the 1920s remained similar to previous decades. Assimilationists, or Americanizers, aimed their policies at making Indians into American citizens. The Bureau of Indian Affairs (BIA) tried to turn Indians into small farmers as it had since its creation a century before. To fight against assimilation, which many Indians rejected, preferring to maintain their traditional way of life and heritage, several Native American rights groups emerged and began to organize resistance to the efforts to take away their cultures. In 1921, the American Indian Defense Association (AIDA) became the most important group in this drive for self-determination.

Led by John Collier, a white social worker and community organizer from New York City, AIDA led the fight for Indian religious and cultural freedom. Collier became commissioner of Indian Affairs in 1933. He loved living with and learning about Indian beliefs and practices. He felt that the Indian way of life was far superior to the white world of greed and violence. As executive secretary of the AIDA, he established an office in Washington to lobby Congress to grant Indians sovereignty. The group opposed assimilation because Indians deserved to live according to their own traditions on reservations that they controlled.

In its first campaign, the association led the fight against a bill introduced in Congress in 1921 by Senator Hiram Bursum (Republican of New Mexico). The Bursum Bill favored a new approach to the Indian question and received support from real estate developers, oil companies, and western cattlemen and ranchers. If Congress adopted this new policy, the government would take away all land given to Indians in previous decades. Bursum's goal was to dispossess the Pueblo Indians of New Mexico and Arizona from land they had lived on since before the coming of Spanish explorers. His bill required Indians to produce legal titles to the lands; if they could not the government would take over and sell the property to private developers. Because many Pueblo peoples had occupied their villages since the 1200s, producing any legal documents showing original ownership would have been impossible. Indians never had deeds or titles; they just lived on the lands they farmed and hunted and had no concept of private ownership.

Collier's fight against the Bursum Bill caught the imagination of many Americans, especially those who saw Indians as a nature-loving, innocent, and happy people who would now suffer the loss of their homes because of greedy landlords and corrupt politicians. Few white Americans actually had any idea about the true conditions on Indian lands and reservations. To them Indians represented a pure, noble people, uncontaminated by the evils of modern industrial society. This image of the "noble savage" about to be cheated of his lands encouraged

Appointed Indian affairs commissioner John Collier, 1933. Courtesy of the Library of Congress, LC-USZ62-111222.

many people to write their representatives and the Senate defeated the bill. In its place, Congress passed legislation that created a Pueblo Lands Board to sort out the tangled problem of ownership.[57]

In 1923, the AIDA merged with two smaller groups creating the Indian Rights Association (IRA). In its first act, the IRA published a series of pamphlets that exposed fraud and mismanagement on reservations. In Oklahoma, for example, oil companies had cheated hundreds of elderly Indians out of their property and their life savings. In another instance, an oil company paid for the murder an entire family of Osage Indians after they refused to sell their oil rights. Indian police never found the killers. In the aftermath of these revelations, Secretary of the Interior Hubert Work appointed a "Committee of One Hundred" to look into the scandals and other reservation problems. The committee worked for more than a year before issuing a report to President Calvin Coolidge, but it had little impact on Indian policy.

In 1924, Indians became American citizens by act of Congress, but for most native peoples the only change meant that they were responsible for paying federal taxes. States with large Indian populations continued to treat Indians like second-class citizens. They could not vote; they could not serve on juries, and in Arizona, Utah, and New Mexico, Indians did not attain those privileges for another 25 years. Citizenship for Indians simply was another part of the goal of remaking Indians into Americans. Once again it did not work.

The desperate conditions facing most Indians on reservations came to public attention with publication of the Meriam Report, officially titled *The Problem of Indian Administration*, in 1928. Lewis Meriam, an anthropologist, and nine other social scientists worked for one year gathering information concerning the health, education, economic conditions, and community life of Native Americans. One Indian, Henry Roe Red Cloud, a Winnebago, served on the committee. Their findings revealed conditions among Indians that shocked the nation. "An overwhelming majority of the Indians are poor, even extremely poor," the report began, "and they are not adjusted to the economic and social system of the dominant white civilization."[58]

Indian health, the investigators concluded, "as compared with that of the general population is bad." Tuberculosis, pneumonia, and measles killed thousands of Indian children and adults every year. Living conditions on reservations were deplorable; inadequate housing made life more difficult and unhealthier. "There is great overcrowding, so that all members of the family are exposed to any disease that develops," the researchers concluded, and the houses built by the BIA were no more than "small shacks with few rooms and with inadequate provision for ventilation." Most reservation housing lacked "any toilet facilities whatever," and women and children often had to carry water for "considerable distances from natural springs or streams, or occasionally from wells."[59]

While visiting reservations across the country, the social scientists observed, "it was almost always possible to tell the Indian homes from the white by the fact that the white person did much more than the Indian in keeping his house in condition." For this, however, they refused to blame the Indians. The quality of the land they lived on was so bad that "a trained and experienced white man could scarcely wrest a reasonable living" from it. Very few jobs existed on reservations and few of them were close to cities where Indians might find employment. Adding together the conditions faced by reservation Indians—poor health, low standards of living, inadequate housing, poor quality of land, and lack of job opportunities—could only yield one result, "real suffering and real discontent." Indians did not want to live as they were living, as some critics argued. They were not happy "in their idleness and irresponsibility." When Indians lost their children to hunger and disease, they suffered that loss with the same sense of despair as "the white man."[60]

What caused the poverty of the Indians? The Meriam Report issued a full-scale criticism of government policy. After the U.S. Army moved Indians to reservations, the government began issuing rations to them. Many Indians took the rations because they felt the government owed them something for taking away their lands and the culture. This "pauper point of view" made them think that the government now supported them, so they would no longer have to make their own living. This attitude created laziness and dependency. The allotment system did not improve the quality of life for Indians. Again, they could live without working simply by leasing their land to whites. Even worse, reservation agents kept most of the lease money and doled it out to Indian families only if they needed it. Why? Because Indians "were ignorant of money and its use," the agent believed. This view resulted only in creating more dependency.

The Meriam Report found Indian schools "grossly inadequate." The Indian Service allotted 11 cents per day to feed children in boarding schools, an amount that kept them hungry, unhappy, and sick. A poor diet led to an extremely high rate of trachoma, an eye disease that usually led to blindness, among Indian boys and girls. Lack of fruit and vegetables guaranteed that tuberculosis disabled many others. Indian children suffered from a rate of tuberculosis 17 times higher than that of whites. A few more dollars could have greatly reduced these afflictions, but Congress could never seem to find those dollars in its annual appropriations.[61]

A serious problem involved the vast amount of labor demanded of Indian children. Generally, children worked half-day and went to classes during the other half. Laundry work seemed to predominate. The investigators concluded that if the government enforced its child labor laws, which it did not do, it could shut down many of these laundries. The curriculum did not fit the needs of the students; vocational training programs emphasized what the report called "vanishing trades," and many of the teachers lacked basic teaching qualifications. In addition, once they completed their education, students were on their own. They received no help in finding jobs, moving on to colleges or universities, or in returning to their homes. The BIA based the entire educational process on the false idea "that the shortest road to civilization is to take children away from their parents and insofar as possible to stamp out the old Indian life."[62] That notion had not worked in the past and many Native Americans hoped that it never would.

Although many Native Americans did not apparently know it, a Kaw Indian, Charles Curtis (1860–1936), served as vice president of the United States from 1929 to 1933. His father, a non-Indian, had married Curtis's mother, of the Kaw or Kansa tribe, shortly before the Civil War. His mother died before Charles reached the age of four, and his white grandmother raised him for two years before he returned to his Indian grandmother. From age 6, he lived on the Kaw Reservation in eastern Kansas where he attended a Quaker mission school.

After completing high school, Curtis studied law and was admitted to the Kansas bar. He had inherited a 40-acre allotment from his mother and turned it into a profitable business. Elected county attorney as a Republican in 1885, he enforced the state prohibition laws with vigor. In 1892, voters sent him to the U.S. House of Representatives where he would remain until 1907. He had never participated in Kaw tribal affairs on the reservation; he had his membership in the tribe taken away in 1878. In 1903, however, he became chair of the House Committee on Indian Affairs. Here he worked to abolish tribal courts and to protect Indian orphans. Elected to the Senate in 1907, he served in that body until Herbert Hoover selected him to be vice president in 1928.

As vice president, Curtis advocated improving conditions on reservations but took little action to help that cause. He had little influence in the Hoover White

House and the president rarely consulted him on any matter. As vice president, he attended cabinet meetings and hosted official dinners but otherwise did nothing of importance. Nevertheless, Curtis has the distinction of being the highest-ranking Native American politician thus far in United States history.[63]

LATINOS

In 1920, a total of 486,418 Mexicans lived in the United States according to the Census Bureau. They had more than doubled their numbers since the previous census in 1910. The 1920s recorded an even faster population growth, reaching more than 850,000 by the middle of the decade. Historians refer to this as the "Great Migration" in Mexican American history. More than half of that population (56 percent) were American-born and lived in the southwestern United States in the territory acquired by the United States after the Mexican American War (1846–1848). The newcomers crossed the Rio Grande during World War I when the draft caused a labor shortage on American farms and in industrial cities. Farmers and ranchers in states bordering on Mexico, including California, Arizona, New Mexico, and Texas, had relied on a supply of cheap agricultural laborers from south of the border for decades. They worked in the sugar beet and cotton fields of Colorado and Texas and moved up and down the West Coast picking fruits and vegetables. On American farms they could earn 10 times as much as they could doing the same kind of work in their homeland.[64]

Most of these migrant workers entered the United States legally because few restrictions existed. Farmers needed workers and Mexico supplied them. In 1921, during the discussion of immigration restriction all proposals to limit Latin American migrants—Latin America included all the nations from Mexico to Argentina—met intense opposition from representatives from Texas, Arizona, California, and other western agricultural states. Agricultural interests in those states wanted and received unrestricted immigration for their supply of migrant workers. Prices for food would rise dramatically if the law placed restrictions on Latinos, a California senator warned. The farmers had the support of the State Department on this issue because any limit on Latin American immigration would severely harm attempts to improve trade relations with those nations. Hence, the 1921 bill reduced immigration from every area of the world except Latin America and Canada (where French Canadian shoemakers and textile factory workers played a major role in the New England economy).[65]

Congress discussed limits on Mexican migrant workers three years later during debate on the 1924 bill establishing a quota system for immigrants but again refused to impose any restrictions on migrants coming from Latin America or any nations of "the New World," meaning Canada and the islands of the Caribbean. Those favoring restriction warned that an open border with Mexico posed a terrible threat to American civilization. Unrestricted access to the United States allowed a racially inferior people an open opportunity to flood into the country and take away American jobs by the thousands. If Congress did nothing to stop the flow, within two generations the United States would become a Spanish-speaking nation.

More than 40,000 Ku Klux Klansmen marched on Washington to support the restriction legislation. The American Federation of Labor also joined the cause. Its president, William Green, told a Congressional committee that Latin Americans usually took jobs for far less pay than Americans would accept. Eugenic scientists provided "evidence" demonstrating without a doubt that Mexican "blood" was mostly Indian "blood," and both races scored much lower than whites on intelligence tests. Secretary of Labor James J. Davis, who had recently ordered all unemployed Latinos to leave the country a directive he had absolutely no authority to enforce, testified next. He explained that unrestricted Mexican migration to the United States had resulted in a sharp rise in unemployment in the previous two years.

Congress took one step toward controlling migration from south of the Rio Grande when it created the United States Border Patrol (USBP) in 1924. Before this agency took over the task, the only federal law officers patrolling America's borders were 75 agents of the Mounted Guards of the Immigration Service, in those days part of the Department of Labor. They rode along the Mexican border from Texas to California looking for Chinese workers who were trying to enter United States territory in violation of the 1882 Chinese Restriction Act. The Border Patrol began with 450 officers assigned to the Mexican and Canadian borders. Possible problems that might emerge in dealing with Spanish-speaking people did not seem to influence the selection process. One high-ranking agent expressed a view held by many English-speaking border residents: the people of Mexico and Latin America were "extremely pathetic specimens of the human race." Luckily, "nature has protected them by endowing them with the stupidity and apparent insensibility to pain [just like] a mule. . . . So, I regard the Mexican as a mere machine, or a clod of clay."[66]

Agricultural and migrant workers in Mexico averaged about 12 cents a day picking crops. Farmers in the United States paid as much as $1.25 for the same amount of work. One section of the 1924 immigration bill established a $10.00 fee for obtaining a visa. That fee seemed enormous to Latinos seeking to escape the grinding poverty of their native lands. This requirement dramatically increased the number of people who crossed the Rio Grande illegally. The Border Patrol estimated that more than 100,000 Latinos entered the United States in 1925 without purchasing a visa. When news of this reached Congress, it doubled the number of Border Patrol agents.

The immigration problem along the Mexican border grew worse every year despite the increase in Border Patrol officers. Eventually, farmers and patrol agents in the Southwest reached what they called a "gentlemen's agreement." It required Latino farm workers to register with the USBP, whether or not they entered the country legally, and then they would get an identification card that allowed them to work. The card cost $18.00, but the workers could buy it for $3.00 a week.

Congress reacted with fury when members learned about this unauthorized program. John Box, a rabidly anti-Mexican representative from Texas, called it "immigration on the installment plan" that allowed "blood-thirsty, ignorant bandits" cheap access to the United States where they were already threatening to become a majority of the population, at least in his home state.[67] The Labor Department reacted quickly to Congressional complaints and revoked the "agreement" only a few months after it had been negotiated. It ordered Border Patrol agents to collect the entire $18.00 at one time, more than one-third of a year's pay for many Latinos wishing to migrate.

Representative Box introduced a bill in 1926 imposing a quota system for Latino immigration. Big business and the powerful agricultural bloc in Washington, D.C. fought hard to defeat the Box Bill. The United States Steel Corporation fought vigorously to maintain an open border. During the war, it had recruited thousands of Mexican laborers to work in its mills to replace drafted steel workers. They worked hard and well and for less money than the people they replaced and they did not go on strike. Farmers and growers kept up their traditional opposition to any restriction on labor from south of the border and the Box Bill was defeated.

By 1929, illegal entry from Mexico reached its highest level of the decade, and Congress decided to double the size of the Border Patrol once again. Then the Great Depression hit and anti-immigrant attitudes grew as rapidly as unemployment rates. In 1930, the Immigration Service initiated a repatriation program that returned thousands upon thousands of Latin Americans to their homelands. Some lived here legally; many others were American citizens. Such things mattered little, and the point was to throw Latinos out so that more jobs would be available for "real Americans," the whites who had lost their jobs.

The growing political influence of Mexican Americans in the southwestern states was illustrated by the career of Octaviano Larrazolo (1859–1930). Voters in New Mexico elected him governor in 1918, and in 1928, he became the first American of Mexican descent to sit in the U.S. Senate. Born in Mexico, he came to the United States in 1871 intending to study for the priesthood. He changed his mind, however, and became a schoolteacher and later a principal in a small town in Texas. Larrazolo became increasingly upset at the mistreatment of Mexican Americans and decided to study law so that he could fight in the courts against prejudice and discrimination.

He moved to New Mexico in 1895 and joined the Democratic Party. After three straight losses for local offices, he quit the party, blaming it for lack of support, which he attributed to anti-Mexican hostility on the part of party leaders. In 1911, he switched to the Republican Party where he found similar hostility to the problems of Mexican citizens among the leadership. Nevertheless, he and several other Hispanic Republicans attended the New Mexico constitutional convention. Through their efforts, the new constitution outlawed all forms of discrimination and prohibited separate schools for Mexican students. Efforts to end segregated schools for African Americans failed, however.

In 1918, voters sent Larrazolo to the governor's mansion where he served a single term. He promoted bilingual education while governor, but the state legislature rejected this cause. As governor, he enacted laws that created the Child Welfare Board and the State Board of Health. He also supported an income tax bill despite opposition from his own party. The Republicans decided not to slate him for a new term in 1922. Later in the decade, he lost an election for the state supreme court, although he eventually served a term in the New Mexico House of Representatives. In 1928, he won a special election to fill out the remaining year of the term of Senator Andrieus A. Jones who had died in office. Because of his own illness, Larrazolo served in the Senate for only six months before he returned home and died on April 7, 1930. He continued his efforts to support the political and educational rights of Latinos until the end of his life.[68]

ASIAN AMERICANS

The Asian population of the United States had reached 332,432 according to the 1920 census. That total included 220,596 Japanese, 85,202 Chinese, 26,634 Filipinos, and 6,181 Koreans. Most of this population lived on the West Coast, with California having the largest Asian population of any state. Asians faced discrimination and mistreatment almost from their first arrival, and California led the way.

Beginning in the 1850s, with the arrival of several thousand Chinese laborers, a series of laws made life difficult and dangerous for Asians. Whites blamed the Chinese for taking away their jobs by working for much lower wages, stealing their land, and spreading disease. California's Constitution of 1879 made it a crime to employ Chinese workers in any state or local government jobs. Anti-Asian hostility grew so intense throughout the United States that Congress prohibited the immigration of Chinese workers for 10 years. The Exclusion Act of 1882 also denied citizenship to Chinese who had entered the United States at any time before passage of the legislation. Congress extended the law's provisions for another decade in 1892 and made them permanent 10 years later.

The Chinese were not the only Asians excluded from the United States. The "gentlemen's agreement" of 1907, negotiated by President Theodore Roosevelt and Japanese Foreign Minister Hayashi Tadasu, kept all Japanese from entering the United States and becoming citizens. Then in 1917, Congress created a "barred zone" denying entry to the United States to people living on the continent of Asia and included most of the islands of the Pacific Ocean, excluding only the Philippines and Hawaii because those islands belonged to the United States, and its people had certain rights under the U.S. Constitution.

These laws accomplished their goal—effectively keeping Asians out of the United States until the end of World War II. Those who had entered the country before passage of the laws could remain in the country but faced widespread discrimination. California passed a law in 1913 denying to "aliens ineligible for citizenship" the right to own land. Asians were the only Californians denied the right to become citizens, so this law was aimed only at them. By 1921, more than a dozen states, from Minnesota to Texas to Washington, followed California's initiative.[69]

California voters approved even tougher additions to the Alien Land Law by passing a ballot measure (Proposition 1) in 1920 that made it illegal to "sell or lease" any land to noncitizens (Asians). In addition, it prohibited the purchase of land with money "from an Asian alien." The California *Voter's Guide* explained that the law's "primary purpose is to prohibit Orientals who cannot become American citizens from controlling our rich agricultural lands. . . . Orientals and more particularly Japanese [have] commenced to secure control of agricultural lands in California." Seventy-five percent of the voters supported the proposition showing the intense anti-Asian racism felt by many of its citizens. Three years later, the Supreme Court of the United States upheld the constitutionality of the act in *Porterfield v. Webb* (1923).[70]

The Supreme Court issued a series of decisions in the 1920s supporting the notion that Asians should not become American citizens. The Court's key decision came in *Ozawa Takao v. the United States* (1922); in this case, a unanimous court declared that Takao, an American-born college student married to an American-educated Japanese woman who spoke only English, could not become an American citizen because he was not "white." The Court upheld a lower court ruling that Takao was "in every way eminently qualified under the statutes to become an American citizen" except for his race. The 1790 Naturalization Act limited citizenship to only aliens "being a free white person." Asians did not fall under that category, according to Justice George Sutherland writing for the Court, they were "clearly" not Caucasian—racially, in the jargon of the times, Asians belonged to the Mongoloid race.

The Court reiterated this view early in 1923 in *United States v. Bhagat Singh Thind*. Thind had been born in India, but he argued that people born in his native country (especially those of high caste such as he was) belonged to the white race and therefore were covered by the 1790 act. The Court rejected this claim despite expert testimony from an anthropologist who provided "scientific evidence" that Indians of Southwest Asia were part of the "Caucasian race." Justice Sutherland once more presented the Court's opinion and argued that in 1790 "white" referred only to immigrants from Great Britain, Ireland, and northern Europe. To defend this opinion, he referred to the view of the public, not to that of the expert. And "common people" in 1923 held that Indians were definitely not white. The "common man's" definition of white person should prevail; therefore, Thind was ineligible for citizenship because he was "not a white person."

Immigration authorities, Congress, state legislatures, and the courts went out of their way to make sure no Asian became a citizen. In 1923, the Naturalization Service revoked a certificate of naturalization it had previously granted Sergeant Major Tokutaro Nishimura Slocum, a severely wounded veteran of World War I. Asians could not become citizens even if they were critically wounded while fighting the enemies of the United States. Sergeant Slocum continued his fight and, in 1935, President Franklin Roosevelt signed a bill granting him citizenship along with 500 other Great War veterans of Asian ancestry.

When President Calvin Coolidge signed the Immigration Act of 1924 into law, it severely reduced immigration to the United States from everywhere by establishing a quota system based on a person's nationality. Every nation in the world, except Asian states, received a minimum quota of 100 people per year who could legally enter the United States. Asian nations received a quota of zero, as Congress reaffirmed the ban on immigrants from the barred zone. In response, the Japanese government called for a national day of mourning. Thousands of Japanese stood in silence in Tokyo and other cities on that day to protest American "racism."[71]

In the United States, Japanese Americans took no action, believing that any protest would probably go unheard anyway. Instead of political protest, they decided to put their money and their energy into educating their children and building their businesses. Then in a few years, their children would earn the respect of white Americans by achieving academic and economic success. Issei parents (those born in Japan) believed their Nisei children (those born in the United States), would quickly win acceptance into the mainstream of American society through hard work and effort. A few Issei wanted their children to receive a Japanese education and sent their children to Japan to learn about the culture of their ancestors, but a majority sent their children to American schools, segregated schools in California, Oregon, Washington, and other states with large Asian populations.

The movement for respect through educational achievement did not lead to acceptance. Highly educated Japanese mathematicians, engineers, scientists, and doctors had difficulty finding employment. Many times Nisei applicants were told to "go back to their own country" when they applied for jobs. Many highly educated Nisei professionals ended up working for Japanese-owned banks and businesses. A small group of college graduates in Seattle began talking about these problems and organized the American Loyalty League. They established a political committee to register Japanese Americans to vote. They advocated "One Hundred Percent Americanism" seeing super-patriotism as the quickest road to equal rights in America. By 1923, the League had virtually disappeared and no similar group appeared until 1930 when the Japanese American Citizens League (JACL) was born also in Seattle.

Chinese Americans faced conditions and attitudes similar to those that challenged the Japanese in the United States. White Americans saw little difference between the two groups; they only saw "Asians." The stereotypical Asian was unhealthy, unclean, and fiendishly criminal. "Orientals" spent their lives crowding into opium dens and gambled their lives and fortunes away. They did not intend to adopt American culture and American ways. Asians preferred to live in separate communities, whether in Chinatown, Koreatown, "Little Tokyo," or "Little Manila"; it made no difference. In these parts of the city, vicious gangs ("tongs") killed each other for no good reason; life was "cheap" in the Orient, a place where drug-addicted "coolies" wasted their lives away, and where prostitution and female slavery flourished. No wonder Asians were poor—they knew no other way of living.

Fewer than 6,200 Koreans lived in the United States in 1920, almost all of them in California. In 1923, a judge in Los Angeles ruled that Koreans were "of the Mongol family" and therefore could not become citizens. They could not become citizens, but they still had to work. Koreans worked in low-paying jobs in restaurants and as gardeners, janitors, and house cleaners; however, many others owned farms and picked crops. The Korean community rejected any alliances with other Asian groups. They preferred to remain quiet and accommodating. They remained extremely interested in events in their homeland. Korea was unique among Asian nations because the Japanese controlled it. They had conquered Korea in 1910 and almost immediately began to mistreat, enslave, and abuse its people. In the United States, signs in Korean-owned stores read simply, "We hate the Japanese; all Japanese."

Much like the Japanese, however, Korean parents stressed education for their children as the best road to success in America, but for a unique reason. Korean children educated in the United States, their parents hoped, would use their knowledge to return to the land of their ancestors and join the fight for independence from the hated Japan. In Korean communities, parents sent their sons to military training schools especially set up to prepare students for the "armed struggle" against the oppressors of their homeland. Hence, Koreans in the United States remained a small but united group, with that unity built on an intense hatred of the nation occupying their homeland.[72]

Another Asian group in the United States, Filipinos, confronted many of the same problems of prejudice and discrimination faced by the Japanese, Chinese, and Koreans but with one difference. The Philippine Islands, their homeland, belonged to the United States. Thus Filipinos did not qualify as "immigrants" and they could not be designated as "aliens." Filipinos coming to the United States called themselves *pinoys*. The majority worked picking fruits and vegetables in the fields of California. In 1920, about 27,000 Filipinos lived in the United States; most were young men. Like other peoples from Asia, they took the jobs white Americans would not take: picking cucumbers, lettuce, and tomatoes; washing dishes in restaurants; cleaning the houses of the wealthy; and working in Alaskan fish canneries. By the end of the decade, about 15 percent of agricultural workers in California were Filipinos.

Another much smaller group, the sons of wealthy Filipinos, did not come to work but attended colleges in the United States. These *pensionados* typically returned to their homeland after graduation and worked in various colonial offices of the American-controlled government.

Because their homeland was a territory of the United States, did Filipinos have the same rights as American citizens? This question caused much confusion. The Philippine Islands became a territory of the United States in the aftermath of the Spanish-American War of 1898 (as did Puerto Rico and Guam). The 1924 immigration bill defined Filipinos as "colonial subjects" of the United States. They were not covered by the various exclusion laws, or the "barred zone." They could not, however, buy land in states with Alien Land Laws, and in many states, as was true of other "Mongols," they could not marry whites. To make their status official, in 1930, a California state judge ruled that Filipinos belonged to the "Mongolian race."

"In many wars it was a crime to be a Filipino in California," wrote Carlos Bulason, a writer, labor organizer, and poet who eventually quit American society and returned to his homeland.[73] Farm laborers worked from 6:00 A.M. to 6:00 P.M. for less than $3.50 a day. They lived in filthy huts, for which they were charged high rents, and worked in dangerous jobs, without healthcare or any opportunity for education. The American Federation of Labor prohibited Filipinos (and other Asian) membership from joining their union affiliates. To make things worse, they faced constant discrimination. Because of a widespread belief concerning their "animalistic" urges, newspapers portrayed them as dangerous sexual predators always on the prowl for white women. Anti-Filipino riots struck Stockton, Dinuba, Fresno, and Watsonville, California in the late 1920s. The American Legion inspired and provoked the attacks in which Filipinos were beaten and sometimes killed, especially if they danced with white women.[74]

All Asians suffered from discrimination and prejudice. Asians in the United States made up less than 1 percent of the American population. They could not become citizens. They worked in the lowest paying jobs. They had little legal protection. The Supreme Court ruled that Asians belonged to an inferior race and barred them from citizenship. Congress prohibited Asians from immigrating to the United States. They lived in separate communities, whether "Chinatowns" or migrant labor camps, usually not by choice but because of local racist ordinances and attitudes. The "yellow peril" (bringing up images of the deadly yellow fever) threatened white American ideals and beliefs. Asians already in the United States were isolated from the rest of society, much like other people carrying a deadly disease. Despite these obstacles, many Asian families believed that whites would eventually accept them, or at least their children, as Americans, if they demonstrated their intelligence and ability to work hard. By the end of the decade, that dream still appeared a long way off.

LAW AND GOVERNMENT

AFRICAN AMERICANS

In 1923, the United States Supreme Court issued a major decision concerning the legal rights of African Americans in *Moore et al. v. Dempsey, Keeper of Arkansas Penitentiary* 262 U.S. 86. The case came out of a 1919 race riot in Arkansas during which 200 or more African Americans and five whites died. The state tried 12 black men for murdering the whites, and a jury found them guilty and sentenced them to death. During the trial, mobs of hostile whites surrounded the courthouse demanding death for the accused. Under appeal, NAACP lawyers presented evidence that the prosecution denied the defendants a habeas corpus hearing and that witnesses had been tortured to give false testimony against the accused. State courts and a federal court rejected that appeal. In a 6–2 decision, however, the U.S. Supreme Court overruled the lower courts and ordered a new hearing and a new trial. The "mob-dominated" atmosphere during the first trial violated the "due process" clause of the Fourteenth Amendment. It took another year but eventually Arkansas authorities released all 12 men from prison.

In *Corrigan v. Buckley* 271 U.S. 323 (1927), the Supreme Court took a step backward in promoting equal rights for all. It upheld a "restrictive covenant" agreement among white homeowners that prohibited them from selling their property to African Americans. After a white woman contracted to sell her home to a black family, she was brought to court for violating the agreement. The Court rejected her appeal saying that federal law did not cover private agreements. The Fourteenth Amendment prohibited discrimination by government agencies but did not apply to individuals. (In 1948, in *Shelby v. Kraemer* 334 U.S. 1, the Court reversed its 1927 decision upholding that such covenants were not legally enforceable.)

The Court in *Nixon v. Herndon* 273 U.S. 536 (1927) took a modest step toward improving voting rights when, in a unanimous decision (9–0), it ruled that a Texas law limiting voting in Democratic primaries to whites only was unconstitutional. Dr. Lawrence Aaron Nixon, who had paid his poll tax, brought the case after election officials had turned him away when he tried to vote in a primary election. The Court rejected the argument made by Texas that primaries were not state-run elections but private contests sponsored by private institutions—political parties—and thus not subject to federal law.

ASIAN AMERICANS

In general, federal and state laws and Supreme Court decisions removed the civil and legal rights of Asians bowing to the prejudices of white Americans. The Cable Act of 1922 took away the citizenship of women married to aliens ineligible for American citizenship, in other words all Asians. Women with European or African husbands would retain their citizenship but only if they divorced their spouse or their spouse died. Then in the same year in *Ozawa v. U.S.* 260 U.S. 178, the Supreme Court ruled that the Naturalization Act of 1790, which allowed only "free white persons" to become citizens, was constitutional. Therefore Ozawa Takao, who had been born in Japan but lived in California where he had graduated from high school and attended college, could not become a citizen. Asians were not white—meaning Caucasian according to the justices—so they were ineligible for citizenship under any circumstances. A few weeks later, it advanced anti-Asian discrimination in *United States v. Bhagat Singh Thind* 261 U.S. 204. The Court ruled that Thind, a native of India, could not be naturalized because he was not white, contradicting the scientific experts who testified that Indians belonged to the Caucasian race. The justices determined that the "common man," not scientists or anthropologists, defined the meaning of "white." The principle that the "understanding of the common man" prevailed among the justices; hence natives of India were Asian, and they could not become citizens under the 1790 Naturalization Act.

The Court addressed the Alien Land Laws in three cases, each time affirming the right to discriminate. In *Terrace v. Thompson* 263 U.S. 197, *Porterfield v. Webb, Attorney General of California,* 263 U.S. 225, and *Webb v. O'Brien* 263 U.S. 225, the justices upheld the right of states to enforce Alien Land Laws. "No constitutional right of the alien is infringed," the court concluded because states had "wide discretion" in determining who could or could not own property. If they wanted to discriminate based on race, they had that right. Then, in another decision defining the meaning of "white," the Court reaffirmed a limited view of that term. In *Gong Lum v. Rice* 275 U.S. 323, a Chinese couple in Mississippi sued the state because it would not let their daughter attend a "whites' only" school. The Supreme Court ruled in favor of the state, defending the idea that anyone of the "yellow race" was "colored" and therefore not eligible to attend a "white" school.

EUROPEAN AMERICANS

The laws aimed at immigration had their greatest impact on Europeans wanting to come to America. For the most part, Congress made it difficult for anyone to enter the United States. The once open door policies on immigration ended in 1921: Congress passed and President Warren G. Harding signed the first bill limiting immigration to the United States on the basis of ethnicity. The Emergency Immigration Act established a quota system—based on nationality—for the nations of Europe, the Middle East, Africa, and the southwest Pacific (Australia and New Zealand). China, Japan, Korea, and India remained within a "barred zone." Congress continued the total ban on immigration from Asia. The law excluded Canada, Mexico, and other nations in the Western Hemisphere from the quota system. Because farmers in the United States relied heavily on cheap labor from these countries and Spanish- and French-speaking migrant workers played an important role in keeping American food prices low, these immigrants faced no restrictions. The Act gave special preference to relatives of American citizens and the commissioner of immigration had the authority to make sure that family unity remained a priority in deciding who could enter the United States. Congress extended the Emergency Act in 1922 for two more years before adopting even tougher restrictions in 1924.

In a rare victory for freedom of choice and the right to privacy, the Supreme Court in *Meyer v. Nebraska* 262 U.S. 390 (1923) struck down a 1918 Nebraska law that prohibited the teaching of any modern language other than English in public schools. A product of the anti-German hysteria of World War I, the law, according to the Court, violated the liberty of parents who "privately and alone" could determine what language their children should speak or learn.

Then in 1924, Congress passed the most restrictive immigration bill in American history. The National Origins Act, also called the Quota Immigration Act, limited the total number of legal immigrants to the United States to 164,447 per year. Each "nationality" would be restricted to no more than 2 percent of that group's population in the United States as of the 1890 census. Use of that census as a benchmark severely limited immigration from Italy, Poland, and Eastern Europe, as mass migration from those places did not begin until the mid-1890s. Supporters of restricting immigration wanted to keep these people out of America because "scientific evidence" presented during committee hearings by eugenic scientists proved the biological and mental inferiority of southern and Eastern Europeans. Congress maintained open borders for migrants from Mexico and Canada.

The U.S. Supreme Court approved sterilization in *Buck v. Bell* (1927). "Buck" was Carrie Buck, a 19-year-old Virginian, and Bell was John H. Bell, superintendent of the Virginia Colony for Epileptics and Feeble-minded. Carrie Buck, according to Bell, qualified for sterilization because she was the "probable potential parent of socially inadequate offspring." She already had one child who a Red Cross nurse testified was of "below average" intelligence and "not quite normal."

In its argument before a lower court, the state of Virginia said that Buck came from a family of "the shiftless, ignorant, and worthless class of anti-social whites of the South." Her mother, Emma, had a criminal record and the police had arrested her several times for prostitution; she also probably had syphilis. After hearing this evidence, the judge ordered that the authorities had the right to sterilize Carrie to prevent her from giving birth to more children that were "defective." After a series of appeals, the Court ruled 8–1 that Carried Buck met the definition of "feeble-minded" and "promiscuous" and that it was in the interest of the health and safety of the people of Virginia to have her sterilized. Judge Oliver Wendell Holmes wrote the majority opinion. Although one judge, Pierce Butler, dissented from the majority, he chose not to write an opinion.

Holmes's opinion concluded: "It is better for all the world, if instead of waiting to execute degenerate offspring for crime, or to let them starve for their imbecility, society can prevent those who are manifestly unfit from continuing their kind." He ended with the pronouncement that "three generations of imbeciles are enough." Doctors at the state colony operated on Carrie Buck. A few years later, she received a parole and worked as a domestic servant until her death in 1983. Apparently, neither Carrie Buck nor her daughter Vivian was feeble-minded or morally degenerate. Carrie had not been promiscuous. A nephew of her stepparents had raped her. They then confined Carrie to the state hospital for shaming the family by getting pregnant out of wedlock. She would not be allowed to do that again, her stepfather explained, as he signed her admission papers. The Supreme Court ruling affected many more people than Carrie Buck, however, because in Virginia alone state medical authorities authorized more than 8,300 sterilizations until the operations stopped in the 1970s.[75]

In 1942, the Supreme Court ruled again on sterilization in *Skinner v. Oklahoma* (316 U.S. 535). This time, however, the court tossed out an Oklahoma law that called for sterilization. Under its provisions, the Oklahoma Habitual Criminal Sterilization Act of 1935 called for the sterilization of persons convicted of three "felonies involving moral turpitude." Jack Skinner had been arrested three times, twice for stealing chickens and the last time for armed robbery. In a unanimous decision, the Court ruled that the law violated Skinner's rights because a clause in the act excluded sterilization as a punishment for persons convicted of "embezzlement or political offenses." That exclusion violated the equal protection clause of the Fourteenth Amendment. In all other respects, the punishment for embezzlement or taking bribes to pass a law (or other "political offenses") was no different from the penalty for larceny and burglary. Why single out the latter two crimes for a punishment as devastating and irreversible as sterilization but exclude embezzlement, the Court wondered. No valid reason for that distinction existed, so the judges declared the Oklahoma statute unconstitutional.

NATIVE AMERICANS

Congress provided badly needed money to improve the health and education of Indians living on reservations in the 1921 Snyder Act. With better healthcare and schooling, congressional supporters hoped, Native Americans would quickly become "civilized." Later investigations found that even this increased spending failed to improve living conditions on the reservations.

The General Citizenship Act made all Native Americans citizens of the United States if they had not already attained that status by other means. Indians could now vote in federal elections (and pay taxes), but several western states still prohibited them from voting in state and local elections. Citizenship had little impact on the difficult lives faced by many Native Americans.

MEDIA AND MASS COMMUNICATIONS

African American newspapers in the United States grew dramatically in circulation in the 1920s, led by Georgia-born Robert Abbott's (1870–1940) *Chicago Defender*. Between 1917 and 1930, its number of readers grew from 90,000 to almost 300,000 weekly. More than half of the paper's readers lived outside of Chicago, many in the South. During the decade Abbott continued to attack segregation, racism, lynching, and disfranchisement in the South. Even after the 1919 race riot in his city, he continued to advocate that blacks abandon the South and move to the North where opportunities for a better life existed.

Another major black-owned northern newspaper, the *Pittsburgh Courier*, had a circulation of 100,000 in the 1920s. It became one of the first newspapers to have a national readership. By the 1930s, it published editions in 12 states around the country including Louisiana and Texas. It took a steadfast stance against racism everywhere. The paper's editor and publisher, North Carolina-born Robert Lee Vann (1879–1940), denounced lynching and racism but also offered advice to his readers on resolving financial problems, how to improve their children's education, and which movies to see. A third important paper was the New York City-based *Amsterdam News*. Its founder (in 1909) and editor James Anderson adopted a militant stance against racism. He called on blacks to defend themselves rather than meekly accepting discrimination, which he charged the NAACP and Urban League with advocating. By the end of the 1920s, the paper's circulation reached more than 100,000, even though it criticized blacks in Harlem and across the United States for their apathy.

From 1920 to 1930, the most influential African American magazines were the NAACP's *The Crisis: A Record of the Darker Races*, edited by W.E.B. Du Bois, and the National Urban League's *Opportunity: A Journal of Negro Life*, edited by black sociologist Charles S. Johnson. The NAACP had established *The Crisis* in 1910 to instruct black people on the problems of lynching and racial violence, as well as to be a forum for African American social and political thought. In the 1920s, Du Bois began sponsoring monthly literary prizes for emerging black writers in 1921 and also published *Brownies' Book*, a magazine for children. *The Crisis* literary editor and novelist Jesse Fauset helped launch the Harlem Renaissance by publishing stories, plays, and poems by Langston Hughes, Jean Toomer, Claude McKay, and Countee Cullen. At the beginning of the decade, *The Crisis* had a circulation of about 50,000, but by 1930 that readership had dropped to about 13,000, probably because of the economic impact of the Great Depression. Many readers simply could not afford the subscription rate by this time.

The Urban League's monthly magazine made its debut in January 1923. Under Johnson's direction, *Opportunity* quickly gained a readership almost as large as *The Crisis*. Its prizes for literature and poetry, first awarded in 1924, helped spark the Renaissance. Johnson believed that publishing distinguished works of art and literature would help bring an end to racism and inequality. In 1928, *Opportunity* had a circulation of about 11,000, the highest it had achieved. The magazine sold for 15 cents a copy and during the Depression changed its focus from literature to economic development for African Americans.

A third magazine specifically aimed at an African American audience, the proudly socialist *Messenger*, did not survive the 1920s. Edited by labor leader A. Philip Randolph, the "World's Greatest Negro Monthly," as he subtitled it, criticized *Crisis* and *Opportunity* for being too moderate in their goals and too cowardly in calling for an end to segregation. Although founded in 1917, *The*

Messenger published regularly every month only from 1921 to 1928 and then went out of business. Randolph stressed politics over literature, although beginning in 1925 he began devoting more space to art and theater. His goal continued to be the creation of a strong socialist movement in the United States. The magazine boasted 100,000 subscribers at the beginning of the decade but folded in 1928 because of growing financial problems. Its primary contribution to the Harlem Renaissance was its uncompromising call for militant opposition to inequality in American society.

The radio series *Sam 'n' Henry* made its first appearance in January 1926. Two years later, it transformed into the more famous *Amos 'n' Andy* and became one of the most popular shows of the era. Created by Freeman Gosden and Charles Correll, the broadcasts shared one feature with minstrel shows of the 1880s—both were shows about blacks created by white men for white audiences. Gosden and Correll came from North Carolina and moved to Chicago to work on radio shows. Their show about "colored folks," as they described it, became enormously successful, reaching an audience of 40 million nightly listeners (at a time when about 120 million people lived in the United States). The show captured almost three-quarters (74 percent) of the national radio audience.

The white creators acted most of the parts and used an accent that many of their audience considered "black." The cast of characters included the whole range of African American stereotypes. George "Kingfish" Stephens represented one type of "coon," as he schemed endlessly trying to find a way to get rich without having to work too hard. He was loud, bumbling, and stupid. Amos is the Uncle Tom type, wise, philosophical, and long-suffering. Andy Brown usually helped The Kingfish find some way of tricking people out of their money. He would rather be fishing and drinking beer, or eating watermelon than doing anything else. The NAACP, which issued several complaints about the show, found two characters particularly offensive, "Lightning," the Stepin Fetchit twin and the slow-as-molasses janitor, was the most demeaning character in the cast with the possible exception of Calhoun "the lawyer." The NAACP bitterly attacked the portrayal of "Negro lawyers . . . as slippery cowards, ignorant of their profession and without ethics." "Mammy" actually appears twice, as the character Sapphire, Kingfish's wife, and as her mother, called simply "Mama" in the show. Both women constantly yell and scream at the Kingfish, reminding him how useless and ridiculous his get-rich-quick schemes are.[76]

Amos 'n' Andy never addressed the problems of racism, segregation, and prejudice in American society. Even though the characters allegedly lived in Harlem, they inhabited a world unknown to the New Negroes struggling for political rights, freedom, and social equality. Many blacks expressed outrage at how they were portrayed in the media. When Stepin Fetchit appeared before an all-black audience during World War II, they booed him off the stage. The black-owned Pittsburgh *Courier* launched a petition campaign in 1931 to remove *Amos 'n' Andy* from the air. It received several hundred thousand signatures, but nothing came of the effort. The show remained the most popular in its time slot for a dozen more years. Its white audience loved the message: racism and second-class citizenship did not exist. The African American population lived happy, if sometimes mildly troubled, lives, just like everybody else. They hated to work, were quite stupid, and talked with a very funny, mumble-mouthed dialect. White Americans therefore had nothing to fear; race relations were fine because blacks showed no signs of suffering from prejudice, degradation, and many years of second-class treatment by white society.

EUROPEAN AMERICANS

Stereotypes of European ethnic groups filled newspapers in the 1920s. The press filled the public mind with images of dangerous, radical immigrants beginning with the Sacco and Vanzetti trial in 1921. The judge and the prosecutor resorted to every negative stereotype they could find to convince the jury that the accused were Italian "aliens" who had no intention of becoming American citizens. The prosecution encouraged the jury to disregard any testimony from defense witnesses mainly because they were "Italians" and their words could not be trusted. Presiding Judge Webster Thayer demonstrated an intense hatred for Italians throughout the trial. Boston newspapers echoed his views and crusaded for the death penalty throughout the trial. The image of the crazed, bomb-carrying "agitators" from Italy remained in the American mind for years after this trial. The 1920s also introduced the "Italian mobster" image into American society. Although gangsters came from every ethnic group, Al Capone became the most famous and richest mobster of them all. His name left a lasting impression on the public because he killed more and destroyed more than any other gangster of his time. The alleged connection between Italians and crime received a further boost from the eugenics movement, which presented statistical evidence to Congress that Italians had a higher rate of imprisonment than any other European group.

German Americans had a difficult time recovering from the assault on their loyalty during World War I. Images of "The Hun," the savage pack of brutal killers who had raped their way through Belgium, proved hard to forget. The German stereotype had a positive side to it, however. Even before the war, Americans had respected Germans for their intelligence, discipline, and cultural achievements. American students seeking the best universities in Europe went to Germany. For many Americans, Germany served as the center of European science, philosophy, and music. Then the war came and the image changed rapidly. A more positive view gradually replaced the Hun image, as illustrated by Congress's decision to give Germany a high quota of immigrants under the 1924 Immigration Restriction Act. For German Americans, however, the more positive profile they received in the press had little impact. The vast majority had been so frightened by the anti-German hysteria of the war years that they did everything they could to hide any public displays of ethnic identity.

Army IQ tests given to recruits during the war had a devastating impact on the image of Poles and other East European groups. Their relatively low scores on the tests gave rise to the notion that they were less intelligent than the German, Scandinavian, and English test-takers. But the groups that suffered the most from negative stereotypes in the decade were American and European Jews. Anti-Semitism had a long history in the United States, but it took a particularly ugly form in the 1920s. Much of the renewed hostility toward Jews came from *The Dearborn Independent*, a Michigan newspapers owned, published, and edited by the great auto magnate Henry Ford.

From 1920 to 1922, Ford conducted an unending campaign of hate through publication of pamphlets, books, and editorials condemning Jews for almost every wrong that affected civilization. The *Independent* had subscribers around the world, including a young Austrian war veteran named Adolf Hitler. (After becoming German chancellor in 1933, Hitler placed a photograph of Ford on his office wall.) Hatred of Jews in Ford's paper and in many other parts of the United States increased after the Communists took over Russia in 1917. *The Independent* called the new communist government of Russia "the present Jewish government of Russia." Jews and Communists worked together, and more Communists lived in the United States than in the Soviet Union, Ford wrote, seeking the destruction of private property and capitalism. Both groups advocated powerful unions, according to the auto manufacturer, and wanted to bring Communist terror to America.

In 1920, Ford published *The International Jew*, a collection of essays that accused Jews of controlling the world's banks, secretly conspiring to destroy Christian civilization, and taking over American public schools so they could twist the minds of American children into accepting "communistic ideas." When sales of his cars started to decline in 1927, Ford issued an "apology" to Jews for his previous attacks and he stopped publication of *The Independent*. His publishing company continued to send out anti-Jewish books, however, and he never apologized for that.[77]

NATIVE AMERICANS

Once again, the media presented severely contrasting views of an ethnic group: good Indians or bad Indians filled newspapers, magazines, and films. "Good Indians" had appeared in books and literature almost since the time Columbus first described the people he met on his first voyage in 1492. This stereotype came down through times as the "noble savage." They lived with nature and rejected the hard-driving and vulgar materialistic values of whites. They had an "inner peace" unknown to Europeans or Americans because of their direct contact with the gods of creation. In the Jazz Age, this image attracted poets and artists who felt lost in the world of business and banking.

A film by Robert Flaherty, *Nanook of the North* (1922), captured the "noble savage" image in the person of Nanook, an Inuit (Eskimo) hunter. The documentary followed Nanook through blizzards and ice fields in his struggle for daily existence. The manly struggle against the elements for food and shelter, amidst the purity of the Arctic snows, contrasted greatly with the day-to-day lives of office workers in noisy, congested cities. The noble savage provided an image through which victims of modern progress—people tied to their desks and machines—could escape into a free, primitive environment. The positive Indian stereotype gave Americans an alternate world into which they could escape for a dime or less.[78]

Future Commissioner of Indian Affairs John Collier preferred Pueblo life to anything he experienced as a social worker in New York City. He saw the communal lifestyle of Pueblo Indians as a model for reforming American society. "Only the Indians," he wrote, "were still the possessors and users of the fundamental secret of human life—the secret of building great personality through the instrumentality of social institutions."[79]

"Bad Indians," on the other hand, dominated popular culture in the 1920s. Native Americans can be lazy, drunk, and degraded, while living on government handouts. Unlike the past generations, Indians no longer appeared as dangerous, wild, war-loving, savages in real life, but in movies this image prevailed. The United States Army had confined Indians on reservations by 1890, so whites no longer needed to fear them. Their population continued to decline, however, from alcoholism and other diseases, and many still stubbornly refused to enter the modern world. In the press, when Indians received coverage, the stories emphasized the "degraded savage" and their troubles because the "noble savage" had disappeared. As investigations of reservation life would eventually show, reservation life was indeed terrible for most Native Americans.

The media hit Indians with two negative stereotypes in the 1920s. In movies, they often came across as hostile and violent with painted faces. Photographs of Indians in blankets and feathered headdresses made them look like "exotic savages." They always made war or danced the war dance or appeared with war paint on their faces—a brutal, nasty people. Investigations of reservation life depicted a people on the verge of disappearing because of their weakness for alcohol and addiction to violence. They were poor and diseased yet they still danced, which upset officials in the all-white Office of Indian Affairs in Washington, D.C.

In a heavily reported story, Commissioner of Indian Affairs Charles Burke began a campaign in 1923 to limit traditional dances on the reservations to one each month. The office also prohibited anyone less than 50 years old from being present or taking part in the dances. Reservation superintendents and missionaries needed to devise a "propaganda" campaign against the dances. The "moral welfare" of Indians depended on this action. In a directive given to all Indians, Burke explained what they needed to do, "What I want you to think about very seriously is that you must first of all try to make your own living, which you cannot do unless you work faithfully and take care of what comes from your labor and go to dances or other meetings only when your home work will not suffer by it." He then encouraged them to stop doing "evil or foolish things," such as the dance performances that wasted their time and energy.[80]

The conflict between "good Indians" and "bad Indians" symbolized the vast division between defenders of Indian culture and those who believed that only if Indians learned white ways would they survive. An official with the Office of Indian Affairs explained to the *New York Times* that unless Indians adopted American ways quickly they were doomed. "Thousands of these people are still in a state of quasi barbarism . . . Civilization has barely breathed on many of them." On one point, however, advocates of both positions could agree: Indians were childlike and innocent. They filled their days with "worry and childlike confusion," a critic of Indian dancing wrote.[81] Defenders of traditional dances concluded that these "children of nature" needed to retain their ways and ceremonies, if only to protect them from the real savagery of the outside (white) world of buying and selling. "Good" or "bad" Indian stereotypes both stood in the way of accepting Native Americans as mature, interesting people who had as much to offer white society, in terms of values, ideas, and equality, as white society had to offer them.

LATINOS

The *siesta* stereotype appeared frequently in American mass media when Hispanics appeared in the press or the movies. Hispanics allegedly slept two hours every afternoon and they were lazy, ignorant, and corrupt. Images from the Mexican Revolution (1911–1920) also appeared frequently, especially in the forms of Pancho Villa and Emiliano Zapata. More often than not, these images showed them as vicious, dirty, rebellious, and cruel bandits riding through the countryside rather than the revolutionary heroes they were hailed as in their homelands. American newspapers used terms such as *greaser, bandito*, and *macho* when referring to people from south of the Rio Grande.

Hispanic men and women filled a more romantic role in the movies. Here, the "Latin lover" model was Luis Antonio Damaso Alonso, otherwise known as Gilbert Roland (1905–1994), who first appeared in 1927 in *Camille* with Norma Talmadge, one of the most successful white stars of the silent screen era. Ramon Novarro (1899–1968), born Jose Ramon Gil Samaniegos, another of the Latin lovers, became even more popular than Roland. The star of successful films such as *The Prisoner of Zenda* (1923), *The Arab* (1924), and *Ben-Hur* (1926), Novarro like his friend the Italian-born (and much more famous) Rudolph Valentino had the dark-haired, dark-eyed, exotic look that producers and audiences found so romantic next to European blondes such as Greta Garbo. The source of moviegoer's fascination with Hispanic leading-men remains a mystery, although it might have been related to an interest in interracial love. Dark-skinned but definitely not black, Latin lovers provided a touch of the illicit and in some places illegal contact between men and women of different colors.

Latin American women also appeared as very romantic characters in the movies of the 1920s. Many movie fans considered Dolores Del Rio (1905–1983), born Lolita Dolores Martinez Asunsolo Lopez Negrete in Mexico, the most glamorous of the Hispanic stars of the era. As with Latin lovers, Hispanic actresses had that dark-skinned, exotic allure that appealed to mainly white audiences. The

Latin "spitfire" stereotype she played in movies beginning in *Joanna* (1925) and continuing through *The Whole Town's Talking* and *The Loves of Carmen* (1928) reassured white-Anglo viewers that those Spanish women, at least the upper class ones, acted in ways (usually overtly sexual) that white women would never consider doing. Hispanics were not pure, but *they* were! Unfortunately, some of Del Rio's performances proved so insulting to Hispanics that countries from Mexico to Argentina banned them.[82]

CULTURAL SCENE

THE HARLEM RENAISSANCE

In the 1920s, African American art and literature flourished during the Harlem Renaissance as the decade witnessed the emergence of the "New Negro." During this time the term signified pride and dignity and signaled a declaration of independence from white ideas about art, politics, history, music, and literature. Several new organizations emerged, such as the National Urban League and the Brotherhood of Sleeping-Car Porters and Maids (the first major independent black union), to join the NAACP in the fight for equal rights.

"Renaissance" means "rebirth" in French, and Harlem refers to the two-square mile section of New York City that became the center of the revival of African American culture. Leaders of the Renaissance, especially poet and journalist Langston Hughes along with novelist Claude McKay and the philosopher Alain Locke, believed that they had the job of explaining and illuminating "the Negro condition in America." They also believed that producing great literature and music would help convince whites that African Americans were their equals in all aspects of life and thereby deserved respect and acceptance into the community of Americans.[83]

Jean Toomer, born Nathan Pinchback Toomer in Washington, D.C. (1894–1967), a light-skinned black, produced the first great novel of the Renaissance, *Cane*, in 1923. Although it sold fewer than 500 copies, this mystical portrait of six southern women passing through a dying society, while black people in the North seek new life and hope, received glowing reviews from critics. One critic called it "a book of gold" and celebrated Toomer as a "bright morning star of a new day of the race in literature." Toomer, however, rejected his labeling as a "Negro" writer and told his publisher to "never use such a word" again. Toomer never published again throughout his life. He moved to New Mexico where he became involved in Native American religion.[84]

Countee Cullen (1903–1946) is remembered mainly for his poetry, although he also produced a novel, several plays, and children's books. He graduated from New York University and earned a master's degree in English and French from

Harvard. He published his first volume of poetry, *Color*, in 1925. As the title indicates, most of the poems concerned racial subjects, specifically the African experience in the United States. Cullen wanted to be known as a poet—his favorites were John Keats and Lord Byron—not a "Negro poet," and his second volume, *Copper Sun* (1927), dealt mainly with themes of love and loss. The next year he received a fellowship to study in Paris where he produced *The Ballad of a Brown Girl* (1928), dedicated to his future wife Nina Yolande Du Bois, daughter W.E.B. Du Bois, the famous black sociologist, historian, and editor of the NAACP's monthly magazine *The Crisis: A Record of the Darker Races*. The marriage lasted less than two years because Nina sued for divorce after learning that her husband was mainly attracted to men. He eventually married again (in 1940) and continued to write poetry until his death (from high blood pressure) in 1946. From 1934 until his death, he taught English and French at a predominantly white New York City high school.[85]

Langston Hughes (1902–1967), born James Mercer Langston Hughes, became known as the dean of Negro writers. Born in Joplin, Missouri, Hughes came to New York City in 1921 to study engineering at Columbia University. Although only 19 years old, he had already written many poems (including "The Negro Speaks of Rivers," one of his most famous poems), taught school in Mexico, and had learned German and Spanish. After dropping out of school, he spent three years in Paris before returning to his mother's house in Washington, D.C. Many of his poems first appeared in *The Crisis* and *Opportunity*, the magazine of the National Urban League. His first volume of poetry, *The Weary Blues*, appeared in 1926 followed the next year by *Fine Clothes for a Jew*. Hughes believed he should be considered a "Negro poet" who had to raise his voice against racism and prejudice.[86] His goal in writing was to uplift the lives of African Americans by celebrating their culture and history. During his life, he published 16 books of poetry, 2 novels, and 30 plays along with much more including children's books and a weekly newspaper column.

Many of the intellectuals associated with the Renaissance appeared in a special issue of *Survey Graphic: The Magazine of Social Interpretation* devoted to "Harlem: Mecca of the New Negro." Edited by Alain Locke (1886–1954), a Howard University philosophy professor, it included poetry, literature, photography, and historical and political essays. "Youth speaks, and the voice of the New Negro is heard," Locke wrote.

This younger generation could depict "a spiritual wealth" for black people, "which if they can properly expound will be ample for a new judgment and reappraisal of the race."[87] The essays were devoted to explaining and interpreting African American culture and psychology.

A division between the politically oriented "old guard" and the younger advocates of black art and culture for its own sake broke into the open by the end of the decade. The civil rights "elite," led by W.E.B. Du Bois, argued that the right to vote, adequate housing, and jobs were more important for most of the black population than great art or literature. Du Bois's reaction to Claude McKay's

Home to Harlem (1928) typified this attitude. McKay's realistic portrait of life in the ghetto, and the life of a dining-car attendant on the New York Central Railroad, became the first bestseller in the United States written by a black American (McKay came from Jamaica); it made Du Bois feel "like taking a bath."[88] Du Bois felt that portraying the lives of the "debauched tenth" only hurt the drive for constitutional rights led by the people he referred to as the "talented tenth," the doctors, lawyers, professors, and scientists leading the struggle against racism.

Langston Hughes tried to bring the two generations together in an essay he wrote for *The Nation*, a white magazine of liberal opinion. He argued that whether or not white society found black culture acceptable was irrelevant. "If white people are pleased, we are glad. If colored people are pleased, we are glad. If they are not, their displeasure doesn't matter either."[89] Only an art that captured "the spirit of the race" and uplifted its people mattered, he explained. Literature and art had to express the real conditions faced by the masses of men and women, however vulgar and violent their lives might be. "Negro" life had to be depicted as it was lived; art was not created for the pleasure of an elite audience; it had to explore the consequences of discrimination and despair and examine how people triumphed over those evils.[90]

The Harlem Renaissance produced many other great artists and writers including novelist Jesse Fauset; writer, folklorist, and anthropologist Zora Neal Hurston; muralist Aaron Douglas; and painters Archibald Motley and Palmer Hayden. In music, jazz became the most powerful expression of New Negro culture and experience. Bands led by Louis Armstrong, Fletcher Henderson, Chick Webb, Cab Calloway, Fess Williams, and Duke Ellington, along with singers such as Ella Fitzgerald, Billie Holiday, Bessie Smith, Sarah Vaughan, and Ethel Waters, created music that reflected the pain, energy, and struggle toward freedom that exemplified the black experience in the United States.[91]

To think, however, that great art and music would reduce racial hatred in America or would improve the economic and political lives of the 15 million blacks in the United Stated proved to be an unrealistic expectation. Even the greatest black poets, bandleaders, novelists, philosophers, and civil rights leaders faced prejudice and discrimination wherever they traveled in their homeland. The Renaissance saw a rebirth of art, music, and literature, but it had little impact on equality and justice.

The movies of the decade portrayed blacks as Uncle Tom, the Coon, the pickaninny, Uncle Remus, or the Mammy Movies with an Uncle Tom figure showed a black man, usually dressed as a butler or a household servant, who was happy, submissive to whites, long-suffering but still smiling, gentle, kind, self-sacrificing, and properly courteous and respectful to women (especially white women of all ages and types).

"Coons" filled the movies and the airwaves. They were ignorant, lazy, crazy, goggle-eyed fools who wasted their lives away playing dice. They ate watermelon, stole chickens, and talked in a long, lazy drawl while longing for the "good old days when 'massa' took care of his poor old darkies." In other words, the nineteenth-century stereotype of Jim Crow—the minstrel show's happy slave who delighted white audiences by showing just how dumb (but always with an intoxicating happiness shining through his big white teeth and red lips) and childlike whites hoped African American males really were. One difference existed between the Jim Crow character and the movie-made reincarnation—a white man played Jim Crow in the nineteenth century; a black actor portrayed him in the twentieth century. One actor set the standard for this degrading stereotype and he got very rich doing it.

Lincoln Theodore Monroe Andrew Perry (his mother named him after four American presidents) portrayed the image of the "white man's black" so successfully that his stage name, Stepin Fetchit (originally he appeared on stage with a horse in an act called Step—the horse's name—and Fetch It—as he called himself), became a synonym for inferiority and slavishness. Billed as "Stepin Fetchit, the World's Laziest Man," he captured the hearts of an American audience ready to laugh at a half-brained nitwit. He represented what many viewers saw as an inferior race. Lincoln Perry and his imitators (African American actors such as Willie Best and Mantan Moreland) reinforced that degrading view over and over again. Luckily, they could still smile, roll their eyes, smack their lips, and dance no matter what degrading things happened to them. They had no self-respect or dignity and white audiences loved them for that reason. They fit the desired image of black Americans: they were dumb, lazy, and ignorant, and no one needed to fear them. Perry became the highest paid African American in Hollywood where he drove around in a pink Rolls Royce.[92]

The pickaninny represented a subcategory of the "coon." Portrayed by a black child with kinky hair, big eyes, and not much of a brain, "Buckwheat," a character in the dozens of "Our Gang" comedies of the silent and early sound picture era perfectly fit this stereotype. Harmless, blissfully ignorant, and hardly aware of events going on around him, Buckwheat reinforced the view that years of discrimination, prejudice, and segregation had no impact on African American children—if anything it just made them funny to look at and to hear (once sound came onto the scene). Even funnier, his hair stood on end when he got scared, which happened quite frequently. A third type of happy-go-lucky "coon" appeared in the person of Uncle Remus. Harmless, friendly, and wise, this elderly ex-slave had suffered through years of demeaning slavery only to emerge as an amusing teller of philosophical tales.[93]

Black women in film and popular culture, even before the 1939 classic *Gone with the Wind*, filled two roles: "Mammy" or Maid. In the 1920s, few black women appeared in the movies. Still, the image of Aunt Jemima (according to one survey one of the 10 most recognizable product images in the world) filled both stereotypes. She became the symbol of Quaker Oats pancake mixes in 1926, although her career as the stereotypical black servant or slave dates back to the 1890s. Based on a minstrel show character, the always smiling black woman with the red kerchief over her hair clearly was the happy slave toiling away in the kitchen. As with other black images in 1920s' movies and advertisements,

Stepin Fetchit in *Hearts in Dixie*, 1929. © 20th Century-Fox. Courtesy of 20th Century-Fox/Photofest.

the slave experience had no impact on her life except to make her happier and more motherly. The message delivered by her face on the box said quite plainly that black women belonged in the kitchen. As the copy on one add informed its readers, Aunt Jemima learned her recipe for pancakes "on the Old Plantation" and she had not changed it a bit. (Her close relative "Uncle Ben" did not appear on rice boxes until 1943, but the smile on the face and the servant's bowtie and red jacket said the same thing: blacks are happy serving white people; the sting, pain, and humiliation of slavery and second-class citizenship are gone.)[94]

NATIVE AMERICANS

Indian literature in the 1920s centered on two women writers, Gertrude Simmons Bonnin (1876–1938) and Mourning Dove (1888–1936). No movement or revival identified these novelists, although they stressed similar ideas and themes that gave birth to a modern Native American literature.

Gertrude Bonnin, or Zitkala-Sa (Red Bird) in her native Lakota, published *American Indian Stories* in 1921. Born to a white father and Indian mother on the Yankton Sioux Reservation in South Dakota, she lived there with her mother, Ellen Simmons, known as Tate Iyohiwin (Reaches for the Wind) until the age of eight. She then attended a Quaker mission school in Indiana before transferring to Earlham College in that state and then the New England Conservatory of Music in Boston. After graduation, she taught at the Carlisle Indian Industrial School in Pennsylvania (whose motto was "We must kill the savage to save the man") for one year before returning to her reservation. Here she witnessed the unhappiness of her mother who had begun to hate white civilization and the great hardships it had imposed on Indian people.

Zitkala-Sa turned to writing and political action to save her people. Her next book, *American Indian Stories,* appeared in 1921 and tells about her life on the reservation and the immense difficulties Indian children faced when they were placed in boarding schools. On the reservation, she and children like her lived with people they loved and trusted. At the schools, they encountered teachers who believed their job was to destroy all aspects of the "savage" culture they came from so that they could fully participate in American society. Zitkala-Sa rejected this assimilationist ideal and turned to the fight for self-determination for her people.

In 1923, she led an investigation, funded by the General Federation of Women's Clubs, into the mistreatment, murder, and abuse of Native Americans on the oil-rich lands of Oklahoma. Her report, *Oklahoma's Poor Rich Indians: An Orgy of Graft and Exploitation of the Five Civilized Tribes, Legalized Robbery* (1924), created a stir in the press and led to a congressional investigation into the poverty and exploitation she found on the reservations she visited. In 1926, she founded the National Council of American Indians to lead the fight for tribal rights and retaining Native American customs, traditions, and culture. For the last 20 years of her life, Zitkala-Sa lived in Washington, D.C. where she lobbied Congress continuously to improve conditions on reservations. During her long career, she composed an opera "Sun Dance," performed for the first and only time shortly before her death. It received some praise from critics as a successful attempt to depict "the life of a noble people too little understood." Her stories, essays, and autobiographical sketches helped build public awareness of the misery faced by many Indians in the United States.[95]

Mourning Dove (Hum-ishu-ma), born Christine Quintasket on the Colville reservation in eastern Washington State, produced three works of literature, although she published only two during her lifetime. She had a very difficult life. Her mother died when Mourning Dove was 14 and she helped raise her younger brothers and sisters. She had very little formal education and worked as a housekeeper and fruit picker for most of her brief life. She died at age 48 of "exhaustion from manic depressive psychosis," according to her death certificate.

She wrote her first (and only) novel while moving around the Pacific Northwest picking fruit. Scholars believe she completed the work in 1915, although some believe her husband, a white merchant, Lucullus Virgil McWhorter, drastically changed the manuscript to make it more popular and saleable. She barely recognized the novel when he returned it to her with his changes. Not published until 1927, *Cogewea, the Half Blood: A Depiction of the Great Montana Cattle Range* documented the unfair treatment and loss of identity experienced by mixed-bloods. One of the first Native American novels, *Cogewea* also depicts the physical and mental abuse suffered by Indian women married to white men.

Her second work, *Coyote Stories,* appeared in 1933. It is a collection of tribal stories and legends Mourning Dove recorded while interviewing tribal elders. Coyote is an important figure in Salish folklore, both godlike and human. He knows why spiders have eight legs, why badgers are fat, and why mosquitoes drink human blood. The stories, Hum-ishu-ma hoped, would help whites understand one of the Indian ways of thinking, at least the Salish way. Mourning Dove died in 1936 having completed her autobiography shortly before. Fifty-four years later, in 1990, a friend found the manuscript in her attic and saw to its publication. Thus *Mourning Dove: A Salishan Autobiography* became part of Native American literature. It contains a detailed record of Salish culture and a history of the people, as well as the story of Christine Quintasket's life.[96]

Sam Blowsnake, a Winnebago, related his history to anthropologist Paul Radin in 1914. First published as an ethnological document, Radin presented the work to the public in 1926 as *Crashing Thunder: The Autobiography of an American Indian.* Radin, who studied under Franz Boas at Columbia University, lived among the Winnebago people for several years, studying their language and culture. Radin wanted to get an "inside view" of Indian culture by having "a native himself give the account in his own mother tongue." For that purpose he allowed Sam Blowsnake (also known as Crashing Thunder), a member of a prominent Winnebago family, to tell his own story and the story of his people. Radin had Blowsnake's "reminiscences" translated and published without any changes, although he later admitted he had "expanded" on a few of Blowsnake's stories. Nevertheless, critics found the volume "impressive, amusing, and pathetic" as well as a work of "immense importance" to anyone interested in the "mystical life" of American Indians.

Crashing Thunder tells the story of his own life while providing a detailed discussion of Winnebago religious life. He begins with his birth and evolves into the story of many young Indians imprisoned on reservations who find release in alcohol, drunkenness, violence, and thoughts of suicide. After the violent death of his brother, he encounters terrifying ghosts in his dreams and they encourage him to seek revenge. He becomes a thief, a robber, and a murderer before he undergoes a religious conversion with the help of peyote. He describes his visions and dreams in detail, and they lead him to God (Earthmaker). As the autobiography ends, Blowsnake marries and begins raising a family. "Before I joined the peyote," he concludes, "I went about in a most pitiable condition, and now I am living happily and my wife has a fine baby."[97]

The most widely read books about Native Americans in the 1920s came from the pen of James W. Schultz (1859–1947), a New Yorker by birth. Schultz attended West Point for a year, but after a hunting trip to Montana he fell in love with the state and joined the Blackfoot tribe. He married Fine Shield Woman of the tribe and lived with her until her death in 1884. Their son, Hart Merriam Schultz, also known as Lone Wolf, became a famous artist and illustrated many of his father's books. Schultz spent several years in Los Angeles serving as the book critic for the *Los Angeles Times.* He also wrote short stories and articles on Indian life for magazines such as *American Boy* and *Forest and Stream.*

His first book, the autobiographical *My Life as a Blackfoot,* appeared in 1907. Eventually he published more than 30 works of fiction. He learned to speak the Blackfoot language and became an expert on their culture. Schultz became a bitter critic of the Bureau of Indian Affairs' assimilation policy and spoke in favor of Native American sovereignty and independence in his novels and short stories. Many of his books were translated into German. Although most of his tales, with titles like *The Trail of the Spanish Horse* (1921), *In the Enemy Country* (1928), and *Skull Head the Terrible* (1929), dealt with nineteenth-century conflicts between Native Americans and white settlers and soldiers, he also wrote about the poverty and wasted lives on reservations.

ASIAN AMERICANS

One major work of Asian American literature appeared in the decade, Indian writer Dhan Gopal Mukerji's (1890–1936) autobiography, *Caste and Outcast,* published in 1923. In the book, Mukerji relates the story of his life as an upper caste Brahmin in his homeland and explains his decision to come to America. In the last part of the book, he describes his impressions of life in the United States and his three years as a student at the University of California, Berkeley from 1910 to 1913. While studying for his degree, Mukerji earned money as a migrant laborer in the fruit and vegetable fields of California's Imperial Valley. He eventually transferred to Stanford University where he married an American, Ethel Ray Dugan, a teacher. After graduation, he remained in the United States for the rest of his life, becoming a noted lecturer and interpreter of Indian religion and culture before American audiences. Among other accomplishments, he authored several best-selling children's books including, *Kari, the Elephant* (1922) and *Gay Neck: The Story of a Pigeon,* winner of the prestigious Newbery Medal for children's literature in 1928. *Gay Neck* tells the story of a carrier pigeon serving with the Indian Army in France during World War I. He loses his courage after several harrowing and life-threatening experiences carrying messages through poison gas and machine gunfire. After the war, Gay Neck flies to a Hindu monastery in the Himalayas where he regains his courage after talking to a lama and meditating.

Caste and Outcast remains Mukerji's most famous work. In it, he tries to explain the Hindu way of life to Westerners. He stressed the great tolerance Hindus had for other peoples and religions including Christianity. Islam, on the other hand, brought only hatred, oppression, and death to Hindu India. Mukerji's experiences in California's agricultural fields produce just as much suffering and prejudice. Indian students in Berkeley faced discrimination everywhere, even on campus from professors and students. In India, he belonged to the elite caste; in America he lived with outcasts—their previous lives of gentility and kindness meant nothing. The only Americans Mukerji liked belonged to the radical Industrial Worker's of the World (IWW) who actually treated all people as equals, regardless of race or religion. Other Americans talked about it but never really acted as if they truly believed in equality and justice.

As a result of the success of his book, Mukerji became a friend and an advisor on India and Hinduism to such writers and poets as Van Wyck Brooks, T. S. Eliot, Theodore Dreiser, Eugene O'Neill, and Lewis Mumford. The famous historical team of Will and Ariel Durant, authors of an eight-volume world history, made him their chief advisor on India and Hinduism. The Great Depression of the 1930s brought financial hardship and ruin to the author's family. In 1931, he published his last work, an English translation of the classic Hindu classic "The Bhagavat Gita," under the title of *The Song of God*. Shortly thereafter, he suffered a nervous breakdown and for the last five years of his life lived in almost total seclusion. At age 46, he took his own life in his New York City apartment, leaving behind his wife and only son.[98]

LATINOS

In the 1920s, the most important literary work by a Spanish writer in the United States came from the pen of Daniel Venegas, a Mexican immigrant. Scholars have been unable to determine his date of birth or of his death. His semi-autobiographical novel, *The Adventures of Don Chipote: Or, When Parakeets May Suckle their Young*, appeared in 1928. It tells the story of a young, naïve Mexican immigrant coming to the United States in search of cities paved with streets of gold. He finds poverty, despair, prejudice, and almost slavelike conditions while working in railroad construction and as a migrant farm worker (*campesino*). Venegas obviously wrote the book to serve as a warning to Mexicans—stay in your home country. Life in the United States offers migrants little more than hunger and starvation wages, and "*los mexicanos se haran ricos Estados Unidas: cuando los pericos mamen*" (Mexicans will only become rich in the United States when parakeets suckle their young [in other words, never.])

Venegas produced other works, mainly plays, but none of them has survived. The only information about them comes from reviews in Spanish-language newspapers. Venegas saw himself as a voice for the working-class, and many of the critics seemed appalled by the coarseness of the language he used. In this, Venegas stood apart from other writers, journalists, and community leaders who felt that literature should portray the lives of the "better classes" of immigrants to earn the respect of English-speaking Americans. Venegas, on the other hand, blamed the Anglos—especially the wealthy railroad companies and farmers—for victimizing their workers and making their lives miserable. Their "shameless deeds" made migration to the United States a terrible option for Mexicans and they should avoid it at all costs.

Any conclusions about minority group artists and writers during the 1920s should emphasize their criticisms of white society and their alienation from it. Assimilation—"becoming American"—was not a goal for African Americans, Asian Americans, Native Americans, or Latin Americans. Assimilation meant accepting or ignoring years of brutal mistreatment, second-class citizenship, violence, and discrimination. Most artists and intellectuals defiantly resisted joining the white mainstream in the United States until its members backed away from, apologized for, or repented of a long history of injustice and inequality.[99]

INFLUENTIAL THEORIES AND VIEWS OF RACE RELATIONS

Eugenics comes from a Greek word that means well-born. In the 1920s, a science of "eugenics," which taught that racial traits and characteristics were inherited through a person's genes, emerged. Key scientists associated with the eugenics movement included Charles Davenport (1866–1944), Harry Laughlin (1880–1943), and Henry Fairfield Osborn. They taught that a person's health, intelligence, and moral character came from their genetic inheritance. Eugenics had much in common with animal husbandry, the breeding of stronger and bigger horses, cows, chickens, and pigs. Just as experts in hog breeding knew how to manipulate genes to produce better pigs, experts in the gene structure of human beings wanted to create a more intelligent breed of people. One thing eugenicists agreed on was that the human race was in decline. They traced this decline to defective genes from unhealthier races from Africa and Asia. Immigration laws let them come into the country and, with few restrictions, they rapidly mixed into the population of the stronger people of European descent. The greatest threat came from interracial marriage.

Miscegenation, a word referring to mixed race marriages, threatened the future of the United States It did not apply only to "black/white" marriages, however, because "race" had a far broader meaning than the color of a person's skin. People talked of the "German race," the "Russian race," the "Greek race," and they believed these terms described different species of humanity that had importance beyond an individual's place of birth. Race determined a person's intelligence, morality, physical powers, and even things like someone's tendency to commit criminal acts. Color, of course, had great importance and, like everything else, derived from an individual's genetic inheritance. Genes made human beings different from each other and those derived from an individual's mother, father, and the chromosomes they carried. The "darker races," or "Negroid," carried genes that made them biologically inferior to "Nordics," a "scientific" term used to identify white-skinned people. Because of the vast influx of inferior breeds of people, white Americans faced the threat of degeneration. Bad genes mixed with good ones led to evolutionary decline. The more one came in contact with Africans, or other inferior breeds of people such as Asians, Hispanics, Native Americans, Italians, Poles, or Greeks, the greater the potential of interracial "mixing" and the final collapse of civilization.

Unlike other animal species, human beings seemed to violate the ordinary rules of evolution. Darwin taught that weaker species of animals gradually died away in their competition with stronger rivals for the food available to them. The strong thrived and the weak did not according to the laws of evolution and natural selection. Among competitors in the human species, however, weaker, less energetic individuals had more offspring than did fitter, healthier more intelligent mothers and fathers.

The eugenics movement in the United States emerged out of the American Breeders' Association (ABA). This group organized in 1903 to study the scientific breeding of livestock. The ABA created a Committee on Eugenics chaired by Stanford University president David Starr Jordan. Other active members included Robert Decoursey Ward and Prescott Hall, founders of the Immigration Restriction League. Psychologists Edward I. Thorndike and Walter Fernald, both active in the development of intelligence testing, and Henry H. Goddard and Alexander Graham Bell, members of a committee studying "feeblemindedness," added their prestigious names to the eugenics crusade.

English scientist Francis Galton, Charles Darwin's cousin, coined the term *eugenics* in 1883. He wrote that his new term expressed "the science of improving the stock . . . to give the more suitable races or strains of blood a better chance of prevailing speedily over the less suitable than they otherwise would have had." In America, the eugenics movement declared its goal, "to stem the tide of threatened racial degeneracy." That could be accomplished by protecting the United States against "indiscriminate immigration," which was leading to the "complete destruction of the white race."[100]

Tests given to soldiers during World War I provided solid evidence that most members of the human race fell below the level of intelligence needed for surviving in the complex, modern world. According to the Stanford-Binet Intelligence Test, the first "IQ" test, developed shortly before the war began and given to all soldiers, American men walked around in a constant state of ignorance. Test scores of 46 percent of whites were "morons"; 90 percent of blacks fell into that category. That the test-makers' questions might have been flawed—how many adults who averaged perhaps three years of schooling, not unusual for the time in some areas of the country, would know the capital of New York, or who composed the opera Aida—did not seem to occur to them. What could be done with this evidence? Eugenicists recommended sterilization of "morons." They could not be permitted to have children. If stronger horses were bred by weeding out weaker ones, why not use the same methods with people? The world did not need more ignorance. The statistical evidence from the test scores told the story; the "African" race did not have the intellectual capabilities needed to survive in the modern, scientific world. Should degenerates populate the globe?

Eugenic scientists sought to reverse the movement toward barbarism in two ways: so-called negative and positive eugenics. "Negative" eugenics stood for reducing human "degeneration" by passing laws restricting marriage only to those couples with favorable genes. Other advocates of negativism wanted to sterilize people with defective genes to prevent them from passing unwanted inherited attributes (for example blindness, feeblemindedness, moral degeneracy) to another generation. These ideas had wide support among scientists, social workers, mental health officials, and even heads of state. Presidents Theodore Roosevelt, Warren G. Harding, Calvin Coolidge, and Herbert Hoover all spoke in favor of sterilization. A third approach involved removing citizens with unwanted diseases or inherited characteristics from any contact with "normal" people by committing them to prisons or hospitals for the "feebleminded." (In Germany, Adolf Hitler's Nazis followed this prescription to the ultimate extreme by killing anyone deemed "mentally" defective, physically "handicapped," or "racially" impure.)

Negative eugenicists supported an extreme method for reducing the number of children born to parents of low intelligence or low moral character. Sterilization of the "feebleminded" was a necessary policy for the betterment of humanity. The Army IQ tests showed how many ignorant people lived in America. Another survey of the population, financed by the Eugenics Research Association, found that at least one-tenth of Americans needed sterilization so that they would not pass defective genes to another generation. By 1925, 27 states legalized forced sterilizations for various categories of degeneracy. Ten years later more than 20,000 Americans had been sterilized. Many of these people were poor and black. They lived in state-run mental hospitals and homes for the mentally retarded. More than 500 of them died during the operation. From a genetic viewpoint, the drive to save humanity from degeneracy had at last begun.[101]

Sterilization might be considered too negative of a method of saving the future of the human race. "Positive" eugenicists suggested less violent methods for accomplishing the same goal. They thought that the key to America's future lay in encouraging the "better stock" of citizens to have larger families. Financial incentives might encourage the "best and brightest" to have more babies. Whether through tax breaks for decent, middle class families having lots of children, financial bonuses for mothers giving birth to many offspring, or simply giving blue ribbons at state fairs to the "fittest" families with the healthiest children (a method adopted in more than 20 states) did not matter. The then current practice among middle class families of having no more than two children doomed the white race to oblivion. Eugenicist Madison Grant argued in *The Passing of the Great Race* (1916), one of the classics of eugenic "science," that the white race would disappear unless the United States took drastic measures to increase the numbers of its most superior racial stock.[102]

Leaders of the eugenics crusade included Charles Davenport, a zoology instructor at Harvard University, and the most prominent biologist of his time. He established the Cold Spring Harbor Research Laboratory to study human genetics in 1910. Located in New York State and financed by the Carnegie Institute of Washington, D.C., the laboratory published many books on eugenics and gathered statistical and biological evidence that supported the eugenicists' agenda. Davenport's major work, *Race Crossing in Jamaica*, appeared in 1929. The book provided data warning white America about the dangers of race mixing and interbreeding. The "low" level of intelligence, high rate of crime, and lack of initiative found among the Jamaican population proved that the African race and white race should never be allowed to mix.[103]

Davenport believed that all human traits were inherited. He included eye color, hair, skin, height, weight, musical ability, literary skills, mathematical skills, body energy, mental ability, strength, nomadism, insanity, criminality, speech defects, blindness, cancer, pneumonia, and many other traits. Environmental conditions, education, home life, poverty, even childhood beatings by violent parents influenced nothing. "No doubt poverty and crime are bad assists in one's early environment," David Starr Jordan wrote. "No doubt these elements cause the ruins of thousands who, by heredity, were good material of civilization. But again, poverty dirt, and crime are the product of those, in general, who are not good material. . . . The slums are at once symptom, effect, and cause of evil." As another eugenicist put it more simply, it is "not the slums which make slum people, but slum people who make the slums."[104]

Harry H. Laughlin, a friend and colleague of Davenport, had a Doctor of Science degree from Princeton University. He specialized in cytology—the science of cells. He had a keen interest in the excessive rates of insanity he found among immigrant populations in the United States. At Cold Harbor, he became the superintendent of research, a position he retained until his death in 1939. His interest in, and publications on, immigrants led to his appointment as an expert witness to the United States House of Representative Committee on Immigration and Naturalization in 1923. Evidence he presented, mainly gathered from statistical analyses of intelligence test scores, prison populations, and the racial and ethnic background of patients in hospitals for the mentally ill, helped gain passage of the national-origins quotas established in the 1924 immigration law. Members of the Eugenics Research Association had elected Committee Chair Albert Johnson their president only the year before.

Laughlin advocated "negative eugenics" and published a study called *Eugenical Sterilization in the United States* in 1922 that had a major impact on American law and social policy. When Laughlin published his study, 12 states had already approved sterilization laws. These laws allowed for the sterilization of the "feebleminded, insane, criminalistic, epileptic, inebriate, diseased, blind, deaf, deformed, and dependent." That last category included "orphans, ne'er-do-wells, tramps, the homeless, and paupers." In 1933, the Nazi government of Adolf Hitler adopted a law modeled on the American laws that led to the sterilization of more than 350,000 Germans. Three years later, Laughlin received an honorary degree from a German university for his contributions to "the science of racial cleansing."[105]

Laughlin and his supporters believed they had scientific proof that children of "defective persons" were a "menace to society." He asserted that heredity played the major role in creating "insanity, idiocy, imbecility, epilepsy, and crime." Sterilization would prevent what he and former President Theodore Roosevelt had called "race suicide."[106] If the fitter families of Nordic stock had fewer babies, then society had to make sure that "degenerate" people had none. Sterilization was a painless operation according to its advocates and the goal was pure—the reduction of human misery. In 1907, Indiana had enacted the first sterilization law. Virginia passed its law in 1924, shortly before the legislature passed the Racial Integrity Act outlawing miscegenation.

The major challenge to eugenics came from social scientists Robert Park of the University of Chicago and Franz Boas at Columbia University in New York City. Both argued for an environmentalist view. Historical and social circumstances determined human behavior not skin-color or other inherited characteristics. Park started teaching at his university in 1913 after serving several years as the personal secretary and public relations manager for Booker T. Washington. Before his work at Tuskegee Institute, he wrote for newspapers in Detroit, Denver, and New York City. As a student, he had studied philosophy at Harvard and at a university in Germany.

Park (1864–1944) became interested in the sources of racial hatred, which he felt led to racial segregation. He believed separation by skin color had a positive and a negative outcome. Racial separation based on ideas of white superiority made African American assimilation into the mainstream of society impossible. On the other hand, segregation forced blacks into their own communities. Here they developed a sense of solidarity and racial pride. Forced by white prejudice into their own areas of a city or town, they came to value their own culture and developed their own businesses, churches, schools, music, literature, and values. In this community, they could build their own history, their own language, and even their own religion. Park pointed to Marcus Garvey and his followers as proof of his theory of upward mobility based on racial pride.

Cultural and economic achievements helped create a sense of self-confidence and self-worth necessary among all blacks if they wanted to move forward in a white world. In Park's analysis, the Harlem Renaissance showed that African Americans could produce great works of art. Knowing that they could create great works of art, establish successful businesses (including a class of black millionaires), and make major scientific discoveries would help blacks become a unified people.

A spirit of black nationalism would develop because of racial segregation and prejudice. This feeling of racial solidarity would eventually replace religion as the key unifying force in African American society, for it, too, provided answers to troubling questions of the meaning of life. Blacks had little opportunity for participating in a meaningful life in white American society, Park argued. What modern society denied them a national identity would replace—dignity, pride, a sense of well-being and self-worth, and a measure of order to a fear-filled, chaotic existence. Group identification would prevent mental disorganization and despair among individuals.

Blacks were not economically and socially inferior to whites because of their genes, Park believed. Instead, inequality came from the discrimination, prejudice, poor schooling, and lack of opportunity they faced in American society.

Park offered reasons to hope for a better future, however. Racial inferiority existed in people's minds not in their chromosomes or genetic inheritance, and minds changed more quickly by education and experience than by altered human genes by scientists (if they ever showed that they could). Over time, racial animosity would decrease because as blacks moved up the social and economic ladder through their own efforts, whites would learn to respect them. Park's views echoed those of the National Urban League, which he helped found, and of his old friend Booker T. Washington.[107]

Franz Boaz (1858–1942), a German-born anthropologist who taught at Columbia University, probably did more than any other person in the United States to challenge the eugenic interpretation of human intelligence and abilities. Sometimes called "the father of American anthropology," he challenged the "scientific" idea that "education and environment do not fundamentally alter racial values," as eugenicists believed. Beginning with *The Mind of Primitive Man* (1911) through *Anthropology and Modern Life* (1928), Boaz argued that culture, by which he meant everything human-made, played a far more important role in determining a person's life chances and capabilities than did his or her genes or skin color.

In his 1928 work, Boas outlined his principle of "cultural relativism." Each culture—and in this instance, he meant each human society—was the product of a unique and particular history. Cultures developed in response to geography, environment, and human needs and since these things varied from place to place and continent to continent, each society would respond in different ways to their surrounding. Desert communities produced different types of human cultures than did societies trying to survive in tropical rainforests and thus developed different cultures and personalities. No culture was "better" or "worse" than any other; they were just different. Aboriginal people in Australia had not built great cities or produced great literature but that did not make their culture inferior to Europeans. Cultures, like apples and oranges, could not be compared. A general "human nature" did not exist; a people's history existed and every culture had its own unique culture, generally built in response to the external environment.[108]

Boas supported the NAACP and other African American organizations. He testified before Congress against the 1924 immigration restriction bill and attacked the data collected from IQ tests. He believed that scientists and intellectuals had a responsibility to work toward improving human life. He hoped that people would learn to tolerate differences between cultures and learn that diversity enriched the human spirit. Many of his students went on to challenge the assumptions of the biological and genetic theories so common at the time. His students included Margaret Mead, author of the ground-breaking *Coming of Age in Samoa* (1928); Alfred Kroeber, who put together the *Handbook of Indians of California* (1925); Ellen Chews Parsons, who lived with Indians in the Southwest and produced the epic *Pueblo Indian Religion* (1929); Melville Herskovits, who founded the study of African history in the United States; and Ruth

Benedict, especially in her *Race: Science and Politics* (1940). They all studied under Boas and spent their careers challenging the "scientific racism" of the eugenicists.[109]

Boaz's influence grew in the 1930s, although eugenic views remained popular among natural scientists and medical doctors, especially in Adolf Hitler's Germany. Many of the principles of American eugenics found their way into Nazi science. The German dictator acknowledged that he learned many of his ideas on race from reading publications of American eugenics researchers. He subscribed to American industrialist Henry Ford's rabidly racist newspaper *The Dearborn Independent*. Eugenic theories eventually led to the killing of millions, as "Life Unfit for Life" became a popular slogan in Germany.[110]

RESOURCE GUIDE

SUGGESTED READING

Avrich, Paul. *Sacco and Vanzetti: The Anarchist Background*. Princeton, NJ: Princeton University Press, 1991.

Baldwin, Neil. *Henry Ford and the Jews: The Mass Production of Hate*. New York: Public Affairs Press, 2001.

Black, Edwin. *War Against the Weak: Eugenics and America's Campaign to Create a Master Race*. New York: Four Walls and Eight Windows Press, 2003.

Bogle, Donald. *Toms, Coons, Mulattoes, Mammies & Bucks: An Interpretive History of Blacks in American Films*. New York: Continuum, 2001.

Boyle, Kevin. *Arc of Justice: A Saga of Race, Civil Rights, and Murder in the Jazz Age*. New York: Henry Holt, 2004.

Daniels, Roger. *Coming to America: A History of Race and Ethnicity in American Life*. New York: HarperCollins, 2002.

Dray, Philip. *At the Hands of Persons Unknown: The Lynching of Black America*. New York: The Modern Library, 2003.

Gerstle, Gary. *American Crucible: Race and Nation in the Twentieth Century*. Princeton, NJ: Princeton University Press, 2001.

Gonzales, Manuel. *Mexicanos: A History of Mexicans in the United States*. Bloomington: Indiana University Press, 1999.

Hirsch, James S. *Riot and Remembrance: America's Worst Race Riot and Its Legacy*. Boston: Houghton Mifflin, 2002.

Kuhl, Stefan. *The Nazi Connection: Eugenics, American Racism, and German National Socialism*. New York: Oxford University Press, 1994.

Lewis, David Levering. *When Harlem Was in Vogue*. New York: Penguin Books, 1997.

Schneider, Mark Robert. *African Americans in the Jazz Age: A Decade of Struggle and Promise*. Lanham, MD: Rowman and Littlefield, 2006.

Takaki, Ronald T. *A Different Mirror: A History of Multicultural America*. Boston: Little, Brown, 1993.

Takaki, Ronald T. *Strangers from a Different Shore: A History of Asian Americans* Boston: Little, Brown, 1998.

Thernstrom, Stephan, ed. *The Harvard Encyclopedia of American Ethnic Groups*. Cambridge, MA: Harvard University Press, 1980.

Tolney, Stewart and E. M. Back. *A Festival of Violence: An Analysis of Southern Lynchings, 1882–1930*. Urbana: University of Illinois Press, 1995.

FILMS/VIDEOS

Against the Odds: The Artists of the Harlem Renaissance (1993). Edwards, Amber, director. A documentary from the Public Broadcasting System (PBS). On DVD and VHS.

Marcus Garvey: Look for Me in the Whirlwind. (2001). Nelson, Stanley, director. A documentary from the PBS series "The American Experience." Based on archival footage, it tells the story from Garvey's arrival in the United States in 1916 to his trial in 1925. DVD and VHS.

Nanook of the North. (1922). Flaherty, Robert, director. This great documentary provides a direct study of the lives of Inuit (Eskimo) hunters. DVD released in 2006.

Sacco and Vanzetti. (2007). Miller, Peter, director. Contains artwork, music, poetry, and film clips about the case. Actors John Turturro and Tony Shalhoub read the prison writings of the two Italian immigrants. Commentary is provided by Howard Zinn and Studs Terkel. From Willow Pond Films.

The Vanishing American. (1926). Seitz, George, director. Silent film starring Richard Dix and Lois Wilson. It presents a sympathetic portrait of Native Americans and is based on a story by Zane Grey. DVD and VHS.

WEB SITES

The Eugenics Movement. Eugenics Archive, http://www.eugenicsarchive.org/eugenics/branch.pl. Well documented with biographies, pictures, pamphlets, and other original material.

Harlem Renaissance. Schomberg Center for Research in Black Culture of the New York Public Library, http:// www.si.umich.edu/chico/Harlem/. A page with images and biographies of the artists and poets of the period.

The Indian Citizenship Act. Eugenics Archive, http://www.eugenicsarchive.org/eugenics/branch.pl. Contains the act and background along with images and newspaper accounts.

Library of Congress, http://www.loc.gov/rr/program/bib/harlem/harlem.html.

Lynching in the United States. Long Island University, http://www.liu.edu/cwis/cwp/library/african/2000/lynching.htm. Includes a brief history, a great bibliography, images, and links to many other cites covering the topic.

Marcus Garvey. Marcus Garvey, http://www.marcusgarvey.com/. Life and times are well presented along with hundreds of documents, photographs, and speeches.

Sacco and Vanzetti. University of Missouri School of Law, Douglas Lindner's page, http://www.law.umkc.edu/faculty/projects/ftrials/SaccoV/SaccoV.htm. Includes transcripts, images, biographies, and court decisions.

Tulsa Historical Society, http://www.tulsahistory.org/learn/riot.htm. Provides a wealth of information including photographs, newspaper coverage, and eyewitness accounts.

NOTES

1. Paul Avrich, *Sacco and Vanzetti: The Anarchist Background* (Princeton, NJ: Princeton University Press, 1991), 77–78.

2. Quoted in Avrich, *Sacco and Vanzetti*, 111.

3. Quoted in Francis X. Busch, *Prisoners at the Bar: An Account of the Trials of the William Haywood Case, the Sacco-Vanzetti Case, the Loeb-Leopold Case, and the Bruno Hauptman Case* (Indianapolis: Bobbs-Merrill, 1952), 108.

4. Herbert B. Ehrmann, *The Case That Will Not Die: Commonwealth vs. Sacco and Vanzetti* (Boston: Little, Brown, 1969), 12–13.

5. Francis Russell, *Tragedy in Dedham: The Story of the Sacco and Vanzetti Case* (New York: McGraw-Hill, 1962).

6. Felix Frankfurter, *The Case of Sacco and Vanzetti: A Critical Analysis for Lawyers and Laymen* (Boston: Little, Brown, 1927), 62–63.

7. Quoted in Frankfurter, *The Case of Sacco and Vanzetti*, 65.

8. Quoted in Frankfurter, *The Case Against Sacco and Vanzetti*, 67–71.

9. Quoted in Felix Frankfurter, *The Case Against Sacco and Vanzetti*, 116–21.

10. Katherine Anne Porter, "The Never-Ending Wrong," *The Atlantic Monthly*. June 1977.

11. Marion Denman Frankfurter and Gardner Jackson, eds. *The Letters of Sacco and Vanzetti* (New York: Penguin Books, 1997), xxxi–xxxvii.

12. William Young and David E. Kaiser, *Postmortem: New Evidence in the Case of Sacco and Vanzetti* (Amherst: University of Massachusetts Press, 1985), 202.

13. Felix Frankfurter, *The Case Against Sacco and Vanzetti*, 126.

14. Louis Joughin and Edmund M. Morgan, *The Legacy of Sacco and Vanzetti* (New York: Quadrangle Books, 1964).

15. Francis Russell, *Sacco and Vanzetti: The Case Resolved* (New York: Harper and Row, 1986).

16. James S. Hirsch, *Riot and Remembrance: America's Worst Race Riot and Its Legacy* (Boston: Houghton Mifflin, 2002), 8.

17. Scott Ellsworth, "The Tulsa Race Riot," *Final Report of the Oklahoma Commission to Study the Tulsa Race Riot of 1921* (Tulsa, OK: Tulsa Oklahoma Commission, 2001), 37–38.

18. Quoted in Hirsch, *Riot and Remembrance*, 97.

19. Quoted in Hirsch, *Riot and Remembrance*, 116.

20. Larry O'Dell, "Riot Property Loss," in *Final Report*, 147–48.

21. Larry O'Dell, *Final Report*, 149.

22. John Hope Franklin, "History Knows No Fences," *Final Report*, 131–32.

23. Stewart E. Tolney and E. M. Beck, *A Festival of Violence: An Analysis of Southern Lynchings, 1882–1930* (Urbana: University of Illinois Press, 1995), 4–6.

24. Michael Fedo, *The Lynchings in Duluth* (St. Paul, MN: Minnesota Historical Society Press, 1993), 5–6.

25. Fedo, *Lynchings in Duluth*, 168–69.

26. Fedo, *Lynchings in Duluth*, 175.

27. Philip Dray, *At the Hands of Persons Unknown: The Lynching of Black America* (New York: The Modern Library, 2003), 258–59.

28. Quoted in Dray, *At the Hands of Persons Unknown*, 260.

29. Quoted in, *At the Hands of Persons Unknown*, 260–62.

30. Robert L. Zangranado, *The NAACP Crusade Against Lynching, 1909–1950* (Philadelphia, Temple University Press, 1980), 50–51.

31. Zangranado, *The NAACP Crusade*, 55.

32. Quoted in Dray, *At the Hands of Persons Unknown*, 270.

33. John Egerton, *Speak Now Against the Day: The Generations before the Civil Rights Movement in the South* (New York: Knopf, 1994), 36–38.

34. Dray, *At the Hands of Persons Unknown*, 304.

35. James R. McGovern, *Anatomy of a Lynching: The Killing of Claude Neal* (Baton Rouge: Louisiana State University Press, 1982), 141.

36. Dray, *At the Hands of Persons Unknown*, 359–60.

37. Quoted in Dray, *At the Hands of Persons Unknown*, 366.

38. Gary Gerstle, *American Crucible: Race and Nation in the Twentieth Century* (Princeton: Princeton University Press, 2001), 94–97.

39. Edwin Black, *War Against the Weak: Eugenics and America's Campaign to Create a Master Race* (New York: Four Walls Eight Windows Press, 2003), 185–86.

40. Edwin Black, *War against the Weak*, 188–89.

41. Edwin Black, *War against the Weak*, 194.

42. Marc Reisler, *By the Sweat of Their Brow: Mexican Immigrant Labor in the United States, 1900–1940* (Westport, CT: Greenwood Press, 1976), 247–48.

43. Roger Daniels, *Coming to America: A History of Immigration and Ethnicity in American Life* (New York: Harper/Collins Publishers, 2002), 282–84.

44. Mae M. Ngai, "The Strange Career of the Illegal Alien: Immigration Restriction and Deportation in the United States, 1921–1965," *Law and History Review* (Spring 2003), http://www.historycooperative.org/journals/1hr/21.1/ngai.html.

45. Frances Paul Prucha, *The Great Father: The United States Government and the American Indians* (Lincoln: University of Nebraska Press. 1984), 732–34.

46. Brookings Institution, *Report on Indian Families* (Washington, D.C., 1934), 16–17.

47. Brookings Institution, *Report on Indian Families*.

48. Gregory A. Freeman, *Lay This Body Down: The 1921 Murders of Eleven Plantation Slaves* (Chicago: Chicago Review Press, 1999), 161–62.

49. Alain Locke, "The New Negro," *Survey Graphic: Magazine of Social Interpretation*, Special Edition, *Harlem: Mecca of the New Negro*, March, 1925.

50. Kevin Boyle, *Arc of Justice: A Saga of Race, Civil Rights, and Murder in the Jazz Age* (New York: Henry Holt, 2004), 339–46.

51. Kevin Boyle, *Arc of Justice*, 347.

52. Leslie V. Tischauser, *The Burden of Ethnicity: The German Question in Chicago, 1914–1941* (New York: Garland Publishing, 1990), 67–72.

53. Leslie V. Tischauser, *The Burden of Ethnicity*, 71.

54. Leslie V. Tischauser, *The Burden of Ethnicity*, 75–76.

55. Leslie V. Tischauser, *The Burden of Ethnicity*, 78.

56. Roger Daniels, *Coming to America*, 282.

57. Francis Paul Prucha, *The Great Father*, 791–95.

58. Lewis Meriam, *The Problem of Indian Administration* (Baltimore, MD: The Johns Hopkins Press, 1928), 1–5.

59. Lewis Meriam, *The Problem of Indian Administration*, 8–9.

60. Lewis Meriam, *The Problem of Indian Administration*, 15.

61. Lewis Meriam, *The Problem of Indian Administration*, "Summary of Finding and Investigations," 5–33.

62. Lewis Meriam, *The Problem of Indian Administration*, 27–28.

63. William E. Unrau, *Mixed-Bloods and Tribal Dissolution: Charles Curtis and the Quest for Indian Identity* (Lawrence: University Press of Kansas, 1989), 178–82.

64. Manuel G. Gonzales, *Mexicanos: A History of Mexicans in the United States* (Bloomington: Indiana University Press, 1999), 113–16.

65. Marc Reisler, *By the Sweat of Their Brow: Mexican Immigrant Labor in the United States, 1900–1940* (Westport, CT: Greenwood Press, 1976), 12–15.

66. Marc Reisler, *By the Sweat of Their Brow*, 216.

67. Marc Reisler, *By the Sweat of Their Brow*, 221.

68. Alfred C. Cordova and Charles Burnet Jacob, *Octaviano Larrazolo, a Political Portrait* (Albuquerque: Department of Government, University of New Mexico, 1952), 34, 37, 75–76.

69. Iris Chang, *The Chinese in America: A Narrative History* (New York: Penguin Books, 2000), 171.

70. Ronald Takaki, *Strangers from a Different Shore: A History of Asian Americans* (Boston: Little, Brown Inc., 1998), 223–24.

71. Takaki, *Strangers from a Different Shore*, 242.

72. Ronald T. Takaki, *A Different Mirror: A History of Multicultural America* (Boston: Little, Brown Inc, 1993), 367–72.

73. Carlos Bulosan, *America Is in the Heart* (New York: Harcourt, Brace and Company, 1943), 181–86.

74. Carlos Bulosan, *America Is in the Heart*, 188.

75. J. David Smith and K. Ray Nelson, *The Sterilization of Carrie Buck* (Far Hills, NJ: New Horizon Press, 1989), 79.

76. Donald Bogle, *Toms, Coons, Mulattoes, Mamies & Bucks: An Interpretive History of Blacks in American Films* (New York: Continuum, 2001), 11–12.

77. Neil Baldwin, *Henry Ford and the Jews: The Mass Production of Hate* (New York: Public Affairs Press, 2001), 225–27.

78. Mary Ann Weston, *Native Americans in the News: Images of Indians in the Twentieth Century Press* (Westport, CT: Greenwood Press, 1996), 247–48.

79. Frances P. Prucha, *The Great Father: The United States Government and the American Indian* (Lincoln: University of Nebraska Press, 1984), 375.

80. Frances P. Prucha, *The Great Father*, 389–90.

81. Shari Huhndorf, *Going Native: Indians in the American Cultural Imagination* (Ithaca, NY: Cornell University Press, 2001), 179.

82. George Hadley-Garcia, *Hispanic Hollywood: The Latins in Motion Pictures* (Secaucus, NJ: Citadel Press, 1990), 224.

83. David Levering Lewis, *When Harlem Was in Vogue* (New York: Penguin Books, 1997), 25–26.

84. Charles Scruggs, *Jean Toomer and the Terrors of American History* (Philadelphia: University of Pennsylvania Press, 1998), 89.

85. Blanche Ferguson, *Countee Cullen and the Negro Renaissance* (New York: Dodd, Mead, 1966), 102.

86. David Levering Lewis, *When Harlem Was in Vogue*, 74.

87. *Survey Graphic* (March 1927), 7–8.

88. David Levering Lewis, ed., *Portable Harlem Renaissance Reader* (New York: Penguin Books, 1994), xiv.

89. *The Nation*, January 25, 1928, 114.

90. David Levering Lewis, ed., *Portable Harlem Renaissance Reader*, 221.

91. David Levering Lewis, *When Harlem Was in Vogue*, 171–75.

92. Mel Watkins, *Stepin Fetchit: The Life and Times of Lincoln Perry* (New York: Random House, 2005), 16–18.

93. Mel Watkins, *Stepin Fetchit*, 40.

94. Jill Watts, *Hattie McDaniel: Black Ambition, White Hollywood* (New York: HarperCollins), 131–32.

95. Zitkala-Sa, *American Indian Stories* (Lincoln, NE: Center for Great Plains Studies, University of Nebraska Press, 1980), 93–99.

96. Mourning Dove, *A Salishan Autobiography* (Lincoln, NE: University of Nebraska Press, 1994), xi–xxxi.

97. Paul Radin, ed., *Crashing Thunder: The Autobiography of an American Indian* (Lincoln, NE: University of Nebraska Press, 1983), 204.

98. Dhan Gopal Mukerji, *Caste and Outcaste* (Stanford, CA: Stanford University Press, 2002), 200–210.

99. Daniel Venegas, *The Adventures of Don Chipote, or, When Parrots Breast-Fed* (Houston, TX: Arte Publico Press, 2000), "Introduction," by Nicolas Kanellos, 1–16.

100. Edwin Black, *War Against the Weak; Eugenics and America's Campaign to Create a Master Race* (New York: Four Walls and Eight Windows Press, 2003), 16.

101. Edwin Black, *War Against the Weak*, 35–36.

102. Roger Daniels, *Coming to America: A History of Immigration and Ethnicity in American Life* (New York: HarperCollins, 2002), 222–23.

103. Edwin Black, *War Against the Weak*, 45–46.

104. Edwin Black, *War Against the Weak*, 222.

105. Stefan Kuhl, *The Nazi Connection: Eugenics, American Racism, and German National Socialism* (New York: Oxford University Press, 1994), 21.

106. Edwin Black, *War Against the Weak*, 118.

107. R. Fred Wacker, *Ethnicity, Pluralism, and Race: Race Relations Theory in America Before Myrdal* (Westport, CT: Greenwood Press, 1983), 72–73.

108. R. Fred Wacker, *Ethnicity, Pluralism, and Race*, 98–99.

109. Stanford Lyman, *The Black American in Sociological Thought* (New York: G. P. Putnam's Sons, 1972), 47–48.

110. Stefan Kuhl, *The Nazi Connection*, 85–86.

1930s

TIMELINE

1930

January–June   The Tribal Arts Exposition, sponsored by the Bureau of Indian Affairs, travels the United States. This eventually leads to the formation of the Indian Arts and Crafts Board in 1936.

January 10–22   In Watsonville, California white mobs attack a community of Filipino agricultural workers, burning their homes and killing at least one person.

January 26   A superior court judge in Los Angeles rules that Filipinos belong to the "Mongolian race" and cannot legally marry white persons.

March 31   The National Association for the Advancement of Colored People (NAACP) protests President Herbert Hoover's nomination of John J. Parker to the U.S. Supreme Court, saying that he has racist attitudes.

April 6   The Scottsboro Boys are arrested in Alabama and charged with rape.

April 25   The U.S. Senate issues a report on "The Kidnapping of Indian Children from Parents on Reservations by Indian Administration School Officials." It exonerates the Indian Bureau of any wrongdoing.

May 7   The United States Senate rejects the nomination of John J. Parker to the Supreme Court.

July   Mexican American lettuce-field workers conduct their first strike in California's Imperial Valley; it ends in defeat.

August 29	The Japanese American Citizen's League holds its first convention in Seattle.
December 1	Younghill Kang's *The Grass Roof*, the first Korean American novel, is published.
December 10	The Young Negro Cooperative League is founded by Ella Baker to organize consumer cooperatives.

1931

Green Grow the Lilacs by Native American playwright Lynn Riggs is published. It is later adopted for Broadway by Richard Rodgers and Oscar Hammerstein who call it *Oklahoma*.

Wallace Fard establishes the Nation of Islam in Detroit.

The Brookings Institution sends its "Report on Negro Housing" to President Herbert Hoover, a scathing indictment of housing conditions in black communities.

January–July	Seventy-five thousand Mexican immigrants are forced to leave California in a first wave of mass deportations that hit the United States during the Great Depression.
March 1	The India Society is founded in New York City by Hari G. Govil to promote better understanding of Indian culture.
May 1	In *Independent School District (Texas) v. Salvatierra*, a Texas district court rules that Mexican Americans have been segregated in Texas public schools but that this has not caused them harm. Mexican students learn differently from whites so they are better off in separate classrooms.

1932

Clark Foreman publishes *Environmental Factors in Negro Elementary Education*, a scathing indictment of African American education in the southern states.

Black Elk Speaks by Nicholas Black Elk and John G. Neihardt is published.

April 12	A strike by Mexican beet-field workers in Colorado ends in defeat for the workers.
May 2	In *Nixon v. Condon*, the Supreme Court overturns a Texas law that prohibits African Americans from voting in primary elections.
November 2	In *Powell v. Alabama*, the Supreme Court overturns the conviction of the nine black defendants in the Scottsboro case because the attorney assigned to defend them had not provided a meaningful defense.

1933

	John Collier, an advocate for Indian rights, is appointed commissioner of Indian Affairs by President Franklin Roosevelt.
	Land of the Spotted Eagle by Luther Standing Bear, a Lakota Sioux, is published.
	Native American writer Mourning Dove publishes *Coyote Stories*, a book of Indian myths.
May 11	The Julius Rosenwald Fund sponsors a national conference on "The Economic Status of the Negro," under the leadership of black sociologist Charles S. Johnson.
October	A strike by 12,000 Hispanic cotton-pickers in California ends in defeat after vigilantes killed two striking pickers.
November 30	The Filipino Labor Union is founded in California.

1934

	W.E.B. Du Bois, educator, civil rights leader, and editor, resigns from the NAACP in a dispute over tactics and goals.
	The Southern Tenant Farmer's Union is organized in Arkansas.
	American Indian writer John Joseph Mathews's novel *Sundown* is published.
March 24	The Tydings-McDuffie Act limits Filipino immigration to 50 people per year.
June 18	Congress passes the Indian Reorganization Act giving tribes the option of choosing new tribal governments and writing new constitutions.
	The Johnson-O'Malley Act is passed in Congress giving federal money to state governments to provide education and social services on Indian reservations.
July 7	A strike by the largely Hispanic Sheep-Shearer's Union in West Texas ends in defeat.
July 10	Congress passes the Filipino Repatriation Act allowing Filipinos in the United States a chance to go back to their homeland at government expense.
November 7	Voters in Chicago elect the first African American Democrat, Arthur Mitchell, to Congress.
November 21	The Apollo Theater, a showcase for African American talent, opens in Harlem.

1935

	The National Council of Negro Women is organized, with Mary McLeod Bethune elected as its first president.

	Mexican American author Miguel Antonio Otero publishes *My Life*.
March 19–20	A race riot in Harlem erupts after a rumor is spread that police had beaten a black teenager for shoplifting. Unemployment in Harlem reaches 50 percent.
April 1	In *Grovey v. Townsend*, the Supreme Court says the Texas Democratic Party can keep African Americans from voting in primaries if the party—not state law—authorizes it to do so.
	In *Norris v. Alabama*, the Supreme Court reverses a second guilty verdict in the trial of the Scottsboro Boys because Alabama African Americans were excluded from Alabama juries.
June 16–18	The American Communist Party sponsors a National Negro Conference in New York City hoping to attract African American support.

1936

July 25	A strike by Mexican and Filipino lettuce-field workers in Salinas, California ends in defeat for the union.
	Native American author D'Arcy McNickle publishes *The Surrounded*, a novel about reservation life and the difficulties of assimilation.
August 4–9	African American athletes win 13 medals at the Berlin Olympics.
August 27	Congress establishes the Indian Arts and Crafts Board.

1937

March 26	President Franklin Roosevelt appoints the first African American to the federal bench, William H. Hastie.
December 6	The Supreme Court upholds the constitutionality of a Georgia poll tax in *Breedlove v. Suttles*.

1938

	The Hispanic Civil Rights Congress is founded by Bert Corona.
March	A strike by the mostly Mexican Pecan Sheller's in San Antonio, Texas ends with workers winning an increase in wages.
August 1	The Hilo Massacre in Hawaii during a strike against the Dole Pineapple Company results in the death of 20 workers.
November 6	The first Asian American, Hiram Fong, is elected to the legislature of the Territory of Hawaii.

| December 12 | The Supreme Court issues *Missouri ex rel Gaines v. Canada*, ordering the state of Missouri to admit its first African American student, William Gaines, to its law school. |

1939

February 2	The Daughters of the American Revolution (DAR) refuses to let black soprano Marion Anderson perform at Constitution Hall in Washington, D.C.
March 10	Hattie McDaniel receives an Academy Award for Best Supporting Actress for her role as "Mammy" in *Gone with the Wind*, a first for an African American performer.
May 15	American authorities refuse to allow 800 Jewish refugees from Germany permission to leave the ship *St. Louis* so that they can enter the United States. Most later die in Nazi concentration camps.
July 1	Congress rejects a bill to allow 20,000 Jewish children, refugees from Germany, special permission to come to the United States.

OVERVIEW

The single most important factor affecting the lives of Americans in the 1930s was the Great Depression, the collapse of the economy resulting in the high level of unemployment around the country. The depression reached more than 30 percent by 1932, increasing suffering for Indians on reservations, black and white farmers and sharecroppers in the South, African and Latino Americans in cities and towns across America, as well as for white Americans. Racial and ethnic strife added to the economic woes of American minorities. In the South, segregation and Jim Crow laws, which made it illegal for African Americans and whites to sit, eat, or go to school together, affected everyone. The number of lynchings decreased to an average of 10 a year, but Congress could not pass a law making lynching a federal crime. The Scottsboro affair in Alabama that almost led to the execution of nine wholly innocent young black men illustrated the intense racism of white southerners. Only intervention from the United States Supreme Court kept the nine men falsely accused of rape from the electric chair. In the North, African Americans lived with less fear than those in the South, but a large majority lived in racially segregated communities. Unemployment in black communities was often twice as high as it was in white neighborhoods.

President Franklin D. Roosevelt's New Deal programs, such as Social Security and the minimum wage, contained provisions that effectively prevented African Americans from participating in them. Because of opposition from white southern Senators, most blacks were not covered under the Social Security Act or minimum wage laws. Social Security did not cover farm workers, laundry workers, household servants, and hospital workers. African Americans made up a large number of workers in these areas, and the same categories were excluded from minimum wage provisions. Public housing was built in white neighborhoods first. Southern senators and members of the House threatened to vote against these measures unless those jobs were excluded.

Many African Americans found refuge in religion. In place of Marcus Garvey's Black Nationalism and his Universal Negro Improvement Association came Father Divine's "heavens" on earth and Elijah Muhammad's Nation of Islam. Both leaders promoted black pride and reliance on each other to survive in the struggle against poverty and oppression.

For Asian Americans the new decade meant a renewed fight against Asian exclusion laws and Alien Land laws. Divisions among Asian American, however, made a successful campaign for equal rights difficult. Chinese, Filipinos, Japanese, and Koreans had different agendas and seldom worked together. Many Chinese Americans preferred to stay out of any struggle for equality. Filipinos came to America in large numbers to work as agricultural laborers, houseboys, and servants. They faced harsh conditions in these jobs because of continuing prejudice. Japanese American leaders thought that displays of super-patriotism would quickly lead to equal rights and citizenship, but it did not. Instead it led to World War II "relocation camps." The small Korean community focused most of its attention on liberating their home country from Japanese oppression.

From 1930 to 1933, Latinos were removed by the thousands from the United States and repatriated to the homelands, mainly to Mexico. Perhaps a half-million Latinos were deported by time the program was completed. A large majority of Spanish-speaking workers who crossed the Rio Grande worked in agriculture, picking fruits and vegetables. But growing unemployment in the United States meant that many white Americans were now willing to take those jobs. One goal of repatriation was to create jobs for desperately poor white Americans, but racism and prejudice also played a role in the deportation campaign. Immigration agents often arrested "Spanish-looking" people with little regard for their constitutional rights.

On Indian reservations the depression increased hunger and malnutrition in places where life had been hard for most residents even before the depression hit. After years of struggle, Congress in 1934 granted Indians the right to choose their own reservation governments and write their own constitutions. John Collier, the new commissioner of Indian affairs, had been a longtime fighter for Indian sovereignty and promised to improve education, healthcare, and the reservation economies. By the end of the decade he had accomplished some of his goals. Life for Native Americans was still very difficult; rates of unemployment, poverty, and crime were much higher than in any other communities in the United States. But Indians now had some power to determine their own futures, speak their own languages, and practice their traditional religions.

European Americans continued to feel the impact of the 1924 quota system. Immigration to the United States from Europe dropped to record low levels in the 1930s. For some Europeans the quotas established had a more deadly impact. Thousands of European Jews wanted to immigrate to America after the Nazis came to power and Adolf Hitler began his campaign to rid Germany of all Jews. Because of America's quota system, they could not get to the United States and many of them would perish in the Holocaust. Race and ethnicity continued to influence people's lives, sometimes with deadly consequences.

KEY EVENTS

MEXICAN REPATRIATION

Between 1930 and 1933, the United States "repatriated," or deported, more than 400,000 Spanish-speaking immigrants, principally Mexicans. *Repatriation* means to return to a person's homeland; *deportation* refers to forcing people to return to their place of birth, usually for committing a crime. Many of the people sent out of the country had been born in the United States, making them American citizens by birth. U.S. Immigration Service agents, however, made no distinction between citizens and noncitizens when they swept through Hispanic neighborhoods in Los Angeles, Phoenix, Chicago, and other cities with large Spanish-speaking communities. In many cases they simply rounded up anyone who spoke Spanish or looked Spanish, put them on buses, and returned them to the border.

Although the 1924 immigration restriction legislation did not cover Mexicans or other immigrants from the Western Hemisphere, other laws were used to limit the number of people entering the United States from South America or Canada. President Herbert Hoover ordered that the "likely public charge" provision of the 1891 immigration law (known as the LPC clause) be strictly enforced. This section of the law prohibited entrance into the United States to "paupers or persons" unable to take care of themselves and therefore likely to need public assistance or aid. Rules and regulations defining "LPCs" were tightened in 1928 by order of the president to include any immigrant who did not have a job. The law was retroactive—anyone unemployed for any period of time during their stay in the United States could be sent back home. The depression created huge unemployment problems in every community, not just immigrant neighborhoods. Now, unemployed immigrants could be expelled as LPCs.

Applicants for visas to enter the United States faced other problems. Counselor officials in Mexico could refuse to issue a necessary visa to any person they believed would not be able to find a job in the United States. Even if potential migrants showed that they had a job waiting for them, however, they could be denied a visa under the anticontract labor restriction of the 1885 immigration law. This provision made it illegal for any employer to import or arrange for the importation of laborers for any set period of time. Violators of this law, passed by Congress after pressure from unions afraid that corporations would bring immigrants into the country as strikebreakers, would be arrested and sent back to wherever they came from.

The Mexican removal or Mexican "repatriation plan," as President Herbert Hoover called it, expanded as the Great Depression spread across the United States. By 1931, more than 12 million (almost one-third of the workforce) Americans had lost their jobs. Secretary of Labor William N. Doak who had authority over the Immigration Service at this time blamed this vast increase in unemployment on the presence of millions of "illegal aliens" who had taken jobs away from Americans. Removing the illegals, he claimed, would help restore prosperity.[1] In this case, the secretary's interpretation of illegals included LPCs. Los Angeles had the nation's largest Spanish-speaking community or *barrio*. The Mexican exclusion program began there. According to the Immigration Bureau plan, its agents, along with the local police, would conduct deportation raids by applying methods that would "scare these people out" of the city. Spanish-language radio stations and newspapers were recruited to announce planned raids in the community to spread fear. They would also print the names of prominent *barrio* leaders they arrested. The police targeted young men at first but eventually went after people of all ages as panic spread through the neighborhoods.[2]

The authorities ignored constitutional rights. According to a study released by the Los Angeles Bar Association, the police and Immigration Service agents arrested and deported thousands of people without warrants. They shot one farm worker who tried to run away. They did not inform parents that any of their children born in the United States were legal citizens with full constitutional protections. After protests, immigration officials announced that children who were citizens could stay in the United States, but only if they declared themselves orphans. Entire families were arrested and deported and had their property confiscated. No one told them how or whether they would ever get it back; most never did.

After their arrest, "aliens" had the right to a hearing before a Board of Special Inquiry. Thousands of deportees were sent out of the country without this hearing. The accused could make his or her case for remaining in the United States during this hearing. The "boards" consisted of a single member, often the arresting officer who also served as prosecutor and judge. The defendant had the right to an attorney, but in less than 1 percent of the cases was a lawyer present. High legal fees and the hastiness of the proceedings, often held within 24 hours of the arrest, made legal representation all but impossible. The Bureau of Immigration had established no rules of evidence or procedures for judges to follow. The hearings were conducted in English, as few Immigration Bureau workers spoke

Spanish. The "alien" bore full responsibility for showing why he or she should not be deported. No appeals were allowed. No wonder only a very few of those arrested successfully defended their right to stay in the United States.

An immigrant could be deported for a variety of other reasons including committing a minor crime (such as getting a traffic ticket), having a child out of wedlock, committing adultery, or for "moral turpitude," which could be interpreted in any number of ways including demonstrating "bad character." The "LPC clause" remained a favorite of anti-immigrant supporters. Local officials in Los Angeles, for example, claimed that many illegal aliens came to the United States simply to get relief money that rightfully belonged to "Americans." A study by a private charity found that less than 3 percent of Mexican families in California were getting that aid, and those who did received an average of $61.00 per year from the county relief agency.[3]

The hearings provided little protection for immigrant rights, but the ordeal of the deportees was hardly over. At the border they received humiliating treatment from Border Patrol agents. Upon arrival, they had their clothes removed and were shoved into barbed wire pens before being deloused. Then they had their hair cut off before being marched naked in front of a medical officer. Meanwhile, other agents fumigated any luggage or clothing they had brought with them. So many deportees arrived that the Border Patrol had to hire extra agents. They received minimal training or, as one officer reported about his experience, "they just give you a .45 single action revolver with a web belt—and that was it."[4] Immigrants deported to Europe did not receive this kind of treatment.

The government of Mexico worked closely with American immigration officials during what one Spanish-language newspaper in California labeled the "de-Mexicanization of the United States." Mexico had lost thousands of workers to the United States in the 1920s and now wanted them back, even though its economy had suffered great losses from the global depression. Mexico's leaders wanted to improve relations with the United States, hoping that such an effort would improve trade relations with its neighbor to the north and perhaps eventually help their economy recover. So Mexican consuls in the United States helped identify families they believed were illegally here and helped pay for the transportation of the deportees to whatever place they called home. Once in Mexico many of the people could not find jobs and joined the huge number of homeless, unemployed families already filling the streets of that country's cities and towns. To make life even worse, many of the deportees were in Mexico for the first time in their lives.

Racism fueled much of the "Mexican Go Home" crusade in California and elsewhere. Secretary of Labor William Doak called Mexicans "a mongrel population." They were half-Spanish and half-Indian, making them "unassimilable" into American society. During a congressional hearing on an immigration bill, one witness, a former Border Patrol agent, referred to Mexicans as an "extremely pathetic specimen of the human race." He also observed that Mexicans were as dumb as "mules" and "insensitive to pain," so being thrown out of the country would not harm them. Another witness at the hearing, an expert on "eugenics," testified that in Mexican villages "one meets the same idleness, hordes of hungry dogs, and filthy children with faces plastered with flies, disease, lice, human filth, stench, promiscuous fornication, bastardy, lounging, apathetic peons and lazy squaws, beans and dried chili, liquor, general squalor, and envy and hatred of the gringo."[5]

That the repatriation policy was based mainly on racist assumptions is illustrated by the fact that while more than 250,000 Mexicans were deported in 1932, fewer than 500 Europeans shared that same fate. The repatriation program ended in 1933 when Franklin Delano Roosevelt became president of the United States. The Mexican American community had been badly damaged by that time. Mexican Americans and all Spanish-speaking residents of the United States lived in constant fear that they might be the next victims of "repatriation." Many *repatriados* had lost their property, their jobs, and their dignity as a result of the repatriation program. As an 80-year-old victim, deported at age 6 with the rest of his family, recalled seven decades later, "They just kicked us out with what we were wearing. It left a feeling I will have until I die. The government did a very wrong thing."[6]

THE WATSONVILLE RIOT

On Sunday evening, January 19, 1930, a gang of white men attacked a group of Filipino and Chinese farm workers in a bar called "The Filipino Club" seven miles outside of Watsonville, a town of slightly more than 8,300 people on the Pacific Coast in central California. A newspaper reported that nine white women lived above the bar/gambling casino and were seen dancing with the Asian men. In the agricultural regions of California, this kind of "race-mixing" violated long-held racial customs. White women seen with Filipino or Asian men were called "GooGoo Lovers" and treated like prostitutes.

The white owners of the club tried to keep the mob outside the building and fired several shots at them, wounding two men. The sheriff and his deputies arrived as the rioters attempted to break into the saloon. They fired tear gas canisters into the crowd, which quickly dispersed. The officers then drove the fifty-or-so frightened Asians back to their homes in Watsonville. While these events were taking place seven miles away, however, another mob had attacked a rooming house in downtown Watsonville filled with Filipino and Chinese migrant farm workers. Someone in this crowd of what a newspaper called "high school aged" kids heaved a rock through a window. A message tied to the rock warned the lettuce-pickers to stay away from white girls and to get out of town. For the rest of the night gangs of young white men roamed the streets looking for Filipinos and Chinese who they could threaten and beat.

On Monday morning, Filipinos in the community gathered and marched toward a bridge that separated them from the white neighborhoods. Here a much larger group of whites confronted them. After several tense minutes, another group came on the scene consisting of about 25 knife-carrying Mexicans. They stood between the already shouting mobs but then quickly crossed the bridge to join the whites. The Filipinos quickly dispersed. The anti-Asian rioting continued for three more days, however, although the Filipino community offered no further organized resistance.

Watsonville whites organized "hunting parties" of 50 to 100 men to keep the streets clear of Asians. The police did the best they could to break up these gangs, but in one incident, shots were fired into a house occupied by six Japanese field hands. They escaped uninjured, but later that day police and angry whites exchanged shots in front of a taxi-dancehall in the migrant worker's community. Here Filipino, Chinese, and Japanese men could dance with a white woman for 10 cents a dance, another practice that enraged white men. The police wounded two attackers and shot tear gas bombs before the mob retreated.

The violence reached its peak the next day, Wednesday January 22, when the "hunting parties" ran into Filipino homes dragging out their occupants. They whipped some and beat others. They threw dozens of the farm workers into the Pajaro River. The mob roamed the countryside where they demolished migrant workers' homes on farms and ranches that employed Asians. At one, the rioters fired hundreds of bullets into a bunkhouse inhabited by a dozen Filipinos. One of the bullets killed Fermin Tobera. When news spread of Tobera's death, the rampage ended as shocked rioters returned to their homes. The next day the county sheriff arrested seven whites and charged them with murder. Shortly thereafter, the county dropped all charges against the alleged killers after the judge assigned to hear the case received a death threat. In addition, several prominent leaders of the Filipino community, fearful of arousing further white hostility, called for leniency and supported freeing the prisoners. That same judge whose life was threatened told a reporter that he deplored the killing, but the Filipinos were "only ten years removed from savagery" and should be kept out of the county.[7]

The events at Watsonville were hardly new experiences for California's Asian community. Racial hatred in the state had flared many times before. A few days after the violence in Watsonville had faded, vigilantes dynamited a Filipino club in nearby Stockton, and a mob attacked a Filipino labor camp near the small town of Reedley, severely beating the workers before they could get out of bed . . . That summer anti-Filipino riots swept through California cities from San Francisco to Salinas and San Jose. Filipinos were blamed for taking jobs belonging to Americans and for accepting wages far below those whites were willing to accept. The Great Depression's effects were just beginning to be felt as unemployment rose sharply throughout the United States after the stock market collapse of 1929.

More than conflict over jobs, however, led to the anti-Filipino riots in 1930. Violence toward Filipinos, Chinese, and Japanese had afflicted the nation during good times and bad. *Pinoys*, the Philippine term for immigrants to America, faced racial discrimination and mistreatment since their first arrival in the United States at the beginning of the century. Recruited to do the "jobs white men won't do," mainly picking crops—or stoop labor as it was called, washing dishes, or cleaning houses ("houseboys"), they worked in the lowest paying jobs available. California growers claimed that *pinoys* were built for laboring in their fields. They were short, built close to the ground, and used to working in heat and intense humidity. They were also used to working for very cheap wages, although a cheap wage in the United States was a high wage compared with standards in the Islands. That is why thousands of Filipinos, 95 percent of them male, migrated to the United States after their homeland became an American colony in 1899. Money made here would make them rich when they returned home.

A popular stereotype pictured *pinoys* (Filipino Americans) as sexually crazed, brown-skinned predators always lusting after white women. Philippine writer, poet, and labor organizer Carlos Bulosan experienced the consequences of this prejudiced and false image firsthand. After leaving his small village in the Islands, he worked in the California fields picking lettuce, celery, dates, and whatever else was being harvested. Here in small towns throughout the West Coast "the lives of Filipinos were cheaper than those of dogs." In America, he suggested, "it was a crime to be a Filipino. I came to know that the public streets were not free to my people . . . We were suspect each time we were seen with a white woman." In his view, he and his fellow *pinoys* were considered by the police as dangerous as "negroes" were looked upon in the South. The fear of mixed race contacts between men and women played as great a role in anti-Filipino and anti-Asian riots in California, he felt, as it did in stirring up lynch mobs in Mississippi and Alabama.[8]

Shortly after the violence in Watsonville, U.S. Senator Hiram Johnson (Republican, California) introduced legislation calling for the total exclusion of Filipino laborers from the United States. They deserved no better treatment than other Asians did. Chinese workers had been excluded since 1882 and the Japanese were added in 1907. Why should the little "brown skinned men" from the jungles of the southwestern Pacific be treated differently? Congress would wait five years before fully adopting Johnson's measure and by that time, a great change had taken place in California's fields. As a first response to the 1930 riots, the growers had turned to Mexico for cheap labor. By the mid-1930s, when jobs became even scarcer and Spanish-speaking Californians were being deported by the thousands, however, they did not have go even that far from home to get cheap stoop labor. The depression had driven huge numbers of hungry, unemployed whites ("Okies" from the dust bowl in the Great Plains) into the state, and they were desperate enough to work for whatever little money they could get and in jobs that even white men now took whether they wanted to or not.

THE SCOTTSBORO "BOYS"

On March 25, 1931, a freight train rumbled through northern Alabama. On one of the boxcars, a fight broke out between white and black men riding the train looking for work wherever they could find it. The Great Depression had thrown millions of Americans out of work, and thousands of them took to the rails traveling from town to town hoping to find some kind of job. Nine blacks fought with an equal number of whites, each side claiming their right to the boxcar. The African Americans overwhelmed the whites and threw them off the train. The angry losers complained to the local sheriff who telegraphed the news of the fight to a stationmaster in nearby Stevenson, Alabama. He wired the news to the railroad clerk in Paint Rock, a town of barely 500 residents a few miles down the line.

By time the train approached Paint Rock, a mob of angry whites, swinging ropes and chains, had gathered at the station. They dragged the blacks off the train and threatened to lynch them all. Just then two white girls emerged from another boxcar. The women, Ruby Bates and Victoria Price, shouted that they had been "assaulted" on the train and pointed to the nine blacks as their attackers. The local sheriff took the girls to a doctor who examined them and reported that he had found no signs of rape. Nevertheless, the sheriff piled the nine young blacks in the back of a truck and drove them to the county seat of Scottsboro where they were charged with rape and jailed.

The accused rapists were Clarence Norris, Olen Montgomery, Haywood Patterson, Ozie Powell, Willie Roberson, Charlie Weems, Eugene Williams, and two brothers, Andrew and Leroy Wright. They ranged in age from 13, Leroy Wright the youngest, to 20, Charlie Weems the oldest. None had police records. All came from Georgia and were on their way to Memphis looking for work. That night a lynch mob gathered in front of the jail. It became so loud and agitated that the sheriff wired the governor asking for help. The next morning a unit of the Alabama National Guard arrived on the scene. The mob did not reappear.

When the trial of what now were being called "The Scottsboro Boys" began on April 6, however, more than 10,000 people gathered in the street as the

Scottsboro boys, with Juanita E. Jackson from the National Association for the Advancement of Colored People (NAACP), January 1937. Courtesy of the Library of Congress, LC-USZ62-116731.

National Guard surrounded the courthouse. Norris and Weems faced the judge and an all-white jury first. Because none of the boys' parents could afford legal representation, black church leaders from northeastern Alabama had raised money to hire a lawyer. The attorney they hired had never tried a case before because he handled mainly real estate transactions. During the trial he never talked to the defendants and showed up drunk at the courtroom his first morning in town. The presiding judge quickly appointed an elderly local attorney to assist the defense council, but he was on the verge of senility, had never been involved in a death penalty case, and like the lead attorney never talked to any of the accused either. This "team" called no witnesses during the trials, asked no questions of any of the witnesses, and made no closing argument.

The state tried the defendants in four different trials before four different juries over a period of three days. At all four proceedings, Price and Bates described how the boys held them at knifepoint and ripped off their clothes, then pushed them to the floor and raped them. Price testified that the assailants screamed "they were going to take us north and make us their women or kill us." A farmer who had been working in his hayloft about a quarter-of-a-mile from the tracks told the juries that he saw "a bunch of negroes take charge of the two girls." The defense attorneys had no questions for this witness.

The boys gave conflicting testimony that only helped the prosecution. Clarence Norris turned on his colleagues and testified that he had witnessed all eight of them raping the white women; however, he was innocent. More confusing testimony followed with Haywood Patterson testifying he had seen only five of the accused committing rape. According to Leroy Wright, "nine" blacks had raped two white women. He later told the *New York Times* that during a break in the trial, a deputy sheriff took him into a back room where another deputy whipped him repeatedly until "I couldn't stand it anymore." The beating stopped only when Wright agreed to testify against his co-defendants. Andy Wright and Eugene Williams insisted that no one had been raped.[9]

Rape was a capital offense in Alabama and the state sought death sentences for the nine accused. In his many summations, the prosecutor reminded the jurors that as a matter of the honor of white women everywhere, they had to return a guilty verdict. The only just punishment was death. The defense attorneys stood silent.

The four juries returned with nine guilty verdicts and eight recommendations for execution. In the case of 13-year-old Leroy Wright, the jury reported an inability to reach a decision. Eleven of the jurors had found him guilty and favored executing him, but one juror could not go along with killing a young boy and favored life imprisonment. He refused to change his mind. Therefore in the case of Leroy Wright, the judge declared a mistrial and ordered a new trial.[10]

After the juries rendered their verdicts, the Communist Party U.S.A., (CPUSA) headquartered in New York received a telegram from two of its members in Alabama. They had attended the trials and expressed shock and dismay at the outcome. They thought the case would provide the party with a recruitment opportunity among blacks in the South. Party leaders decided that its legal arm, the International Labor Defense Committee (ILD), should go to Alabama and prepare an appeal. The National Association for the Advancement of Colored People (NAACP) rejected an appeal from a defendant's mother to get involved in the case. The association's leaders doubted the boy's innocence and feared that any association with the case, now that communists were involved, would hurt its image as a pro-American institution.

To raise money for the appeal and awareness of "a legal lynching" in Alabama, communist parties around the world, from New York to Chicago to San Francisco, to Moscow, Paris and London, sponsored huge marches and demonstrations. More than 150,000 Germans marched through Dresden demanding justice in Scottsboro, and 300,000 Americans in more than 100 different cities did the same on May 1, 1931. The party brought two of the boys' mothers north to speak at the rallies and plead for support.

The CPUSA sent Samuel Leibowitz, a noncommunist and one of the most respected defense attorneys in New York City, to handle the appeal. He had handled 78 trials in his home state and had won 77 "not guilty" verdicts. The Alabama Supreme Court rejected his first appeal but did order a new trial for Eugene Williams because he was still a juvenile when the case was heard. Leibowitz took the appeal, based on the inadequacies of the defense lawyers, to federal court. Eventually the case got to the U.S. Supreme Court where on November 7, 1932, it set aside the convictions and ordered new trials for all nine defendants. In its decision in *Powell v. Alabama,* the Court ruled that in death penalty cases, the accused have a Fourteenth Amendment right to due process, which could only be provided by an adequate attorney. The Scottsboro Boys had obviously been denied that right.[11]

The state of Alabama took little time to retry the case. The defense demanded that the next trial be moved to Birmingham, the state capital. Instead, it was moved to Decatur, Alabama, a town not far from Scottsboro. On March 27, 1933, presiding Judge James E. Horton opened the proceedings against Haywood Patterson, the first of the Scottsboro Boys to be retried. "The courtroom was one big smiling white face," Patterson recalled. The judge quickly dismissed a defense motion to drop all charges because no black person had ever served on a jury in Alabama.[12]

Alabama Attorney General Thomas Knight led the prosecution. Victoria Price appeared as the first witness and stuck to her story of how nine blacks had raped her on the floor of the boxcar. He also showed her a scale model of the train built for the defense by the Lionel Corporation. He asked Price if the model looked like the train she had been riding when the alleged rape occurred. "That is not the train I was on," she protested. "It was bigger, lots bigger." Leibowitz felt that these types of answers and the numerous "I don't remember" responses he got from Price would make her look foolish even in the eyes of an all-white male southern jury. But he was wrong. The reaction of a local newspaper editor caught the spirit of the white response much more precisely when he wrote that even if Victoria Price lied, "we don't want a Jewish lawyer from New York, especially one hired by the Communist Party, treating our women—even our poor, white trash—like this."[13]

The star witness for the defense turned out to be Ruby Bates. She had been missing for several weeks and surprised the prosecution by her appearance. Under Leibowitz's guidance, she repudiated her testimony from the first trial and denied having been raped. Under harsh cross-examination by the prosecutor, however, she broke down and changed her story several times. He got her to admit that during her disappearance she had been in New York City and that the Communist Party had paid for her trip. Party members had even bought her a new dress and coat. She had been bribed, the prosecutor told the jury. She had changed her story only because communists had paid her to tell lies. And by changing her testimony, she showed just how unreliable a witness she had become. Leibowitz presented a witness who testified that he and Victoria Price had intercourse the night before the alleged rape and that the girls, both poor, badly educated cotton mill workers, had been prostitutes in Chattanooga, Tennessee.

The defense lawyers thought they had a case they could not lose. Toward the end of his four-hour summation, Leibowitz asked the jury to "give this poor scrap of colored humanity (Haywood), a fair, square deal." In his summation, Attorney General Knight, soon to become Alabama's lieutenant governor, called for "death in the electric chair" for "that thing" who raped Victoria Price. The jury obliged. They found Patterson guilty of rape after only a few minutes of deliberation and demanded his electrocution.[14]

To the surprise of everyone, Judge Horton rejected the jury's verdict and set it aside. He questioned Victoria Price's testimony and suggested that what she said just could not be squared with the facts. Her testimony "bares on its face indications of improbability and is contradicted by other evidence," the judge declared. He ordered a new trial date. Even Haywood Patterson expressed surprise at Judge Horton's ruling, but he declared that the decision "made me feel good. I saw that there could be white folks in the South with the right mind."[15] Judge Horton paid a bitter price for his decision. He lost his reelection bid the following June.

In the next trial, an all-white jury convicted Patterson a third time and once more sentenced him to death. The presiding judge this time proved openly hostile to Leibowitz. He told him several times to "shut up" and denied all of his motions. Shortly thereafter, Clarence Norris faced an all-white jury that quickly convicted him and called for his execution. An appeal to the Alabama Supreme Court failed but the U.S. Supreme Court reversed the conviction of Patterson and Norris once again. This time in *Norris v. Alabama* (1935), the Court ruled that the exclusion of African Americans from the state's jury rolls had deprived the defendants of their Fourteenth Amendment right of equal protection under the law. It sent the case back to Alabama once more for yet another trial.

The fourth (and final) round of trials began in 1936. By this time, the Communist Party had turned the case over to the NAACP. It organized The Scottsboro Legal Defense Committee and chose a new lawyer, Alabama-born Clarence

Watts, to head the team, although Leibowitz remained as an assistant counsel. "Do not quibble over the evidence," the prosecutor implored the jury, "Say to yourselves we're tired of this job and put it behind you. Get it done quick and protect the fair womanhood of this state."[16] On January 21, 1936, a jury that contained one black member found Patterson guilty for a fourth time but recommended a 75-year sentence rather than execution because one of the jurors objected to the death penalty for religious reasons. Shortly before Ozie Powell was to appear in court, he used a concealed knife to cut the throat of a guard, and then another guard shot Powell in the head. He survived but suffered permanent brain damage. Alabama did not try him again for rape. It did, however, convict him of assaulting a prison guard for which he received a 20-year term.

The state dropped all charges against Leroy Wright, Olen Montgomery, Willie Roberson, and Eugene Williams after they had spent six and one-half years in prison. They agreed to leave the state as part of this agreement. After they left Alabama, none was heard from again. In the cases of Andy Wright and Charlie Weems, juries convicted them of rape for which they received 99-year sentences. Clarence Norris received another death sentence, although Alabama Governor Bibb Graves commuted it to life imprisonment. Weems, Norris, and Wright received paroles in 1944 with the understanding that they would leave the state and never return. They did leave but when they came back a year later seeking paroles, the police promptly arrested them and returned them to prison. All three were released again in 1946 and this time they did not return to Alabama.

Patterson remained in prison until 1948. Guards frequently whipped him and placed him in solitary confinement in a dirt-floored cell filled with poisonous snakes, for days at a time. At one point, guards paid another prisoner 50 dollars to kill him. He stabbed Patterson more than 20 times, puncturing his lung, but he survived. After 11 years in jail, he escaped from a chain gang and eventually made it to his sister's home in Michigan. He published a book about his ordeal in 1950. A few days after its publication, FBI agents arrested him. Alabama authorities demanded his return, but Michigan's Governor G. Mennen Williams refused to extradite him. Less than two years later, however, he died from cancer at the age of 39.[17]

What happened to the other Scottsboro Boys? Leroy Wright was arrested and convicted of raping a 13-year-old girl and died in prison. Olen Montgomery became an alcoholic and just disappeared. Roy Wright killed his wife and the man she was with and then killed himself. Patterson killed a man in a knife fight and ended up in prison. Charles Norris ended up in New York City where he got a job with the sanitation department. He led a relatively normal life, although police arrested him several times for illegal possession of a gun. The rest just disappeared.[18] (Ruby Bates disappeared, too. She was never heard from again after the trials ended. Victoria Price, long thought dead, resurfaced in 1976 bringing a libel suit against NBC for airing a documentary that declared her a "known prostitute." She secretly settled the case out of court and died shortly thereafter, insisting to the end that she had told the truth.)

In 1976, Alabama Governor George Wallace pardoned all nine men, but only one, Clarence Norris, was still alive. He accepted the pardon with a great deal of sadness on behalf of the other eight whose lives had been ruined by racism, lies, fear, and ignorance.

INDIAN SOVEREIGNTY

Native Americans had been granted American citizenship in 1924, but they still were not in charge of their reservations. The Bureau of Indian Affairs (BIA) in Washington, D.C. continued to control and police their lives, still banning their dances and religious performances and outlawing the use of their languages in Indian education. The BIA had always operated on the principle that Indians were absolutely ignorant.

This view led to a situation in which Indian reservations were among the poorest communities in the nation. The 1928 Meriam Report, officially known as *The Problem of Indian Administration*, offered a devastating critique of conditions on the reservations and suggested a series of reforms to improve the quality of lives of American Indians. The key change needed, the Report concluded, was to listen to Indians and allow them to have a say in their futures.

The U.S. Senate's Committee on Indian Affairs followed up the Meriam Report with a survey of its own. Committee members toured more than 350 reservations in 1928 and 1929. Many of these reservations were on land considered among the least fertile in the western states. It was badly eroded, weed infested, and dry. On many reservations if Indians wanted to buy anything, whether food, clothes, or tools, they needed to ask the agent for permission. Even if the agent approved the purchase, Indians received a purchase order rather than money to buy the item at the agency store. Indians simply could not be trusted with money, in the eyes of the agents; if they had any they would quickly waste it on alcohol or gambling. If Indians became sick, Bureau agents determined whether or not they really were and only then sent them to a doctor.

In its report, the committee found living conditions so terrible that it shocked many of its members. It offered such withering criticism of the BIA that its commissioner resigned. The new commissioner appointed by President Herbert Hoover was Charles Rhoads, a Quaker and a former president of the Indian Rights Association (IRA), one of the oldest groups (founded in 1882) promoting equal status for Native Americans in the United States. Rhoads announced that he supported the recommendations in the Meriam Report and would try to implement them. He advocated a clear path to assimilation for Indians that included better schools on reservations, an end to corruption in local agencies, and an expansion of programs to improve the transition of Native Americans into the job market.

In pursuit of these goals, the BIA closed most of its off-reservation boarding schools and opened vocational schools on reservations geared to training students skills needed in the local job market. Unfortunately, reservations had among the highest unemployment rates in the country and very few new jobs were being created. To show its commitment to reform, Congress added several million dollars to the BIA budget for 1929. Then the Great Depression hit. The already terrible economic conditions on the reservations became even worse. President Hoover vetoed a bill providing $15 million for Indian food relief in 1930. He feared it would discourage people from seeking work. Congress cut appropriations for the BIA the next year as part of its overall program to reduce government spending during the economic crisis. The Red Cross finally stepped in with aid that prevented outright starvation on those reservations hardest hit by the cutbacks.

In response to the collapse of the entire economy, voters elected Franklin D. Roosevelt president in 1932. (In all, 90 percent of Indians voted for Roosevelt.) Roosevelt's New Deal reforms of 1933–1934 included a bill that would radically change American policy toward Indians. Shortly after taking office the new president appointed John Collier, a longtime advocate of Indian rights and religious freedom, as Commissioner of Indian Affairs. Collier, a white social worker from New York City, had led the American Indian Defense Association (AIDA) since its founding in 1923. Collier brought enthusiasm and a lifelong love of Indian arts and religions to his new position and insisted that "anything less than to let Indian culture live on would be a crime against the earth itself."[19] In his view, white European civilization suffered from too much worship of material goods and not enough respect for the natural order of things.

In the spring of 1934, Collier met with his key advisors in the BIA to draft legislation that would promote economic development and education on Indian lands and also give them some degree of self-government. After much discussion and consultation with legal experts and social scientists interested in Indian culture, including anthropologists Franz Boas and Ralph Linton and Pulitzer Prize winning novelist/anthropologist Oliver La Farge, Collier presented the bill to Congress. Officially titled the Indian Reorganization Act of 1934 (also called the Wheeler-Howard Act after its key sponsors in the Senate and House), the legislation called for self-government including new constitutions for the tribes and local control over education and training. Indians would also be able to get jobs with the BIA, which had very few Native American employees, without passing a civil service test. Opponents of the bill argued that self-government would hinder efforts to assimilate Indians into American society. The effect of the bill, according to a South Dakota Congressman would be to "segregate the Indian and isolate him and make it impossible to ever become an assimilated part of the citizenship of our country."[20]

Collier responded that Indians should be given a choice; some might desire assimilation into American society and improvements in education would help them accomplish that goal. Others who wanted to retain their traditional cultures, however, should be permitted to make that decision and continue to study their tribal languages and follow their customs. Collier believed that a large majority of Indians would choose the second option, but he wanted Indians to make this decision without pressure from Washington or anyone else.

Congress adopted several amendments to the Reorganization Act. The most important mandated that all Indian tribes hold an election within two years to decide whether or not it wanted to become self-governing. If a majority of voters said no, however, the tribe would not be eligible for the $20 million dollars in economic development loans provided for in the act. Congress passed the final bill early in June and President Roosevelt signed it into law shortly thereafter. The final legislation ended the allotment system, in place since 1887, under which individual Indian families had received 160 acres of reservation land from the government. In return, Indians would give up membership in their tribes, learn to become farmers or ranchers, and finally join the modern American world. Instead of individual ownership, title to remaining reservation land would now be held by the tribe.

The new law excluded Oklahoma Indians from its provisions at the behest of the state's congressional delegation. They expressed fears that sovereignty would interfere with assimilation, which in their view was well underway. Congress also excluded Alaskan Indians from coverage because it was a territory and the Inuit (Eskimos) and Aleuts technically were not Indians. A 1936 law, however, extended coverage to these peoples.

A majority of tribes voted in favor of local self-government in 1935 and 1936. The BIA offered guidance on writing the new constitutions. Thus most followed a single model with a chairman, vice-chairman, secretary, and treasurer, and a council elected by eligible voters on each reservation. Once created, these new tribal governments had the authority to review reservation budgets created by the BIA and suggest changes. The councils would represent the tribes in dealing with federal, state, and local governments and hire attorneys to represent them in their dealings with these governments. The new constitution would give native peoples power to police their reservations up to a point. Tribal courts, for instance, would have jurisdiction over most crimes, although major crimes committed on reservations, such as bank robbery or murder, would remain under the jurisdiction of the federal courts.

Despite this lack of total sovereignty, the new Indian governments now had some control over local police matters, education, and healthcare. These new powers reduced the influence of often hostile local county and state governments and employees of the BIA. With passage of the Wheeler-Howard Act, many of the reforms advocated in the Meriam Report had been accomplished. Indians were asked what they wanted. Indian religious beliefs, languages, and other traditions would be respected. BIA appropriations averaged $48 million a year during Collier's tenure (1933–1945), four times as much as it had been in the 1920s. The Indian Reorganization Act changed the course of American policy toward Indians. Instead of assimilation, it became one of independent cultural development. The BIA followed this policy until 1945 when Collier resigned his job after Congress demanded yet another return to a policy of assimilation.

CONGRESS REFUSES TO SAVE 20,000 JEWISH CHILDREN FROM NAZI TERROR AND THE FATE OF THE *ST. LOUIS*

On February 9, 1939, Senator Robert Wagner, Democrat of New York, introduced legislation that called for the admission of 20,000 German Jewish children from refugee camps in Europe. Wagner's bill, presented to the House of Representatives by Edith Nourse Rogers, Republican of Massachusetts, established a special quota for children less than 14 years old that would be spread over two years. Since 1924, the United States had based its immigration policy on a strict quota system based on nationality. Germany's normal quota had been set at about 25,000 immigrants per year, but that number had seldom been met even as the Nazi persecution of Jews intensified between 1933 and 1938. In 1936, for example, the quota allowed 25, 957 immigrants from Germany, but only 6,346 entered the country.

In the wake of *Kristallnacht* ("The Night of the Broken Glass," November 9–10, 1938 when Nazi thugs murdered more than 400 Jews and burned down 300 synagogues), the British and Dutch governments made special provisions to allow several thousands Jewish refugees into their countries. This action inspired introduction of the Wagner-Rogers Bill in the American Congress. Something had to be done, Wagner told his colleagues, to save as many Jews as possible from Nazi terror. Wagner singled out children because he thought this would eliminate the argument that immigrants would take jobs away from Americans. Children under 14 would not pose this threat.

President Franklin Roosevelt responded to *Kristallnacht* by recalling the American ambassador to Berlin and extending the visas of the 12,000 German Jewish refugees already in the country. He also announced, however, that he would not seek any changes in the immigration quota system. A public opinion poll published in *Fortune Magazine* found that 83 percent of Americans agreed with the president on this issue—they opposed any attempt to increase immigration for any reason. Since 1930, applying for even a temporary visa had become increasingly complex. That year President Herbert Hoover asked the Immigration Service and the State Department to begin vigorous enforcement of a provision of the 1917 Immigration Act that excluded any persons "likely to become public charges." This was the "LPC clause" (likely public charge). It meant that potential immigrants needed to show evidence that they had a job promised to them in the States, a difficult thing to do with the onset of the Great Depression before any application could be considered. If they did not have a job, immigrants needed a "sponsor" who would guarantee that they would never seek "relief" or public assistance. Beyond these impediments immigration authorities also insisted that the required several-page applications had to be typewritten in triplicate before being accepted at U.S. embassies. These strict requirements would keep immigration down and thereby protect jobs for Americans, Hoover had insisted.[21]

Eleanor Roosevelt tried to persuade her husband to support the Wagner-Nourse Bill, but he refused, telling her that "it is all right for you to support the child refugee bill, but it is best for me to say nothing." Without the president's support, the bill remained tied up in committee. Opponents of the bill carried out a national campaign to prevent its passage. The American Immigration Conference Board, an anti-immigrant group, sent out thousands of pamphlets proclaiming that "Charity Begins at Home." Passage of the bill would take food out of the mouths of America's children, the Board proclaimed. "Shall we sentence these slum children to crime, poverty, and hopelessness while we import children from a foreign country?"[22] Several congressional opponents argued that if the United States made exceptions for Jewish kids, it would set an unhappy precedent for the future. What happens to the quota system when and if other groups in Europe or anyplace else faced abuse and mistreatment—would we have to change the numbers for them, too? And then where would it stop?

Some of the opposition came from people with distinct anti-Jewish prejudices. Assistant Secretary of State Breckinridge Long and the person in charge of immigration enforcement in the State Department sent a memo to American diplomats in Europe calling on them to do everything they could to keep Jewish refugees out of the United States. He insisted that they "put every obstacle in the way, which would postpone" granting them visas. Secretary of State Cordell Hull showed little sympathy for the plight of German Jews, opposing a boycott of German-made products proposed by White House advisors in 1939. Franklin Roosevelt's cousin, Laura Delano Houghteling, happened to be married to the commissioner of immigration. She openly expressed her views in a comment to the press, "Twenty thousand charming children would all too soon grow into twenty-thousand ugly adults," she warned, if the bill got through Congress.[23]

Opposition of a different sort came from Jewish American groups. The General Jewish Council, which represented the four largest Jewish organizations in the United States, argued that support for Senator Wagner's bill would provoke an anti-Semitic reaction in Congress and among the public. Samuel Rosenman, President Roosevelt's closest advisor on Jewish affairs, echoed that view telling the president that support for the bill "would lead to a Jewish problem in the United States."[24]

The Wagner-Rogers refugee aid bill never made it to the floor of the House or Senate. In the House, an amendment had been added that would admit 20,000 children but only if the regular German quota was reduced by a similar number. The bill died after Senator Wagner refused to add this provision to the Senate bill. It was not introduced again.

The experience of 937 passengers on the German transatlantic liner *St. Louis* showed once more how little the American government and the American people were prepared to do to save Jewish lives. Most of the passengers were German Jews who had bought landing permits for several hundred dollars from the Cuban embassy in Berlin. They planned to get to Cuba from where they would apply for visas allowing them to enter the United States. Eight days before their trip began, the Cuban government—for reasons still unknown—revoked all landing permits. To enter Cuba, immigrants now had to post a $500 bond and get written authorization from the Cuban secretary of state to enter the country. When the ship sailed on May 13, 1939, for Havana no one told the passengers of these new requirements. When the *St. Louis* reached its destination on May 28, Cuban authorities told the passengers that they could not leave the ship.

Everyone remained on the ship for one week while a representative from an American aid committee unsuccessfully negotiated directly with Cuban President Federico Laredo Bru. The Cuban navy kept several "suicide prevention boats" alongside the ill-fated vessel. One passenger cut his wrists and jumped overboard, but most of the passengers remained quietly in their cabins. In early June, the ship's captain grew tired of waiting and headed for Miami, Florida, where he hoped the American government would let him land. But it did not; instead the State Department sent a telegram to the ship informing the passengers that they "must await their turns on the waiting list and then qualify for and obtain immigration visas before they may be admissible into the United States."[25] This procedure normally took several years. President Roosevelt had authority to grant additional refugees by issuing an executive order, but he chose not to do so.

While waiting off the Florida coast, the U.S. Coast Guard kept one of its cutters close by to make sure that no one swam to shore. After receiving this refusal, the *St. Louis* sailed back to Europe. The American Jewish Joint Distribution Committee asked the governments of Great Britain, the Netherlands, France, and Belgium to admit the passengers, but none did. Most of the passengers soon found themselves back in Nazi Germany. Hundreds of them died in concentration camps. A few survived, however, and 50 years later met in Miami to commemorate their ordeal. The fate of the Wagner-Rogers bill and the experience of the *St. Louis* illustrate that hundreds of lives could have been saved had someone with political courage led a drive to change America's extremely restrictive immigration laws. Such was not the case, however.

VOICES OF THE DECADE

CARLOS BULASON (1913–1956)

Carlos Bulosan was a Filipino writer, poet, and union activist. He worked as a farm laborer in California and became interested in union organizing. His *America Is in the Heart* (1943) describes his experiences as a boy and young man in the Philippines and his journey to the United States. In America he found that Filipinos were subjected to discrimination, exploitation, and prejudice. In this passage he argues that America is not only for whites and the rich because being

American does not depend on race, color, or wealth. Instead, it is a feeling, an attitude, and a grand statement of equality.

> America is not a land of one race or one class of men. We are all Americans that have toiled and suffered and known oppression and defeat, from the first Indian that offered peace in Manhattan to the last Filipino pea pickers. America is not bound by geographical latitudes. America is not merely a land or an institution. America is in the hearts of men that died for freedom; it is also in the eyes of men that are building a new world. America is a prophecy of a new society of men: of a system that knows no sorrow or strife or suffering. America is a warning to those who would try to falsify the ideas of free men.
>
> America is also the nameless foreigner, the homeless refugee, the hungry boy begging for a job and the black body dangling from a tree. America is the illiterate immigrant who is ashamed that the world of books and intellectual opportunities is closed to him. We are that nameless foreigner, that homeless refugee, that hungry boy, that illiterate immigrant and that lynched black body. All of us, from the first Adams to the last Filipino, native born or alien, educated or illiterate—We are America!
>
> From Carlos Bulason, *America Is in the Heart, A Personal History* (Seattle: University of Washington Press, 1991), 109–10.

LUTHER STANDING BEAR (1868–1939)

Luther Standing Bear lived in two worlds, Indian and white. He was educated at a government boarding school and later was elected chief of his people, the Oglala Sioux. He acted in dozens of Hollywood westerns and performed in Buffalo Bill's Wild West Show for several years. He began writing at age 60 and published four books on Indian culture and history before his death. In this excerpt from *Land of the Spotted Eagle* (1933), he identifies key differences between Indians and whites.

> The white man does not understand the Indian for the reason that he does not understand America. He is too far removed from its formative processes. The roots of the tree of his life have not yet grasped the rock and soil. The white man is still troubled with primitive fears; he still has in his consciousness the perils of this frontier continent, some of its fastnesses not yet having yielded to his questing footsteps and inquiring eyes. He shudders still with the memory of the loss of his forefathers upon its scorching deserts and forbidding mountain-tops. The man from Europe is still a foreigner and an alien. And he still hates the man who questioned his path across the continent.
>
> But in the Indian the spirit of the land is still vested; it will be until other men are able to divine and meet its rhythm. Men must be born and reborn to

belong. Their bodies must be formed of the dust of their forefathers' bones. The attempted transformation of the Indian by the white man and the chaos that has resulted are but the fruits of the white man's disobedience of a fundamental and spiritual law. The pressure that has been brought to bear upon the native people, since the cessation of armed conflict, in the attempt to force conformity of custom and habit has caused a reaction more destructive than war, and the injury has not only affected the Indian, but has extended to the white population as well. Tyranny, stupidity, and lack of vision have brought about the situation now alluded to as the "Indian Problem."

There is, I insist, no Indian problem as created by the Indian himself. Every problem that exists today in regard to the native population is due to the white man's cast of mind, which is unable, at least reluctant, to seek understanding and achieve adjustment in a new and a significant environment into which it has so recently come. The white man excused his presence here by saying that he had been guided by the will of his God; and in so saying absolved himself of all responsibility for his appearance in a land occupied by other men. Then, too, his law was a written law; his divine Decalogue reposed in a book. And what better proof that his advent into this country and his subsequent acts were the result of divine will! He brought the Word! There ensued a blind worship of written history, of books, of the written word, that has denuded the spoken word of its power and sacredness. The written word became established as a criterion of the superior man—a symbol of emotional fineness. The man who could write his name on a piece of paper, whether or not he possessed the spiritual fineness to honor those words in speech, was by some miraculous formula a more highly developed and sensitized person than the one who had never had a pen—in hand, but whose spoken word was inviolable and whose sense of honor and truth was paramount. With false reasoning was the quality of human character measured by man's ability to make with an implement a mark upon paper. But granting this mode of reasoning be correct and just, then where are to be placed the thousands of illiterate whites who are unable to read and write? Are they, too, "savages?" Is not humanness a matter of heart and mind, and is it not evident in the form of relationship with men? Is not kindness more powerful than arrogance; and truth more powerful than the sword?

True, the white man brought great change. But the varied fruits of his civilization, though highly colored and inviting, are sickening and deadening. And if it be the part of civilization to maim, rob, and thwart, then what is progress?

From *Land of the Spotted Eagle* (Lincoln: University of Nebraska Press, 1978), 248–50.

JOHN COLLIER (1884–1968)

John Collier became commissioner of Indian Affairs in 1933 and served until 1945. He had been active in the Indian rights movement since the early 1920s.

At the Bureau of Indian Affairs he oversaw major reforms, including providing Indians with economic, political, and educational reform. Here he summarizes the achievements of his administration after its first five years.

We, therefore, define our Indian policy somewhat as follows: So productively to use the moneys appropriated by the Congress for Indians as to enable them, on good, adequate lands of their own, to earn decent livelihoods and lead self-respecting, organized lives in harmony with their own aims and ideals, as an integral part of American life. Under such a policy, the ideal end result will be the ultimate disappearance of any need for government aid or supervision. This will not happen tomorrow; perhaps not in our lifetime; but with the revitalization of Indian hope due to the actions and attitudes of this government during the last few years, that aim is a probability, and a real one. . . .

In looking at the Indian picture as a social whole, we will consider certain broad phases—land use and industrial enterprises, health and education, roads and rehabilitation, political organization—which touch Indian life everywhere, including the 30,000 natives of Alaska for whose health, education, and social and economic advancement the Indian Service is responsible. Lastly, this report will tell wherein the Indian Service, or the government's effort as a whole for the Indians, still falls short.

The Indian feels toward his land, not a mere ownership sense but a devotion and veneration befitting what is not only a home but a refuge. At least nine out of ten Indians remain on or near the land. When times are good, a certain number drift away to town or city to work for wages. When times become bad, home to the reservation the Indian comes, and to the comparative security which he knows is waiting for him. The Indian still has much to learn in adjusting himself to the strains of competition amid an acquisitive society; but he long ago learned how to contend with the stresses of nature. Not only does the Indian's major source of livelihood derive from the land but his social and political organizations are rooted in the soil.

A major aim, then, of the Indian Service is to help the Indians to keep and consolidate what lands they now have and to provide more and better lands upon which they may effectively carry on their lives. Just as important is the task of helping the Indian make such use of his land as will conserve the land, insure Indian self-support, and safeguard or build up the Indian's social life. . . .

In 1887, the General Allotment Act was passed, providing that after a certain trust period, fee simple title to parcels of land should be given to individual Indians. Individual proprietorship meant loss—a paradox in view of the Indian's love for the land, yet an inevitable result, when it is understood that the Indian by tradition was not concerned with possession, did not worry about titles or recordings, but regarded the land as a fisherman might regard the sea, as a gift of nature, to be loved and feared, to be fought and revered, and to be drawn on by all as an inexhaustible source of life and strength.

The Indian let the ownership of his allotted lands slip from him. The job of taking the Indian's lands away, begun by the white man through military expeditions and treaty commissions, was completed by cash purchase—always of course, of the best lands which the Indian had left. In 1887, the Indian had remaining 130 million acres. In 1933, the Indian had left only 49 million acres, much of it waste and desert.

Since 1933, the Indian Service has made a concerted effort—an effort which is as yet but a mere beginning—to help the Indian to build back his landholdings to a point where they will provide an adequate basis for a self-sustaining economy, a self-satisfying social organization.

From *Annual Report of the Secretary of the Interior for the Fiscal Year Ended June 30*, 1938 (Washington, D.C., 1938), 209–211.

FATHER CHARLES COUGHLIN (1891–1975)

Father Charles Coughlin was a Roman Catholic priest who had one of the most popular radio programs of the 1930s. Speaking from the National Shrine of the Little Flower in Royal Oak, Michigan, he reached 40 million listeners with his weekly Sunday sermons. His major themes included praise for Adolf Hitler and anti-Semitism. His open hostility toward Jews is conveyed in the following excerpt from one of his sermons. His praise for Nazis led to the cancellation of his radio program in 1939.

Since 1923 when communism was beginning to make substantial advances throughout Germany, a group of rebel Germans—under the leadership of Austrian-born war veteran Adolf Hitler by name—organized for two purposes. First to overthrow the existing German government, under whose jurisdiction Communism was waxing strong and, second, to rid the Fatherland of Communists whose leaders, unfortunately, they identified with the Jewish race. Nazism was conceived as a political defense mechanism against Communism and was ushered into existence as a result of Communism. And, Communism itself was regarded by the rising generation of Germans as a product not of Russia, but of a group of Jews who dominated the destinies of Russia. (November 26, 1938 broadcast excerpt.)

The three outstanding leaders in the world today are the three Jews, Leon Blum, the radical of France; Maxim Litvinov, the reddest of red Russians; and Leslie Hore-Belisha, minister of war in England. . . . Must the entire world go to war for 600,000 Jews in Germany who are neither American, nor French, nor English citizens, but citizens of Germany?

From *Detroit News*, January 9, 1939.

Father Coughlin addresses a large Cleveland rally, May 1936. Courtesy of the Library of Congress, LC-USZ62-111027.

RACE RELATIONS BY GROUP

AFRICAN AMERICANS

The Great Depression of the 1930s brought distress, both economic and social, to the lives of many Americans. The vast unemployment and poverty caused by the collapse of the American economy hit the African American community especially hard. Statistics for New York City provided just one example of the stark disparities between white and black Americans. A total of 50 percent of adults in Harlem were unemployed (nationality the figure was about 60 percent)—while white unemployment in the city and nation averaged about 30 percent. Blacks had a five times greater chance of having tuberculosis than did whites; black babies had a death rate twice as high as white babies; twice as many black mothers died giving birth than white mothers; black families paid twice as much for monthly rent than white families in Manhattan paid; and the median income for black families had dropped by 46 percent compared with their incomes before the Great Crash, a rate double that of white incomes. The only people hit harder by the depression than African Americans in the North were African American farmers and sharecroppers in the South.[26]

The decade began with a rare political victory for African Americans. The National Association for the Advancement of Colored People (NAACP) campaigned successfully against the appointment of a racist judge to the U.S. Supreme Court. In March 1930, President Herbert Hoover nominated Judge John J. Parker of North Carolina, a prominent Republican, to replace a justice who had recently died. The NAACP led the opposition to the nomination because of the judge's previously expressed racial views. Ten years earlier, while Parker was campaigning for governor of his home state, his Democratic opponent charged that if elected Parker would encourage "Negroes" to register to vote and become politically active. Parker responded that "the participation of the Negro in politics is a source of evil and danger to both races and is not desired by the wise men in either race or by the Republican Party of North Carolina." The American Federation of Labor (AFL) joined in the campaign against the nomination because the judge had once ruled that workers did not have the "right to unionize." The Senate eventually voted to reject Parker's appointment to the Supreme Court by a narrow margin. The defeat of Judge Parker's nomination by the NAACP was an important victory for the organization, which for the first time showed it had some influence in national politics.[27]

During the controversy over Judge Parker's nomination, an incident on a freight train traveling through northern Alabama led to the arrest of nine young black men outside the town of Scottsboro. Falsely charged with raping two white women on top of a boxcar, "the Scottsboro Boys," as they came to be called, ended up spending a decade in prison—and for some even longer—for a crime that one of their accusers testified had never been committed. Twice their case reached the U.S. Supreme Court and twice the Court ordered a new trial because the defendants had been denied their basic rights as American citizens, first because they had been denied the right to a competent attorney (their first counsel turned up drunk the opening day of the trial and after that never asked a single question of any witness), and second because no black person had been called for jury service in the entire history of the state. After another trial, a local Alabama judge threw out the all-white jury's guilty verdict because he simply could not believe the testimony of several key witnesses, even though the jurors did. Tragically, the "Boys" lives were ruined by these events, even though they eventually some had the charges against them dropped and the others received pardons (in 1976)—but only after they, except for one, had died.

In other areas of the South, black Americans faced increasingly desperate economic circumstances as the depression and the racism of most white Southerners destroyed any hopes they might have had for a better life. A survey of three gigantic plantations in Arkansas revealed that sharecroppers had a yearly cash income of $290, but the land owners averaged $132,004 per year. In Alabama and Mississippi, poor farmers (both black and white) did even worse, earning an average of $132 for an entire year's work. When Congress met in emergency session after Franklin Roosevelt's defeat of Herbert Hoover in 1932, the new president sent them an economic reform package that he called his New Deal for the American people. First on the agenda came the problems of farmers, and the first major bill Congress sent to the White House created the Agricultural Adjustment Administration (AAA).

The new programs for agriculture, however, did little to help the people most in need of help—black sharecroppers in the South. The main goal of the AAA was to quickly raise prices for farm products, which had fallen to record low levels by 1933. This placed many farmers on the verge of bankruptcy. If supplies could be limited, however, prices would rise quickly. Under one program, farmers would be paid by the Department of Agriculture to destroy one-third of whatever they grew. If hog farmers killed one-third of their pigs, they would receive a check equal to the fair market value of those animals, if they would bury them and not try to sell them. The AAA established these same guidelines for cotton planters, corn growers, cattle ranchers, sugar beet growers, and all the other kinds of farmers found in the United States. If they plowed under every third row of the crop they had already planted, they would be paid for the crop they destroyed. Of course, the bigger the farm or plantation a person owned, the more money he would get and the check went to the property owner—nothing went directly to the people who worked on the farm or plantation. The landowners were supposed to share some of the money they received with their tenants, but little was done to enforce that provision. Under the AAA programs, then, most of the money aimed at helping farmers went to the people who needed it least.

One section of the AAA contract farmer's signed said that each landlord had to keep the same number of sharecroppers on his land and allow them to grow food for their families and raise livestock. When a group of 40 sharecroppers were threatened with eviction by the owner of a 14,000-acre Arkansas plantation who went to court to enforce this part of the law, the U.S. District Court for the region threw their case out ruling that since sharecroppers had no part in signing the contracts with the Department of Agriculture, they had no legal right to sue for their enforcement.

Shortly after the court made its ruling, local police and sheriff's deputies drove onto the plantation and began arresting the sharecroppers and their families. The leaders of this "revolt" ended up in prison after being convicted of spreading "anarchy and blasphemy." Only after the American Civil Liberties Union (ACLU) and the American Socialist Party leader Norman Thomas launched a nationwide campaign on radio, newsreels, and in newspapers did Arkansas's governor release the prisoners. Out of all this turmoil came the Southern Tenant Farmer's Union (STFU), which, in 1935, organized the first cotton-pickers strike in the state's history. The plantations owners responded with a reign of terror by hiring "night riders" to terrorize the local population. They burned the homes of union members, beat and whipped dozens of strikers, killed at least two men, and drove many others out of the county. This first strike failed but the next one—in the fall of

1935—did not. After another round of beatings, shootings, attempted lynchings and arrests, the governor sent in the National Guard and the strike ended.

The plantation owners, perhaps fearful of more violence and another long strike, granted the union a modest wage increase. The "plight of the sharecroppers" had attracted national attention in the press, newsreels, and the radio. The U.S. Department of Justice became directly involved in 1936, charging one of the areas most prominent landowners with keeping his cotton-pickers with "debt peonage," a condition that was close to, but not quite, slavery. A federal judge convicted him and sentenced him to prison. Gradually, it seemed, economic conditions among the nation's poorest citizens were improving, largely because of the STFU.

The AAA gave millions of dollars to white planters in the South and hardly a dime to black sharecroppers. It was not the only New Deal program that failed to help African Americans, however. Southern members of Congress supported Franklin Roosevelt's reform agenda but only at the cost of protecting white supremacy and segregation. They controlled most of the key congressional committees because of the seniority system. Under this longtime practice, the senior member of the majority party—after 1932 the Democrats until 1946—automatically became committee chairs. Because the Republican Party barely existed in the South, few Democrats faced any opposition in their reelection campaigns. Therefore they could expect long careers in Washington, giving them a great advantage over northerners in achieving senior status. At least 90 percent of African Americans in the states of the Old Confederacy could not vote because of poll taxes, literacy tests (in Alabama, for instance, potential voters had to pass an 80-question test of their knowledge of the American Constitution before they could register), and other devices used to prevent them from voting.

Southern senators and representatives loudly opposed any program that threatened to treat blacks and whites equally. Republicans and most northern Democrats, on the other hand, showed little interest in issues involving race. President Roosevelt thought he needed southern support to pass his economic reforms, so he did not challenge them on the race question. The president said nothing when Congress considered an anti-lynching bill because as Representative John Rankin (Democrat, Mississippi) warned, if he said anything favorable about the proposal, "it will ruin him in the South." Southerners dominated positions of power in Congress and as Senator Richard Russell of Georgia assured his Democratic colleague Sam Ervin of South Carolina, on questions of race and segregation "we are not going to yield an inch."[28] They kept their promise.

The final design of the Social Security Act showed the methods used to prevent African Americans from sharing in the benefits of most New Deal legislation. Coverage under the Old Age Insurance and the Unemployment Insurance programs excluded job categories with large numbers of blacks (and other minorities such as farm workers, hospital workers, laundry workers, and maids). Local authorities set eligibility rules for the Aid to Families with Dependent Children (ADC) program. The legislation allowed states to opt out of this social assistance program so states like Kentucky, Mississippi, and Texas, did not take part in it until the 1940s. States that participated set benefit levels for recipients; hence the elderly poor in Georgia received approximately $18.00 a month to pay for food, clothing, and shelter. The NAACP opposed the Social Security bill for these reasons arguing that "it was like a sieve with holes just big enough for the majority of Negroes to fall through."[29] Yet the little public assistance blacks received enabled many to survive. Most were so desperately poor that even the smallest amount of aid made living a little easier for them.

Southern white opposition to racial equality in Congress did not prevent Franklin Roosevelt from appointing more blacks to important positions in Washington than any previous president had ever done. These African American advisors became known as "Roosevelt's Black Cabinet." Among these appointments were Mary McLeod Bethune, the famed educator and friend of Eleanor Roosevelt, the president's wife, to the National Youth Administration; William H. Hastie, who worked at the Department of Interior until 1937, when he became the first African American appointed to a federal court; and Dr. Robert C. Weaver, a sociologist, to the Federal Housing Authority. (In 1965, President Lyndon Johnson appointed Weaver to head the Department of Housing and Urban Development, making Weaver the first African American cabinet secretary.)

One of the major political changes of the decade involved the movement of African American voters from the Republican to the Democratic Party. In the 1934 congressional elections, black voters in Chicago elected the first African American Democrat in American history to the House of Representatives. He defeated black Republican Oscar DePriest, which meant Congress still had only one African American member. Mitchell, like many other northerners of his race, had been a Republican until he saw the impact of New Deal jobs programs on his community and switched to the Democrats. New Deal job programs employed more than 1 million African Americans—albeit at discriminatory wages in southern states—in 1933 and 1934. This kind of government assistance in a time of need led to a huge outpouring of black support for Franklin Roosevelt in the 1936 presidential election. For the first time since gaining the right to vote, a majority of blacks voted Democratic that year, at least in states where they could vote.

On March 19, 1935, a race riot—the first in the nation since the early 1920s—erupted in Harlem, New York. Modest by historical standards, the number of deaths was few, although hundreds of people were injured and the police arrested hundreds more. The violence began after a rumor spread, later proven false, that a black teenager had been caught stealing in a department store and had been beaten to death by its employees. In reality, he had been caught and released. A crowd gathered in front of the store and broke its windows. Then, what was now a mob rushed into the store and began taking out whatever they could carry. The police arrived and shot and killed a young black male who apparently had not been involved in the looting. Within hours thousands of rioters filled the streets of a major shopping area in Harlem. They raided every store in the vicinity and set several fires. Members of the Young Communist League handed out leaflets carrying the false story of the "killing" by the store employees. The riot ended the next day as hundreds of police moved into the area. When the disturbances ended, the police had killed four people and property damage had reached more than $1 million.

New York Mayor Fiorello LaGuardia appointed a Commission on Conditions in Harlem to study the causes of the riot. Their report pointed to several factors leading to this outbreak of violence such as discrimination in the handling of relief programs. All blacks receiving relief, for example, had to give the state all insurance policies worth more than $500 before getting anything. White families were not required to do this. Blacks, the report concluded, received the most menial and dirty relief jobs. Inadequate schools were another problem faced by African Americans. Classes in Harlem schools averaged 40 to 50 students per room, with most schools holding two or three sessions a day, running from 8 A.M. to 5 P.M. The school buildings were "old, shabby, and far from modern." Many of the children came to school hungry and dressed in rags, according to teachers, although the report noted that many teachers refused to be interviewed because they feared retaliation by their principals if they said anything critical of the system. One school had seating in its lunchroom for 175 students, yet it served more than 1,000 children per day.

Along with reporting discrimination by relief agencies and inadequate schools, the Committee on Conditions in Harlem pointed to fear of police violence as a contributing factor to the March riot. Community residents testified that they feared African American officers as much as they did white ones. The police entered homes and took people out without warrants and they arrested men in the streets without "even having given ground for suspicion." Just six days before the riot, police had gouged out the eye of and killed a man waiting in a relief line because he hesitated briefly when they ordered him to move. The police commissioner found that his officers had done nothing wrong and they were not indicted. These economic and social conditions and prejudices, along with an unemployment rate of 70 percent, finally "snapped the nerves" of the community, according to the commission, making the riot predictable and understandable.[30]

Sharecropper protests in the South and a race riot in the North illuminated the desperation of African Americans during the worst economic crisis in American history. Not all protests took violent forms, however. Many blacks sought other ways out of the racism, poverty, and prejudice that infected American life by turning to religion. Two new religious groups grew rapidly in black communities in the United States as the depression wore on: the International Peace Mission Movement of Father Divine and the Nation of Islam.

The riot had exploded close to the home of a popular religious leader, known to his followers as Father Divine. Born George Baker in Maryland in 1880 to former slaves, he began preaching in Baltimore in 1912. Five years later he declared himself God. He carried his message first to Georgia, promoting celibacy and equal rights for women. Local pastors disliked his popularity and charged him with lunacy, but a local judge found him sane in spite of his outrageous beliefs. He moved to Brooklyn in 1914, where he established a commune that outlawed sex, alcohol, tobacco, and gambling. He attracted many followers including dozens of whites who found his message of hope and prosperity satisfying. His community of believers held free banquets every week for all who could attend (sometimes more than 3,000 people) and helped converts find jobs. In the late 1920s, he moved his church to Sayville, a small all-white town on Long Island; local residents resented the crowds who attended his services and also the wealth that he flaunted. He drove a Cadillac, wore silk suits, lived on a large estate in a huge house, and was seemingly always being followed by streams of ecstatic women. (Rumors of his having many affairs with white and black angels filled stories about him in newspapers, but he and his wives always denied them. He married twice, first to an African American woman much older than he was. After her death, he created a greater scandal by marrying a white woman much younger than he was.)

The district attorney had Father Divine and his congregation arrested for disturbing the peace, for which he received a one-year prison term and a $500 fine, the maximum penalty. He entered prison but left two weeks later when an appeals court ordered his release. Shortly after this incident Father Divine moved to Harlem where he established the International Peace Mission Movement. The movement bought hotels, restaurants, clothing stores, and other small businesses. Members lived in the hotels, renamed "Heavens," and work in Peace Mission shops. The banquets continued and the movement opened branches in Los Angeles, Chicago, Washington, D.C. and many other urban centers. By 1934, Father Divine claimed to have two million "angels" (including the daughter of former President Herbert Hoover). His message of positive thinking, communal living, world peace (through following his word), and celibacy appealed to people in distress. In Father Divine's church the needy received food and clothes.

On racial issues he stressed ignoring the idea of race. According to his analysis, African Americans remained poor and oppressed because they thought in terms of skin color. He frequently said he was not black; therefore he could not and did not belong to an abused race. The spirit of brotherhood and compassion found in the Heaven's movement offered temporary relief from the hate and prejudice his followers faced in the world around them. Salvation was here and now rather than in the next world, as promised by mainstream religions. That so many believers accepted George Baker as God and his churches as Heavens revealed the desperation and despair felt by so many during the Great Depression.[31]

Wallace Fard, a door-to-door silk cloth salesman, founded the Lost-Found Nation of Islam (as he first called what would become the Nation of Islam) in Detroit, Michigan, in 1930. Little is known of Fard's background. He may have been part Syrian, or Lebanese, or Palestinian, or something else. He proclaimed that Islam was "the true religion of the Black men of Asia and Africa." In his teachings, he stressed black pride and claimed that Africans were the original human beings. They had been created by Allah (the Arabic word for God) 66 trillion years ago. Whites, on the other hand, had been created by the devil. Fard borrowed heavily from Marcus Garvey's African nationalist teachings in his sermons and writings but never had quite the same success as Garvey. Many members of Fard's first temple had belonged to Garvey's Universal Negro Improvement Association (UNIA) in the 1920s.

Three years after founding the Nation of Islam (NOI), Fard sent one of his disciples, Elijah Muhammad (born Elijah Poole—Fard demanded that his followers give up their "slave names" and take new ones), to Chicago to open a new branch of the church. Fard disappeared shortly thereafter and was never seen again—he may have been killed by the Detroit police or by followers of Elijah Muhammad according to some of his followers, but no one really knows what happened to him. Whatever led to Fard's disappearance is still unknown, but shortly after Elijah Muhammad assumed leadership of the NOI.

The new leader had been born in Georgia in 1897 where his father was a Baptist minister. He joined the UNIA after moving to Detroit in 1923. The deportation of Marcus Garvey four years later deeply disturbed him and increased his bitterness and anger toward white society.

Muhammad moved the headquarters of the NOI to Chicago and proclaimed that Wallace Fard was actually "God." The NOI promoted a message of cleanliness (inward and outward), good manners, strict morality (no alcohol, drugs, tobacco, or gambling), African supremacy over the white race, and total separation from whites. The Muslims would live in a separate state, preferably Alabama. Muhammad attracted large crowds in Chicago and other northern cities whenever he spoke in black communities. By the end of the decade, the NOI had more than 100,000 members. The NOI built schools, businesses, and temples in black neighborhoods throughout the country. For many African Americans membership in the NOI provided security and gave them a feeling of importance—they were now the chosen people of God. This was important to African Americans living in a nation that still treated them as second-class citizens in every part of their lives.[32]

The decade of the Great Depression ended with one more indignity thrust upon African Americans. In 1939, African America contralto Marian Anderson planned to give an Easter Sunday concert in Constitution Hall in Washington, D.C. Many listeners throughout the world considered her one of the greatest singers of the times. Although born in poverty in Philadelphia in 1897, she started singing in her church choir when she was six years old and after years of hard work and concerts around the world, she reached the top of her profession Her father died when she was young, so her mother had to work two jobs, as a laundress and cleaning woman, to support her daughter's singing lessons.

The Daughters of the American Revolution (DAR) owned Constitution Hall and did not seem to care about Anderson's achievements. They refused to let Anderson perform at their Hall, insisting that it had already been reserved by the Washington Symphony for Easter. Anderson's manager requested another date, but the DAR told him no other dates were open for the rest of the year. Finally, the group's president explained that Washington, D.C. laws did not allow blacks to sit in the audience next to whites and that DAR rules did not allow people of color to perform on stage. "I am shocked beyond words to be barred from the capital of my country after having appeared in almost every other capital in the world," Anderson responded.[33] But the DAR stuck to its rules and refused to change its decision.

Howard University, an all-black school in the nation's capital, and the NAACP tried to get the District of Columbia's school board to allow Anderson to give her concert in a high school auditorium. But the all-white board refused; it too had to obey the District's segregation law, according to its president. First Lady Eleanor Roosevelt then got involved. First she resigned from the DAR and wrote about the issue in her daily news column "My Day." The DAR still refused to change its mind, however. Only after Secretary of the Interior Harold Ickes intervened did Anderson get a new site for her concert. Ickes offered her the steps of the Lincoln Memorial for her performance. On Easter Sunday 75,000 people, including Mrs. Roosevelt, turned out to hear Anderson's performance, while millions more listened on their radios. The event received nationwide newspaper coverage and

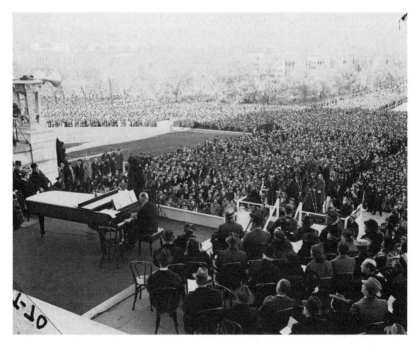

Contralto Marian Anderson performing for a crowd of thousands from the steps of Washington's Lincoln Memorial on Easter Sunday, April 9, 1939, after she was refused permission to perform in Constitution Hall by the hall's owners, the Daughters of the American Revolution. Seated dignitaries included Cabinet secretaries and Supreme Court Justice Hugo Black. Harold Ickes plays the piano. Courtesy of the Library of Congress, LC-USZ62-90448.

opened the eyes, however briefly, of many people to the problem of racial segregation. In her autobiography, *My Lord What a Morning* (1974), Anderson thanked the First Lady for her actions: "There are many persons ready to do what is right because in their hearts they know it is right. But they hesitate, waiting for the other fellow to make the first move—and he, in turn, waits for you. The minute a person whose word means a great deal dares to take the open-hearted and courageous way, many others follow. Not everyone can be turned aside from meanness and hatred, but the great majority of Americans are headed in that direction. I have a great belief in the future of my people and my country."[34] Anderson's feelings express an attitude held by many African Americans at the end of the 1930s—a hope that the future just *had* to be better than the past.

ASIAN AMERICANS

According to the 1930 census, 489,326 Americans of Asian descent lived in the United States. More than half of this population (278,743) came from Japan and most of this community lived on the West Coast. In 1930, James Sakamoto helped found the Japanese American Citizen's League (JACL), an all *Nisei* (Japanese born in the United States) nonprofit civic organization in Seattle, Washington to fight anti-Asian discrimination. Sakamoto had begun the fight for equal rights after graduating from high school when he became active in the Japanese community's efforts to block anti-Asian legislation in his home state. Following the pattern established in other western states, the legislature had passed a law prohibiting Asians from owning, leasing, renting, or sharecropping land in the state. (Some Japanese and Chinese farmers took advantage of a loophole in this act by leasing land on Indian reservations, which were federal property and therefore not subject to the provisions of alien land laws. Here they farmed relatively peacefully.)

In 1923, Sakamoto moved to New Jersey to attend Princeton University. While there he got a job as the English-language editor of a newspaper called *Nichibei shuho* (Japanese-American Commercial Weekly). He soon became a boxer at the Japanese Christian Institute and two years later began a career as a professional prizefighter. In a fight with a much heavier fighter in 1927, Sakamoto took some vicious blows to his head and face. Several of the punches hit him squarely in the eyes, tearing his retinas and leaving him permanently blind. He retuned home to Seattle, borrowed some money from his father, and started his newspaper, the all-English *Japanese American Courier*. As a leader of the JACL, Sakamoto stressed "militant, unquestioning loyalty" to the United States. He advocated self-improvement as the way to acceptance into American society and opposed political activism. "Agitation begets agitation," he argued in his editorials. He also fervently supported the 1931 Japanese invasion of China and took Japan's side in the long, bloody war of conquest that followed.

The JACL won two important victories in its early history. Because of intense lobbying in Washington D.C., Japanese veterans who served in the American army during World War I received citizenship after Congress passed a bill allowing such action. Seven hundred Nisei men became citizens as a result of this effort. The JACL also convinced federal lawmakers to repeal the 1922 Cable Act. That law said that any American woman who married an alien ineligible for citizenship (principally Asians) would no longer be a citizen of the United States. It also said that any Asian woman marrying a Caucasian man would not be considered an American citizen simply because of her marriage. Congress repealed this law in 1931.

Sakamoto wanted complete assimilation and believed one way to accomplish this was through participation in American sports. So he sponsored a Japanese-American baseball league in the Pacific Northwest called the Courier League, which lasted from 1928 to 1941. The game was not unknown in Japan. First-generation Japanese immigrants, *Issei*, had brought the game with them from their homeland. Here baseball had been introduced in elite high schools in the 1880s as part of the Japanese government's commitment to modernizing and westernizing their country. Sakamoto, the Japanese government, and its emperor saw baseball as vital to the Americanization and prosperity of his people. In another editorial he wrote, "The second generation (*Nisei*) are American citizens and through them will be reaped the harvests of tomorrow. Home, institutions, and inalienable rights to live the life of an American, is the cry of the second generation."[35] Through baseball the life chances of Japanese Americans would be greatly improved, Sakamoto argued. And he remained loyal to this vision all the way into the internment camps set up for Japanese Americans forced out of their homes at the beginning of World War II. Even in the camps Sakamoto pleaded for strict obedience to orders and peaceful acceptance of the harsh conditions imposed on the *Nisei* and *Issei* because of their race.

The Courier League proved very popular with Japanese farmers in eastern Washington and the Yakima Valley where hundreds would attend Sunday afternoon ball games and root for their hometown team. Even more came to watch if an all-white team was the opponent. As the Great Depression hit eastern Washington hard in the 1930s, ethnic tensions increased, however. Several Japanese homes were dynamited and at least six others were set on fire in the region, but the major victims of racist attacks were the Filipinos.

In 1930, Filipinos made up 15 percent of all California farm workers. More than 80 percent of the 45,000 Filipinos in the United States were male. As the number of Filipino immigrants increased, so did hostility toward them. Stereotypes were rampant, especially the widespread view among whites that Filipino men were sexual predators (or headhunters coming out of the jungles of Asia, in another misguided popular image) in constant pursuit of Anglo-Saxon women. The Watsonville riot began when a white mob attacked a group of Filipinos dancing with white women. Under California law "Orientals," and this designation included residents of the Philippine Islands, could not marry white women. Neither could "Mongolians," another racial category that included Filipinos according to a Los Angeles judge.

High wages, by Philippine standards, and a constant demand for cheap labor to pick fruits and vegetables, attracted thousands of laborers to the United States and Hawaii in the 1920s. The U.S. Navy provided employment for thousands of Filipinos, mainly because it would not allow African Americans to join. In 1930, 6,000 Filipinos worked as mess stewards, the only occupation open to them. Between 1929 and 1933, as the depression spread, wages for agricultural laborers dropped from $3.50 a day to $1.90 a day for 12-hour days (6 A.M. to 6 P.M.) six days a week. As economic conditions worsened in the United States, Filipino unemployment in California (where 85 percent of that population lived) had reached 75 percent by 1933. White prejudice in agricultural unions organized by the American Federation of Labor (AFL) kept Filipinos from joining. When growers hired nonwhites, including Mexicans, Filipinos, and blacks, to work as strikebreakers, this increased the hostility that already existed between ethnic groups in the lettuce, asparagus, and celery fields of the Imperial Valley.

Then the independent Filipino Labor Union (FLU) led a drive for a 35-cents-an-hour minimum wage, and 8-hour day, and a nondiscriminatory policy in hiring practices in the lettuce fields around Salinas. For a time white and Filipino unions agreed to bargain together and after several weeks, the growers met all their demands. Almost as soon as the strike ended, however, a white mob attacked the offices of the FLU and burned it to the ground. The rioters then set fire to a camp where two thousand Filipino lettuce-pickers lived and subjected the frightened workers "to a reign of terror" bringing a bloody end to that brief period of interethnic cooperation.[36]

In Washington, D.C., Congress had a long history of passing anti-Asian legislation. Chinese, Japanese, Koreans, Southeast Asians, Burmese, Indonesians, and people from India had all been bared from entering the United States by 1933. Because the Philippines had become an American territory in 1899, however, its people were exempt from the anti-Asian exclusionary provisions of U.S. immigration law. They could migrate freely to the United States. Farmers and growers did not mind because the Philippines just added another source of cheap labor for them to exploit. Now that the depression had increased unemployment at home to such a high rate that even white Americans (the "Okies" from the dust bowl, for one example) would work for very low wages, they did not have to depend on outside sources for their field hands anymore. Foreign migrant workers lost their best protectors in Congress—the agricultural lobby—after the depression had done its damage.

Growing pressure from white supremacist "100% American" groups encouraged racists in Congress to sponsor legislation to deal with "the Filipino menace," as a California newspaper put it. The Philippine Independence Act (also called the Tydings-McDuffie Act) of 1934 provided a means to handle the situation. The law allowed the Philippines to become self-governing in 1935 and provided for complete independence from the United States after 10 years. Of course, as soon as the Islands established their new government, Filipinos in the United States would become "aliens" and would no longer be allowed to work in the United

States. Under this reclassification, Filipinos would be subject to the 1924 im-migration quota system. The law set the Filipino quota at 50 per year. Those im-migrants already in the country would be pressured to return to their homeland as quickly as possible. Under the terms of the Filipino Repatriation Act of 1935, the U.S. government would provide free transportation back to their native country.

By 1938, only about 1,900 Filipinos had accepted the free trip back home. Immigration officials estimated that more than 40,000 Filipino farm workers, houseboys, janitors, and cooks remained in the United States. The president of the Filipino Federation of America explained why: "The boys (about 90 percent of this population was male) do not want to go back without money or assurance they will earn a living."[37] If they did return home they could not reenter the United States except as part of the 50-per-year quota. For many that could mean a wait of many years. Of course, a white California judge gave an explanation more in line with traditional prejudices: the boys are "loathe to leave a country" where they boast of enjoying the favors of white girls because they are "a very superior grade of lovers."[38]

Filipinos remaining in the United States continued to work in agriculture, although some found jobs in fish canneries as far north as Alaska. Unlike the Japanese or Chinese, very few ever had enough money to buy their own farms or businesses. Agricultural labor unions continued to discriminate against Asians so they were forced to organize their own unions. The Filipino Agricultural Laborers Association invited Mexicans to join, and in 1939 the integrated Federated Agri-cultural Laborers Association (FALA) emerged. Joining forces across ethnic lines proved a successful strategy. After a one-day strike against the asparagus industry, the growers agreed to shorter hours, an increase in wages, and improved condi-tions in the notoriously foul conditions of the labor camps. FALA had similar success in the celery, brussels sprouts, and garlic fields. By the end of the decade FALA had 30,000 members.

The great cause for the small Korean community in the United States (8,332 according to the 1930 census) during the years of the Great Depression was the continuing struggle to gain independence in their homeland. Hatred for the Japanese, who had occupied their homeland and virtually enslaved its people since 1894, provided a common cause for Koreans in the United States to unify around. Personality disputes between leaders prevented a united front against the Japanese occupiers from emerging. Even Korean churches divided over the issue of how best to win back Korean independence.

Followers of Syngman Rhee (1875–1965) advocated a diplomatic approach to the issue. Born in Korea, Rhee came to the United States in 1904 after spending seven years in a Japanese prison. He studied international relations at Harvard University before eventually earning a Ph.D. at Princeton. He organized the Comrade Society among Koreans in the United States in 1920 to pressure western governments to use their economic power to boycott trade with Japan until it left their homeland. Rhee argued that military attempts to liberate Korea were unrealistic because of the superior military might of Japan. Rhee became the first president of the Republic of Korea after its emergence as an independent nation after World War II. Chang-Ho Ahn (1878–1938), an educator and reformer, championed a guerilla war against the Japanese. In the early 1930s, he left his family in the United States for his homeland to organize military resistance to the Japanese. He died in 1938 in a Japanese prison. Pak Yong-Man (1881–1928), a graduate of the University of Nebraska, also advocated freeing Korea by military means. He organized the Korean National Brigade in Hawaii to train for this mission. While in China recruiting volunteers for the Brigade an assassin, probably sent by the Korean National Revolutionary Party (KNRP), shot him down, killing him instantly. The KNRP, organized in the United States in 1935, was another organization pursuing a military solution to the occupation of Korea, but had little success in achieving its goal of liberation from Japanese imperialism.

EUROPEAN AMERICANS

European groups in the United States faced the same high levels of unemployment and economic distress faced by all Americans during the Great Depression. Many European Americans, whether English, French, Irish, Italian, Polish, Russian, Serbian, or Yugoslav, retained their ethnic consciousness by joining ethnic clubs and societies and followed with great interest events taking place in their old homelands. German American citizens still trying to recover from the anti-German campaign during World War I tended to avoid open expressions of ethnic pride. The Immigration Restriction Acts of the 1920s had virtually cut off migration from anywhere into the United States. For immigrants already here, the languages and customs of the old country were becoming the stuff of memory. The collapse of the American economy increased tensions between groups as they competed for scarce jobs and economic resources. Tensions grew especially between groups that had not yet achieved economic stability, such as the Italians and Jews, because they occupied jobs at the lower end of the wage scale. For others, what was happening in Europe became their only contact with their ethnic heritage. European ideologies, such as fascism and Nazism, transported poorly to groups that had been in the United States for a long time, such as the Germans. And adherents of those totalitarian ideas tended to be recent immigrants with few ties to America. The experience of German Americans during the last war demonstrated how events far away had a direct impact on a group's image in the United States and German Americans who remembered the hysteria tried to stay out of groups with any connection to "alien" ideas.

German Americans had been subjected to vicious abuse during World War I. Their patriotism had been challenged by President Woodrow Wilson and ex-president Theodore Roosevelt and many super-patriotic groups. From 1919 to 1930, German Americans witnessed the defeat and humiliation of their homeland as it struggled through vast inflation, economic instability, bankruptcy, and other catastrophes followed almost immediately by unemployment and depression. Throughout the decade German Americans had no national organization or voice speaking in its name. Then in 1931, the German American Federation held its first meeting in New York City, followed three years later by an organization called the Friends of the New Germany.

Adolf Hitler's coming to power caught the attention of many German Americans. Most hoped that he was right when he announced that he would restore German pride and power. As the Nazis moved closer to total power and began implementing their racial policies, German American newspapers became very defensive. People who criticized the New Germany and its racial policies had no more right to do that than Germans had the right to criticize the United States for its treatment of minorities and its history of segregation and lynching, according to the Chicago *Abendpost*.[39]

The new spirit in Germany aroused new activity in German communities in the United States. More than 500 delegates attended the founding convention of the German American Federation. They agreed to stress the great achievements in art, poetry, and music of Germans, hoping that a rebirth of pride in German culture would help restore respect for their homeland. The Federation began supporting cultural exchange programs for teachers and students. Political questions and debates would be avoided.

The Friends of the New Germany met first in Chicago in October 1933. Delegates to the convention would debate political questions. The group's leaders, most of them recent immigrants, saw fascism as the greatest new idea of the century. They sought to restore pride in Germany by demanding revisions in the "humiliating" Versailles Treaty that had ended World War I. Americans needed to reject the idea that Germany alone had started that war. German pride and self-respect depended on the emergence of a more powerful Germany and the only way to accomplish that would be to support Adolf Hitler.

The first anti-Jewish riots under Nazi rule took place in March 1933; several deaths and significant property damage resulted. The American Jewish Congress (AJC) called for a national protest against Nazi rule. The response of the Central Union of German Citizens of the Jewish Faith, a group claiming to represent all German Jews, surprised many Americans. It asked the AJC to call off the protest. Any such demonstrations would only provoke more violence against the German Jewish community. Despite the appeal the protest went on and eventually led to a full-scale boycott of American stores selling German goods.

A few Germans in America praised the Nazi attacks on Jews, who were often accused of being communists. Hitler's "repudiation of communistic ideas and his unqualified insistence upon a return to the God of its fathers," according Pastor Walter A. Meyer of the Lutheran Church, Missouri Synod, an overwhelmingly German American denomination. Meyer, the Voice of the Lutheran Hour, a popular Sunday afternoon broadcast, held out great hope for "the reconstruction of Germany" under the Nazis. Hitler would save the German people from "pornographic literature, Hollywood films, nudist colonies, and the rampant social evils of a demoralized nation."[40] Many German American newspapers insisted "the reports of Jewish atrocities that have been reported are hysterical fables."[41]

By the end of the decade, pro-Nazi statements of several German American leaders frightened Congressman Samuel Dickstein (Democrat, New York) so much that he called for an investigation of their actions. The House Committee on Un-American Activities (HUAC) chaired by Representative John McCormick (Democrat, Massachusetts) held hearings across the country seeking to expose the threat of Nazism in the United States. The Committee report concluded that "there has been no evidence of any Americans of German blood born in the United States having taken part in the efforts of the Nazi party in Germany." Yet, suspicions about German American disloyalty had been raised by the Congressional investigation once again. The "Hun" image popularized during World War I was making a comeback. The racial and military policies of Adolf Hitler influenced the image of all Germans, so once again they would be portrayed as uncivilized barbarians, whether they supported *Der Fuhrer* or not.[42]

According to opinion polls, Italian American admiration for fascist leader Benito Mussolini exceeded that of German Americans support for Hitler. A journalist spotted pictures of *Il Duce* in Italian neighborhoods, on lampposts and store windows, in cities across the United States. Less than 1 percent of German Americans spoke favorably of the German *Fuhrer*, while a majority of American Italians approved of *Il Duce*. The openly pro-Nazi German American Bund, led by German-born chemist Fritz Kuhn, paraded around New York City and Chicago in swastika-laden uniforms, but it had fewer than 20,000 members in the entire U.S. German Americans were "so completely submerged in the American element," the German ambassador to the United States reported to his government in 1939, "that any appeal to their German heritage will no longer arouse any response in them." The frightening experience of World War I had drained any ethnic consciousness out of them, and they had become too Americanized to become good Nazis.[43]

Jewish Americans responded to the violent anti-Semitism in Germany with a campaign of political activism. The American Jewish Congress (AJC) headed by Rabbi Stephen Wise organized boycotts of German-made products and held rallies protesting the arrests and persecution of German Jews by Hitler's legions. American immigration laws subjected potential Jewish refugees to the requirements of the 1924 immigration quota limits. The law established the quota for Germany at 25,957 per year, but only once in the years after Hitler came to power was that quota ever filled or exceeded (1939 when 33,515 Germans legally entered the United States). Had the quota been filled every year from 1933 to 1940, more than 211,000 refugees from Hitlerism could have reached American shores. Officially, however, only 100,900 of that number entered the United States. Hundreds of thousands more of this persecuted minority would have come, but they had no chance to do so. Every effort in Congress to expand the quota for European Jews went down to defeat. The most notorious incident happened in 1938 when Congress rejected a bill that would have saved 20,000 children from Nazi concentration camps.[44]

LATINOS

The 1930s began with a massive campaign to remove Mexicans, the nation's largest Spanish-speaking group, from the United States. About 2 million Mexicans lived in the United States according to the 1930 census, and almost 50 percent of them had been born within its borders, meaning they were full citizens. Between 1929 and 1935, more than 400,000 Mexicans left the United States and went back to their homeland. Perhaps 200,000 returned on their own while the others were forcibly deported by immigration authorities. Mexicans had been exempted from the 1924 quota system because of pressure from mining, railroad, and agricultural companies. Mexico had been a reliable source of cheap labor for decades to these industries, but the depression created a crisis. Thousands of dust bowl farmers, from Oklahoma, Texas, Kansas, and Colorado (all called "Okies") flooded into California looking for work. The need for Mexican workers declined dramatically. Racists had always opposed immigration from Mexico but as unemployment increased pressure to close the borders and expel "aliens" came from almost everyone in the Southwest, to "protect American jobs."

But more than concern for jobless Americans fueled the campaign to send "illegals" back home. Racism played a major role in the project. For many whites, Mexicans were a lazy, hot-tempered, criminal population that never wanted to become Americanized. They preferred speaking Spanish and took *siestas* in the middle of the day. A white sociologist described Mexicans this way in testimony to Congress, "These people sleep by day and prowl by night like coyotes, stealing anything they can get their hands on, no matter how useless it may be. Nothing left outside is safe unless padlocked or chained down."[45] Hostility reached such a peak in states from Texas to California that many Mexicans started referring to themselves as "Latin Americans."

Immigration agents carried out hundreds of raids in Hispanic neighborhoods of every major city in the United States in 1930. Many times they stopped and detained anyone who spoke Spanish or looked Spanish, not bothering to check on whether they were American citizens. The agents grabbed people and threw them onto buses or trains and sent them back to the border. Here they would be turned over to Mexican authorities who would release them, and then they disappeared into whatever part of Mexico they had come from. Because of this chaotic system, thousands of legitimate citizens ended up looking for homes in a country they had never seen before. According to the Mexican government, many deportees from the United States ended up homeless living in the streets of Mexico City. State governments in Illinois, Indiana, and Michigan where small populations of Hispanics had been recruited by companies to work in the steel mills paid for special trains to carry the "aliens" back to the Rio Grande. In Texas, the state offered free transportation back to Mexico for anyone wanting to leave.

Most of the Mexicans remaining in the United States continued to work in the fields and mines of the American Southwest. In these jobs they came in conflict with farm workers from the Philippines, Japan, and the American dust bowl. For the growers, the abundance of workers became a rush to the bottom. Who could they get to work at the lowest wage? There were plenty of available applicants and they had no union strength to back them up. Farm worker unions in the 1920s had called a series of strikes but most of them had ended in failure. Some of the strikes had been broken where the large growers brought in Mexicans as strikebreakers. This tactic increased hostility between whites and Latinos. The racism that kept Mexicans (and Filipinos) out of whites-only unions meant that prospects for a successful drive for higher wages and better working conditions were dim.

A 1933 cotton strike in California's Central Valley illustrated the problems faced by farm workers (of all races). They often worked 12-hour days, six-day weeks for less than $1.70 a day. California law made public assistance or relief available only to persons who could prove that they had lived in the state for at least three years. In October 1933, the Agricultural Workers Industrial Union (CAWIU) called for a strike against the cotton growers. About 11,800 workers had joined the union, 75 percent were Mexican and the other 25 percent were white. Communist Party organizers had brought the two racial antagonists together, and this soon became the largest agricultural strike up to this point in U.S. history.

The growers had the help of the local police and heavily armed vigilantes from neighboring towns. They attacked the workers' camp, setting it on fire and shooting 11 strikers, two of whom died. The police arrested the strike leaders and jailed them, but hundreds of the union members established picket lines in front of the county jail and demanded the release of their leaders. Out in the fields a group of 100 strikers attacked a field where nonunion employees were working and drove out hundreds of strikebreakers. Then they burned down the field of cotton. The strike ended four weeks later, with the growers giving their field hands an increase in wages. Now they received 75 cents per hundred pounds of cotton picked, almost doubling their previous wages.

The victory proved short-lived, however. The growers organized a Farmers' Association and by the end of the year had successfully lobbied 20 county governments in the region to pass ordinances outlawing picketing. The police arrested the leaders of the CAWIU once again and charged them with criminal syndicalism, the employer's term for union organizing. The arrests destroyed the union.

A short time later the Teamsters, an affiliate of the American Federation of Labor (AFL) arrived in the fields and tried to start a new union. The Teamsters and the AFL, however, refused to allow Mexicans or Filipinos into this union, in accord with their national policy of whites' only membership. The Teamsters effort failed and most Mexicans and Filipinos remained unorganized in California. Passage of the Wagner Labor Relations Act by Congress in 1935 made it a crime to interfere with union organizing but did little to help the pickers because the law specifically excluded farm workers from its protections.

In 1934, Mexican coal miners went on strike in New Mexico and southern Colorado. Again local authorities broke the strike by arresting its leaders and imprisoning them. The mine owners had the miners' leader arrested and charged with terrorism. After his conviction immigration authorities deported him to Mexico and the union he had started quickly collapsed.

One of the largest strikes of the decade took place in San Antonio, Texas. The pecan industry employed thousands of Mexican workers in its plants where they shelled pecans. In 1938, the pecan growers cut the wages of their workers from 7 cents per pound of shelled pecans to 5 cents per pound. (Under this scale the shellers could expect to make at most $2.50 a week.) Five thousand shellers went on strike in protest. They chose 20-year-old Emma Tenayuca Brooks as their leader. As the strike wore on, she joined the Communist Party, which had been active in the area organizing agricultural workers. In her view it was the only political party in the United States willing to help the workers. The San Antonio police did everything they could to break the strike. They arrested picketers and leaders, including Emma Brooks, and charged them with violating a city ordinance forbidding anyone from carrying an advertising sign (in this case "We Want Higher Wages" signs) without a permit. A Texas court said the protest signs were advertisements. Thousands of Pecan Sheller's Union members and their supporters—their families, husbands, wives, grandparents, and children—ended up in San Antonio's unsanitary and overcrowded jails for carrying signs.

After six weeks both sides accepted the arbitration board's recommendations, and the workers returned to their shelling tables even though the options heavily favored the pecan industry owners. The Fair Labor Standards Act went into effect later in 1938. It established a national minimum wage of 25 cents an hour, which would have doubled the sheller's hourly income, but it excluded agricultural workers from its coverage. After the successful arbitration agreement, many pecan companies shut the doors to their facilities or turned to machines to do the job. The union lost so many members it soon went out of existence. Something other than gaining higher wages, however, had been achieved as a result of this conflict. Mexicans and Mexican Americans involved in the strike had demonstrated that the stereotype that they were easily manipulated by "the bosses" and were submissive Spanish-speaking peons who never fought back was false. They had stuck together during the strike, enduring days and weeks of police abuse, and had won a major (if short-lived) victory. Because of these achievements, they encouraged future generations to continue the fight for equality. And this legacy may have been as important as gaining a few extra cents per week in their paychecks. Mexican workers showed they would no longer accept second-class status in America.

Such accomplishments would also be true for Latinos in the American education system where conditions for Hispanic students were truly horrible. A 1928 survey of schools in Texas found that 90 percent of districts separated Mexican and white students and placed them in special classrooms at the elementary level.[46] Segregated school districts for white and African American students had existed since 1876, but people of Spanish descent qualified as white. So the state really sponsored three distinct school systems, one Anglo (white), one black, and one Spanish-speaking. Texas law mandated segregated white and black schools, but no such law separated Mexicans and whites—this segregation was a matter of custom and it many parts of the state this separation had been true since 1845 when Texas became a state.

Segregation of Mexican students usually took place by sending them to a separate building next to or close to the white school. Most districts segregated elementary grades only, because so few Spanish-speaking students went beyond the sixth grade what happened in higher grades did not matter. The school buildings and classrooms for Mexican students were generally small and badly maintained. Worse, most Mexican students did not attend school at all because Texas authorities seldom enforced the state's mandatory school attendance law. Moreover, the school year for Spanish-speaking students going to their classes lasted 1 month less than that for Anglos. "We stop the Mexican school term one month early for cotton-picking," a principal explained. (The same abbreviated term was also true in African American districts.)[47]

The teachers in the Spanish-language schools received less pay and were usually not as well educated and trained as those in Anglo districts. School officials justified the inferior education received by Hispanic students with openly racist arguments. They like most other white Texans, argued that Mexicans were lazy, dirty, and did not want to learn, so why waste better teachers on them. Living conditions in Mexican communities were ignored as a possible explanation for the academic difficulties of Latino students. Impoverished Mexican families often lived in one- or two-room shacks, without plumbing, windows, or beds. The children typically slept on dirt floors while mothers did most of their cooking outdoors and fathers (if present) worked as field hands. They worked only part of a year, usually during planting and harvest season. There were other reasons for the poor state of Latino schools. Many white farmers believed that if their Spanish-speaking laborers got too much education, they would soon move to big cities where they could make more money. For that reason Mexicans had to be kept ignorant, and more importantly they didn't deserve the education because, as a farmer explained, his workers were naturally "inferior, untouchable, and detestable."[48] Any money spent on educating such people would be wasted. It would make no more sense to educate Mexicans than it would to educate monkeys, in this view.

The first court case concerning the segregation of Spanish-speaking students from whites came before a Texas court in 1930. In *Independent School District (Texas) v. Salvatierra*, the court ruled that assigning white and Spanish students into separate classrooms or buildings did not violate the rights of students. The separation took place for educational reasons. School district leaders testified that segregation by language would promote the educational opportunities of Spanish-speaking students. They were not separated for reasons of race but for progressive educational ideals; hence the segregation was legitimate.

In January 1930, the school board in Del Rio, Texas approved a bond issue to build a new high school and remodel its elementary schools. They designated a small portion of the money for expanding the only school for Spanish-speaking students located in a very old two-room building. A group of Mexican parents, with assistance from the recently organized League of United Latin American Citizens (LULAC), sued the district asking a Texas court to close down the separate school for their children. LULAC lawyers argued that the board had deliberately excluded Spanish-speaking students from the white schools in the past and denied them "the right and privilege of mingling with those of the other races in the common enjoyment of the identical school facilities, instruction, associations, and environment." Segregation by language group did great harm to the children by denying them these basic American rights.

The district court ruled that "school authorities have no legal power to arbitrarily segregate Mexican children, assign them to separate schools, and exclude them from schools maintained for children of other white races, merely or solely because they are Mexicans." The Texas Court of Civil Appeals for the Fourth District agreed with that judgment but overturned the lower court decision because no proof had been offered showing that school officials had deliberately intended to discriminate when they separated students by the language they spoke. The segregation came about due to the "wisdom" of educational experts; no harm was intended. The educators segregated the students only because of their language problems. Had the students been separated because of their "national origin" that would have violated their constitutional rights, but they were not. The segregation was imposed for the good of the students. Therefore the schools could remain separate.[49] LULAC appealed to the U.S. Supreme Court, but it rejected the case saying education was a state not a federal matter.

In California, a judge delivered a different verdict on the same issue—the validity of segregating Spanish and Anglo students. The Education Code of California prohibited "Negroes, Mongolians, and (American) Indians" from attending regular (white) public schools. Mongolian referred to anyone of Asian descent including Japanese, Chinese, Filipinos, and Bengali. The code said nothing of Mexicans. In Lemon Grove, a suburb of San Diego, the school board decided to build a separate school building for the approximately 75 Mexican students enrolled in a local grammar school. When school opened after the 1930 Christmas holiday, the Lemon Grove principal stood in the doorway and told all Mexican students that they had to go to the new school, labeled "the barn" (because it looked like one, at least according to Mexican families). When the students told their parents what happened, several families got together and began a boycott, refusing to send their children to a segregated facility.

With the aid of the Mexican consul in San Diego, the parents took the case to a state court. Lawyers for the district argued that Mexican children were educationally "backward" and would benefit from being in separate classrooms, free from the burden of having to compete with better prepared white students. The attorneys for the children, however, presented evidence showing that all but one of the Mexican students spoke English as well as their Anglo classmates. The judge, Claude Chambers, whose judicial philosophy was "justice tempered with mercy," questioned the board lawyers and asked them whether white children were sent to a separate building if they fell behind in their studies? No, they answered and that was enough for the judge. He ordered Lemon Grove to return the Mexican students to their regular school.

Because Mexicans were legally neither Negroes nor Indians—a bill to designate Mexicans as Indians had recently been defeated in the state legislature—and certainly were not Mongolians, the section of the California Education Code mandating racially separated schools did not apply to Mexicans. For the first time in American history, a judge ruled that at least one form of segregation—that by language—was wrong, although the opinion applied only to California. No other district in the state implemented Judge Chambers's decision. In many of these districts, Mexican students went to separate schools until the 1960s.[50]

NATIVE AMERICANS

The Great Depression made living conditions on America's Indian reservations much more difficult then even the Meriam Report's dismal picture presented in 1927. During the Hoover Administration, life for Native Americans had barely improved. Congress refused to appropriate enough money to carry out the changes in healthcare, education, housing conditions, and job training that Meriam and his staff had called for. But then in 1933, when newly elected President Franklin Roosevelt appointed John Collier, a longtime crusader for Indian rights, to head the Bureau of Indian Affairs (BIA), expectations for some sort of assistance rose among reservation Indians.

Collier presented Congress with a series of economic reforms and called for a coordinated effort to improve life on the reservations. But in his first annual report in 1934, the commissioner identified a key problem faced by Native Americans. He pointed out that "the efforts at economic rehabilitation cannot and will not be more than partially successful unless they are accompanied by a determined simultaneous effort to rebuild the morale of a subjugated people."[51]

To accomplish this task, Collier introduced the Indian Reorganization Act of 1934, also known as the Wheeler-Howard Act. It contained many of the ideas suggested in the Meriam Report and by Collier and his staff of anthropologists and Native American leaders. The new legislation returned sovereignty to Native Americans by allowing for elected councils and new tribal constitutions that would govern each reservation. Native peoples had the option, however, of participating in the new system or maintaining their traditional relationship with the government.

The new plan ran into trouble on the largest reservation in the United States, the 40,000-member Navajo reservation in northeastern Arizona. The Navajos rejected the new program by a narrow margin largely because the BIA had implemented an unpopular livestock reduction program. The goal was to raise prices the Indians received for their sheep and goats at local markets by reducing their supplies. In the 1920s, Navajo ranchers had increased their herds to such an extent that overgrazing threatened to destroy what remained of the reservation grassland. The BIA suggested a simple but bloody solution to quickly reduce supplies: half of the Navajo goats and sheep would be killed. In return the Indians would receive temporary jobs from the government to make up for the lost income from the livestock they slaughtered.

From the Navajo point of view this seemed like an appalling waste of property and wealth. Agents from BIA and the federal Soil Conservation Service pressured the Indians to comply with the project, but many refused, especially those with smaller numbers of sheep and goats. So the agents shot the goats and sheep, more than 200,000 of them. Some of the dead animals were given to the Navajo for food, but many others were left to rot or their bodies were covered with gasoline and set afire. When the referendum on whether to accept the provisions of the Reorganization Act took place a few weeks later, the Indians rejected it. As anthropologist, novelist, and longtime admirer of Navajo culture Oliver La Farge observed, "Like it or not, this was a vote of no-confidence in the present administration."[52]

Collier's hope was to make it possible—through local self-government—for Indians to live as Indians. Indian sovereignty would restore their dignity and pride; no longer would they be wards of the federal government, living on rations and handouts. Under their new constitutions, Native Americans would control and manage their own lands and lives and also be self-governing. The old allotment system promoting individual land ownership would end, and most reservation land would come under tribal control. Also, Indians could write their own rules for government; however, the secretary of the interior would have the final right of approval on these new constitutions.

By 1936, about 75 reservations had approved constitutions and set up elected councils. Many tribes became corporations and they created new tribally owned businesses: the Jicarillas (Apache) started running their own trading post, the Chippewa built and ran a tourist camp, the northern Cheyenne established a farm and livestock cooperative, and the Swinomish of Washington created a tribal fishing business. These tribes lived on small reservations with close-knit relations between families and their businesses became successful. The larger tribes, including the Navajo, the Sioux in South Dakota who resided on the giant and sparsely populated Pine Ridge reservation, and the Blackfeet in Montana, experienced greater difficulty in reorganizing their government and economies. Major disputes broke out between various tribal factions, most important between mixed-bloods who were half Indian/half white and full bloods who were pure Indians. They fought over voting rights, distribution of corporate wealth, and what part Native American a person had to be to take part in tribal affairs.

The Hopi of northern Arizona ran into another problem. The nine Hopi villages had lived independently from each other for much of their history. They existed as free city-states, as in ancient Greece, each with its own government, gods, and rules. Therefore they rejected government attempts to reorganize all Hopi under more unified, corporate lines.

On many reservations a large part of the population lived in great poverty and in such a state of despair that they showed little willingness to participate in elections, councils, or establishing new businesses. The very harshness of their lives caused Indians to give up on any possibility of change or improvement. The average income for an Indian family of four in 1937 was less than $600 a year, and most of this money came from government-sponsored work projects or direct relief. Wealthy Indians existed, especially those lucky few who received oil royalties. A vast majority of Native Americans, however, lived in the lowest tenth of the American population in terms of their yearly income.

In 1936, Congress created the Indian Arts and Crafts Board (IACB) to set standards for the sale of items such as Navajo blankets, jewelry, and Pueblo pottery. The popularity and sale of these items had expanded in recent years and a flood of factory-made items had hit the market. The IACB would certify the authenticity of each item and promote their sales through art shows and exhibits across the country. Arts and crafts never provided a large number of Indians with an income, but almost every reservation had a few artists who could make a living through selling their creations.

By the end of the decade, living conditions had improved only slightly on many reservations. Unemployment stood at about 60 percent. A survey of Indian housing and health found that both remained "woefully inadequate." Southwestern tribes fared better than Indians on the Great Plains, however. The Indians in Arizona and New Mexico benefited from a mild climate and access to an abundance of building materials, especially stone and adobe. The Sioux, Winnebago, Cheyenne, Blackfeet, and Arapaho of North and South Dakota, Montana, and Oklahoma, on the other hand, had practically nothing to build with or grow for food. They lived on treeless plains, suffered through bitterly cold winters in tarpaper shacks, tents, and dirt houses, and then faced a furnace-like heat in the summer. For these Plains Indians little had changed because of the Indian New Deal, as Collier's programs were called; there lives were still difficult.

One survey found that health care for Indians had improved a bit by the end of the decade. The incidence of tuberculosis, "the greatest Indian scourge," the investigators reported, had been reduced among Native Americans, and new health clinics had been opened on the Navajo and several other reservations.[53] Morale within the Indian Health Service had also improved. But again health conditions among the plains Indians had barely made any progress. Lung diseases, especially trachoma, had reached epidemic levels. And alcoholism, drug addiction, and suicide rates had increased dramatically.

By 1940, Indian education had moved away from the old "force them to be white" model and federal funds for public schools had grown to an average of $10 million per year, 10 times what it had been before 1933. Collier had closed most of the boarding schools but not all of them as he had intended. There simply were not enough schools on reservations to handle the yearly enrollment of 10,000 children. Religious and private schools taught perhaps 7,000 Indian students. The curriculum had been modernized in the public schools, and the approach now was to give everyone a basic education, but without taking children away from their families. Vocational and trade schools were opened in South Dakota, Kansas, and New Mexico. About 220 Indians had enrolled in colleges and universities by 1938. That was the good news. The bad news was that 10,000 Indian children did not attend schools of any kind.

John Collier's policies included hiring more Native Americans to work for the BIA, and by the end of the decade, about half of the employees were Indians. The number of Indians in the Washington office had increased from 11 in 1933 to almost 100 five years later. Collier repealed the ban on the use of Indian languages in reservation schools and removed most restrictions on religious ceremonies. The BIA report of 1939 concluded that "the government has much less control over individual lives and activities than it formerly had." Indians had achieved more sovereignty. Yet perhaps the most vital change in the Collier years was that the BIA no longer regarded Indians as a dying people, too weak and too stubborn to assimilate into American society.[54]

MEDIA AND MASS COMMUNICATIONS

AFRICAN AMERICANS

White newspapers generally ignored the unusually desperate conditions of black Americans (as they ignored Indians on reservations) resulting from the Great Depression. Pictures in the press rarely showed African Americans anyway, except perhaps after being arrested for some horrible crime. Few northern newspapers had any correspondents or reporters in the South, so the extreme poverty, segregation, and harsh conditions of sharecroppers in Arkansas, Mississippi, or other Jim Crow states rarely entered their readers' consciousness. Lynchings did not receive wide coverage in newspapers outside the South. The "race question" seemed liked a regional rather than a national issue despite the growth of an African American population in many northern cities during the Great Migration. No one on the national scene, except for Eleanor Roosevelt, raised the issue of race relations in speeches or elections, and the white press followed suit. Black newspapers in the North either closed down because of the harsh economic climate or reduced their staff so they could survive.

Amos 'n' Andy was still a popular radio program helping reassure whites that life might be tough in the ghetto, but there was still time for humor and a lot of scheming to get rich without doing too much work (George "Kingfish" Steven's favorite pastime). The smiling face of Rastus, the smiling chef, continued to appear on Cream of Wheat boxes and Aunt Jemima's hanky-covered head reassured buyers that Mammy was still glad to serve them breakfast. More degrading images continued to appear in magazines and billboards. Pickaninny Peanut Butter

Freeman Gosden and Charles Correll perform as *Amos 'n' Andy* in the NBC radio studios, 1935. Courtesy of the Library of Congress, LC-USZ62-119955.

continued to sell well as did a drain cleaner called Cannibal in a can featuring a round-faced black man with big lips on its label under the slogan "Eats Everything in the New Pipe."[55]

ASIAN AMERICANS

The Asian image in American media was strongly influenced by one theme that appeared almost constantly in newspaper stories about the Chinese and Japanese, a great fear of "the yellow peril."[56] This fear—that millions of Asians are waiting to eventually destroy Western societies just by their shear numbers—appears in short stories, magazines, newspapers, and movies in every decade of the twentieth century. In the 1930s, masses of Asians threatened Western civilization in everything from Fu Manchu thrillers to mystical adventures in the Himalayas in James Hilton's *Lost Horizon* (1937). No popular magazine gave a more negative impression of Asian life and religion than *The Saturday Evening Post*, which published many of Sax Rohmer's stories, including *The Mask of Fu Manchu* (1932). It was made into a movie starring Boris Karlov as the title character. Fu Manchu kidnaps a beautiful white girl to sacrifice to Buddha, the god of all Chinese. He demands human blood from his worshippers, specifically that of a girl. In an elaborate ceremony before hordes of chanting, armed Chinese warriors, the white

Boris Karlov, star of Monogram's "Mr. Wong" series, as
Fu Manchu, 1939. AP Photo.

"goddess" appears in flowing robes and is tied to an altar. The priests are ready to
cut out her heart and just before they do, she is rescued by the white hero. Fu's
announced ambition to kill every last white person in the world is foiled.

LATINOS

The media generally ignored the Latin American community, unless Spanish-
speaking migrant workers went on strike or a Latino raped or accosted a white
woman. Immigration raids usually garnered headlines in the local press and
helped create the image of the illegal aliens. That stereotype always had a Latino
face. The press and the public had little sympathy for the plight of deportees; they
were "criminals" and "lawbreakers" because of they way they entered the United
States. Why so many Mexicans and other Latinos left their homelands and took
the risk of coming north was a question seldom raised.

Journalists, outside of California and the Southwest, believed that few white
Americans knew that Spanish-speaking people had lived in the United States
since it became independent. Although Spanish-language newspapers recognized

the problems of language discrimination and were appalled by the negative ste-reotyping of Latino Americans (as in the "lazy Mexican," for example), there was no organized movement to challenge the prejudice or raise awareness of the plight of Latino families and workers. Many Latinos remained hopeful that, if white Americans understood their own history and Latino children were allowed to study in the language of their parents, the stereotypes would gradually go away. Once Anglos began to appreciate the beauty and wisdom of Spanish culture and language, Latino Americans would be one step closer to full equality in their homeland.

NATIVE AMERICANS

In American media the good Indian/bad Indian images dominated. Good In-dians were noble savages and bad Indians were degraded, dumb, and still un-civilized. The "savage" had disappeared from the popular press shortly after the last Indian War in the 1890s, although he would live forever in movie images. In a practice that influenced the lives of many American minorities, the daily press labeled people accused of crimes, as in "Indian Sentenced for Robbery," or "Negro Arrested for Murder," or "Mexican Jailed for Smuggling Heroin." No doubt these front-page headlines conditioned readers to think of violence, drugs, and savagery when they saw a minority person on a bus or in the street. Reporters and Hollywood scriptwriters seemed unable to get away from using words such as "wigwam," "fire-water," "Paleface," and "redskin" in their stories.

These words made many white readers laugh, but they really had nothing to do with Indian life on reservations during the Great Depression. Indian lives had changed greatly since the days of the Old West, but even that concept—that Indi-ans always attacked wagon trains and killed their occupants or attacked and killed homesteaders and farmers every day—had little truth to it. Indian lives had changed since then, but that reality did not come through in movies, magazines, and news-papers. The old stereotypes remained and proved hard to break or challenge.[57]

LAW AND GOVERNMENT

AFRICAN AMERICANS

In a 1931 decision, *Aldridge v. United States*, the U.S. Supreme Court ruled in a case involving an African American killing a white, that the question of racial prejudice in selecting a jury could be raised by the defense. A number of southern states quickly added some black names to their jury rolls. The Court issued two major decisions concerning the Scottsboro Boys that helped save them from the death penalty in Alabama. But the cases had significance beyond that one case, setting the stage for future decisions concerning the adequacy of counsel and jury selection. First, in *Powell v. Alabama* (1932), the Court ruled that the defendants had been denied the constitutional right of due process because their attorney had not provided them with an adequate defense. He had appeared drunk in court the first day of the trial, never interviewed his clients, and had not asked a single question of any witness. The justices ruled that the Sixth Amendment guaranteed defendants in death penalty cases a right not only to counsel but to a more vigorous and competent attorney.

Three years later in *Norris v. Alabama* (1935), the Court overturned another guilty verdict in the Scottsboro case on the grounds that Alabama had deliberately excluded African Americans from its jury selection process. This unfair process had denied the black defendants the right to a fair and impartial jury. The Court ordered a retrial for the accused. At this trial, the state hastily expanded its jury registration process and one black farmer found himself on the next jury. In 1937, the state dropped charges against five of the nine "boys"; another had been killed in prison, and the others were still in prison. By 1959, they were either paroled or pardoned and the last of the accused still in jail finally escaped to the North.

In another decision, *Brown v. Mississippi* (1936), that involved race, the Court overturned a conviction in Mississippi even though the three African Americans charged with murdering a white planter had "confessed" to the crime. At the trial the confessions were the only evidence presented by the prosecution. Under questioning by the defense, several witnesses testified that the confessions came only after the police had whipped and brutalized the accused day –and night for four days. Only then did they sign a confession that had been written for them by a deputy sheriff, The all-white jury presented a guilty verdict despite the evidence of torture, and the judge sentenced the men to death by hanging. The Mississippi Supreme Court upheld the verdict and the death penalty. With the assistance of the NAACP, the defendants appealed to the U.S. Supreme Court, which reversed the conviction. As Chief Justice Charles Evans Hughes wrote for the majority, "the torture chamber may not be substituted for the witness stand."[58]

In a key decision involving segregated schools, *Missouri ex rel. Gaines v. Canada* (1938), the Court attempted to define what constituted equality in the field of higher education. Missouri law excluded African Americans from attending the University of Missouri and its law school. Lloyd L. Gaines, a black college graduate, applied for admission to the law school anyway. The university rejected the application. The state offered to open a law school at its all-black Lincoln University, but as of 1938, Gaines would have been the only student attending. He rejected the proposal. Then Missouri officials offered to pay his tuition to attend law school in another state of his choice.

The NAACP filed suit in state court challenging the exclusionary law but lost on all levels, including at the state supreme court. The NAACP took the case to the U.S. Supreme Court, which, in a major decision, overturned the state court rulings. Speaking for the Court, Chief Justice Hughes argued that true equality—as the 1896 "separate but equal doctrine" established in *Plessy v. Ferguson* mandated—required at least a "parallel education system" for minority students. The fact that Missouri had promised to eventually open a law school at Lincoln University did not provide a sufficient reason to deny Gaines immediate admission to the state university. Likewise, the offer to send him to an out-of-state law school was not a "sufficient expression of equal opportunity" as required by the Fourteenth Amendment. The Court ordered that Gaines be immediately admitted to the all-white law school. It did not happen because Gaines disappeared and no one ever heard from him again. The decision was still important, however, because it represented the first time the Court had ordered desegregation of any school at any level.[59]

In cases involving race and the right to vote, the Supreme Court in *Nixon v. Condon* (1932) ordered the Democratic Party of Texas to allow African Americans voting rights in its primary elections. Texas had given the party's executive committee power to run these elections in response to a 1927 Court ruling in *Nixon v. Herndon* In the 1932 case, the justices said the state could not prohibit minorities from casting ballots in primaries because they were public elections.[60] Three years later in *Grover v. Townsend* (1935), however, the Court reversed *Nixon v. Condon*, finding this time that primaries were private political party functions that could not be regulated by the state. This was an important decision because the Democratic Party was the only political party in most southern states. This meant that the winner in the primary was guaranteed victory in the general election. To be refused the right to vote in a primary excluded African Americans from having a voice in that decision.

In another decision that had a major impact on African American voting rights, the Court decided in *Breedlove v. Suttles* (1937) that Georgia had the right to collect a poll tax. These taxes along with literacy tests had been used by southern states to get around the Fifteenth Amendment, which said that race could not be used as a factor to prevent people from voting. Georgia charged $1 per year to register to vote, which was a burden on citizens with very low incomes or without any income. The Court ruled unanimously, however, that Georgia had imposed a reasonable charge to help pay for elections.

In one important area, the federal government took no action, the crime of lynching. On two occasions in the 1930s, filibusters in the Senate blocked passage of bills making lynching a federal rather than a state crime. In 1930, Southern senators killed an anti-lynching proposal even after several horrible killings took place in Georgia and Texas. Senator Thomas Heflin (Democrat, Alabama), in a long speech against the bill, defended lynching. "Whenever a Negro crosses this line between the white and Negro races and lays his hands on a white woman he deserves to die," he told his colleagues.[61] Four years later, a brutal lynching in Florida sparked another effort to pass a federal anti-lynching law. A mob in Florida pursued Claude Neal into Georgia, where they tortured him before burning him alive. His crime was having a consensual sexual relationship with a white woman. The FBI investigated the lynching because the bloodthirsty mob had crossed state lines. It issued a report to state investigators. It then apparently was lost and no further action took place. Police officials in both states refused to take any action against the lynchers. The House passed anti-lynching legislation; the Senate did not after southern senators launched another filibuster.

In yet another victory (actually a series of victories) for opponents of equal rights in the United States, a coalition of southern Democrats and conservative Republicans successfully blocked all efforts to include equal pay for African Americans and other minorities in every New Deal program that came their way. The Social Security Act of 1935, for example, excluded agricultural workers, hospital workers, hotel and laundry workers, and domestic servants (all job categories with a high percentage of minority employees) from coverage. Three years later, the Fair Labor Standards Act excluded the same job categories from coverage by its minimum wage and maximum hour's provisions. Employers could continue to pay extremely low wages to the people already at the bottom of the U.S. wage scale.

ASIAN AMERICANS

American courts at the state and federal level continued to find ways to define Asians as noncitizens and inferior people. In February 1930, a Los Angeles Superior Court judge decided that Filipinos belonged to the "Mongolian race," because they had come from the continent of Asia. This meant that Filipinos could be subjected to the same discriminatory laws in California as other Asians. Before this ruling Filipinos were considered to be different from the Chinese and Japanese. This decision meant that Filipinos, too, would be prohibited from marrying whites under California law, and they no longer could buy land.

Congress acted on one bill that had troubled Asian Americans for almost 10 years. In 1931, it repealed the Cable Act of 1922. This law took away the citizenship of American women who married any person ineligible for U.S. citizenship, that is, anyone from China, Japan, India, Indochina, or any other part of Asia. White women and African Americans already married to Asians could regain their citizenship only by divorcing their husbands or waiting until their husbands died. After 1931, this was no longer true. The repeal came after two years of lobbying by the Japanese American Citizenship League.

Asian exclusion laws had not applied to Filipinos because their homeland was a territory of the United States. The California congressional delegation, led by Senator Hiram Johnson, called for closing this loophole in restriction laws by promoting Philippine independence. In 1934, Congress passed the Tydings-McDuffie Act, which gave the islands self-government, thereby ended Filipino immigration. The law declared that the Philippines were now a commonwealth and that it would be granted total independence within 10 years. In the meantime, Filipinos in the United States would be considered Asian aliens, subjecting them to the 1924 restriction law. Instead of what had been open immigration, they would now be subjected to a quota of 50 legal immigrants to the United States every year.

The next year Franklin Roosevelt signed the Filipino Repatriation Act into law. It allowed Filipinos in the United States the right to return to the Islands at government expense. Once back in their native land, however, they could come back to the States only as part of the 50 per year quota, which would mean a long wait for most. That is why only a few hundred Filipino Americans accepted the free trip "home."

EUROPEAN AMERICANS

The quota system established by the 1924 immigration law had a major impact on the lives of European Jews trying to escape the Nazis. Congress refused to change the German quota even after *Kristallnacht* (the Night of the Broken Glass) in 1938 when Nazis destroyed Jewish businesses and beat and killed hundreds of Jews in the streets of Berlin and other cities. They set fire to and burned down hundreds of synagogues throughout Germany. Thousands of lives might have been saved if the German quota of 25,957 per year had been increased or even filled, as it had not been in the previous 14 years. In 1939, a bill to allow 20,000 German children outside the quota system into the United States failed to pass the House or Senate. Anti-Semitism in the State Department, Congress, and among the American public played an important roll in blocking passage of this legislation. In his diary, Assistant Secretary of State Breckenridge Long, the man in charge of refugee and immigration services, wrote that he regarded Hitler's *Mein Kampf* as "eloquent in opposition to Jewry and to Jews as exponents of Communism and chaos."[62]

LATINOS

Beginning in 1930, the administration of President Herbert Hoover initiated a program of "repatriation" of Mexican and other Spanish-speaking workers in the United States. Reacting to the joblessness resulting from the worst depression in American history, the secretary of labor and the head of the Immigration and Naturalization Service (INS) called for the expulsion of all "aliens" who were allegedly taking away jobs from Americans. According to the secretary, they added to unemployment in the United States. Because of the new program, between 1930 and 1933, more than 250,000 Mexicans were deported to their "homeland." The INS made little effort to determine how many of the deportees might have been American citizens. For INS agents no proof was necessary; anyone speaking Spanish was considered an alien and shipped back to the border, from where, after being stripped, de-loused, and in other ways humiliated, they were marched back into Mexico. Governments in Illinois, Indiana, and Michigan even paid the transportation costs and procured special trains to hasten the removal of Spanish-speaking residents from their states. After Franklin Roosevelt took office in 1933, the repatriation policy officially ended. At the state and local level, however, and especially in Arizona, California, and Texas, harassment and deportation of Spanish-speaking residents continued.

NATIVE AMERICANS

In 1934, Congress passed the Indian Reorganization Act, also called the Wheeler-Howard Act, giving Native American tribes the option of establishing their own reservation government. They could also draft their own constitutions. The law's major goal was to implement some of the changes advocated by the Meriam Report of 1927. State and local governments, however, received the power to provide social services, education, and healthcare on the reservations under the Johnson-O'Malley Act of 1934. The states signed contracts with the federal government to pay for these services and, as hostility toward Indians remained especially high in states with significant Indian populations, these local governments continued to interfere with true sovereignty.

Two important Supreme Court cases affected the lives of American Indians. First, in *United States v. Creek Nation* (1935), the Court ruled that the government owed the Creek Nation money for land that had been incorrectly left off a survey a century before.

The government had made a mistake and the Indians deserved compensation. The ruling meant that the Department of Interior and the Bureau of Indian Affairs had an inherent obligation to treat Indians fairly and handle their property justly, because Native Americans were dependent on those government agencies for their survival. Then in *United States v. Shoshone* (1938) the Court ruled that Indians had title not just to reservation land but also to the timber and mineral rights on that land. The tribes could lease the rights or sell them, but the money received belonged to the Indians not to the states or counties where the reservations were located.

CULTURAL SCENE

AFRICAN AMERICANS

The Harlem Renaissance came to an end by the early 1930s as the Great Depression turned the interests of black novelists away from creating the New Negro toward depicting the lives of the suffering (and, in many cities and towns with large black populations, starving) poor. Writers such as Richard Wright and Langston Hughes turned to the Communist Party to fight against racism because it seemed to be the only political party in the United States with an equal rights agenda. The Communists had difficulty gaining political support from black workers in the North and the South, but it continued to support the African American struggle for justice, as evidenced by its involvement in the Scottsboro Boys' case. Very few blacks voted for Communist Party candidates in elections, but the party never gave up hoping that fighting against racism would bring the black population into the struggle that would lead to the overthrow of capitalism.

Richard Wright, 1936. Photograph by Carl Van Vechten.
Courtesy of the Library of Congress, LC-USZ62-42502.

Richard Wright (1908–1960) left the South bitter and angry. He hoped to help end the violence and oppression faced by his people. Wright grew up in Arkansas but joined the Great Migration and moved to Chicago in 1927. He worked as a postal clerk, insurance agent, bellhop, waiter, and at various other jobs and read Karl Marx and other Communist thinkers in his spare time. He joined the party in 1932, becoming secretary of the Chicago branch. Three years later he took a job with the Federal Writers' Project of the Works Progress Administration (WPA). Congress gave the WPA authority to create jobs for Americans in every walk of life. It hired schoolteachers, ballet dancers, actors, artists, musicians (jazz and classical), historians, journalists, playwrights, and other jobless Americans. Teachers taught adult education to migrant workers. Dancers, actors, and musicians gave free concerts in small towns and cities where live music was rarely heard. And the Writers' Project produced state and local histories, travel guides, oral histories, and biographies of important politicians and statesmen. Wright became the literary advisor to the Negro Federal Theater of Chicago. At the same time he contributed poetry to the *New Masses,* the Communist Party's arts and literature magazine. While with the Federal Theater, he met Langston Hughes another party member and contributor to its monthly journal.

In 1937, Wright moved to New York City where he continued to work for the Writers' Project. That same year he met Ralph Ellison and Claude McKay, two important black novelists. McKay, one of the major voices of the Harlem Renaissance, had been a Communist since the early 1920s. Ellison, author of *Invisible Man* (1952), worked for the WPA and contributed essays on black life and culture to the *New Masses*. Wright became the Harlem editor of the Communist Party's newspaper *The Daily Worker*. He wrote a "Blueprint for Negro Writing," which tried to establish certain ideas and forms for future black writers to follow. In 1938, Wright published *Uncle Tom's Children*, a collection of four short novels depicting the struggle for life in the Jim Crow South. The success of this book earned Wright a Guggenheim Fellowship and enabled him to resign from the Writer's Project. The money from the fellowship allowed him to work full time on his next and most well-known novel, *Native Son*, published in 1940.

Langston Hughes began the decade with his first novel, *Not without Laughter* (1930), based on his boyhood outside of Joplin, Missouri. It described in colorful detail the lives of a variety of very poor, very abused, but very dignified characters in an isolated African American community in middle America. During the decade Hughes published four volumes of poetry; produced a film, *Black and White*, while on a two-year visit to the Soviet Union; and wrote a book of short stories, *The Ways of White Folks* (1934), and a successful Broadway play, *The Mulatto*. The play ran for three years. Hughes then staged a not-as-successful drama, *The Emperor of Haiti* (1936). In his spare time and with his own money, he established the Harlem Suitcase Theater in 1937. It presented plays that he hoped would inspire the working class to overthrow capitalism. Hughes produced the plays on a minimum budget and without scenery (it was called "Suitcase Theater" because all of its costumes could fit into one suitcase). Tickets cost 10 cents or even less.

Hughes wrote six plays for his Harlem theater in 1938 and 1939. They included *Don't You Want to Be Free?*, a musical history of blacks in America, and *Angelo Herndon Jones*. He based the latter drama on the life of a Communist Party organizer Angelo Herndon, arrested in Atlanta and sentenced to 27 years on a chain gang for leading a protest march of unemployed sharecroppers. Hughes also wrote and produced *De Organizer*, with music by James P. Johnson, a jazz pianist. This "blues opera" told the story of an attempt to organize a sharecropper's strike. The theater closed in 1939 when Hughes moved West and founded the New Negro Theater in Los Angeles.

Other important African American writers of the era included Arna Bontemps (1902–1973) and Zora Neale Hurston (1891–1960). Born in Louisiana, Bontemps grew up in California where he graduated from Pacific Union College. He moved to Harlem where he taught high school English while writing poetry and fiction. His first novel, *God Sends Sunday*, the story of a black jockey from Harlem who earns enormous amounts of money but ends up broke after gambling and drinking it all away, appeared in 1931. Bontemps collaborated with Langston

Langston Hughes, 1936. Photograph by Carl Van Vechten. Courtesy of the Library of Congress, LC-USZ62-92598.

Hughes on two popular children's books, *Popo and Fifina: Children of Haiti* (1932) and *You Can't Get a Possum,* (1934) another story aimed at young readers about a boy and his dog in northern Alabama.

Then in 1936 his most significant novel appeared *Black Thunder: Gabriel's Revolt: Virginia 1800*. Based on fact, it told the story of an attempted slave uprising (sometimes called Prosser's Rebellion) that ended in tragedy after a spy revealed the plot to the authorities. The novel received mixed reviews but enabled Bontemps to get a grant from the Julius Rosenwald Fund. With this money, he worked on his third novel *Sad-Faced Boy* (1937), the story of three boys from Alabama who travel to Harlem where they learn to appreciate the beauties of their home state despite its racism and violence. Two years later, Bontemps returned to historical themes in *Drums at Dusk* (1939), an account of the bloody Haitian slave revolt led by Toussaint L'Overture. The book sold poorly and convinced Bontemps that "it was fruitless for a Negro in the United States to address serious writing to my generation." Instead he turned to "trying to reach young readers not yet hardened or grown insensitive to man's inhumanity to man."[63] During the rest of his life, Bontemps wrote novels for young adults, several children's books, and biographies of Frederick Douglas and Booker T. Washington, always stressing his favorite theme: his people's continuing fight for freedom.

Zora Neale Hurston was a novelist, folklorist, and an anthropologist. Born in Florida, she graduated from high school in Baltimore, Maryland before attending all-black Howard University in Washington, D.C. She graduated in 1925 and entered graduate school at Columbia University in New York City where she studied anthropology with Franz Boas. She returned to Florida where she began collecting stories and tales of slavery days and after from elderly residents of her hometown and its surrounding rural areas. Between 1931 and 1943, Hurston published six novels and an important collection of the folklore of African Americans in the South, *Mules and Men* (1935).

Hurston's *Their Eyes Were Watching God* also appeared in 1935. The novel created a stir among black (and some white) critics, some of whom found its story of the sexual awakening of a black woman too explicit for their tastes. She remained controversial for the rest of her life, at one point being denounced by the NAACP for making statements that seemed to support segregation. Like many

Folklorist and novelist Zora Neale Hurston. Photo by Carl Van Vechten. Courtesy of the Library of Congress, LC-USZ62-79898.

black authors, she wanted to be recognized as a gifted writer not as an African American writer. Facing financial difficulties later in life, she retuned to Florida and worked as a maid before moving into a state home for the elderly where she died in 1960.

African American music in the 1930s moved into the mainstream of American sound. In 1930, *Green Pastures*, the first musical with an all-black cast (although the music and lyrics were written by whites) opened on Broadway. Five years later, another musical featuring an all-African American cast (and also written by a white composer, George Gershwin), *Porgy and Bess*, opened to rave reviews. In the world of classical music, there were two key "firsts" early in the decade. The Eastman Rochester Philharmonic gave the first performance of a major symphony by a black composer, William Grant Still's *Afro-American Symphony*. Three years later the Philadelphia Orchestra performed William Levi Dawson's *Negro Folk Symphony*.

William Grant Still (1895–1978) was born in Mississippi but after the death of his musician father spent most of his childhood in Little Rock, Arkansas, where his mother taught English at a high school. He began studying the violin at an early age and loved to listen to opera on the radio. He attended Wilberforce University in Ohio and the Oberlin Conservatory of Music. After graduation he played violin, cello, and oboe in jazz orchestras led by W. C. Handy, Paul Whiteman, and Artie Shaw before he won a scholarship to the New England Conservatory. Here he studied under Edgard Varese, an important modernist composer.

Considered "the Father of African American classical music," Still composed more than 200 musical works. Many of his earliest compositions have unfortunately disappeared and were never recorded. He contributed an opera, *Troubled Island*, about the Haitian Revolt; several ballets including *Lennox Avenue*, a depiction of life in Harlem; six symphonies; numerous pieces of chamber music; and dozens of arrangements of hymns and spirituals. In 1936, Stills became the first African American to conduct a major orchestra, the Los Angeles Philharmonic. At the New York World's Fair of 1939, Still's music was chosen to represent the United States in its primary exhibit.

No discussion of African American classical music in the 1930s would be complete without a mention of Marian Anderson. Considered by many the greatest contralto of her generation, Anderson came out of a poor, working-class background in Philadelphia. She scrubbed floors for a living while a teenager. A few years later she performed in the greatest concert halls of Europe and North America. Her fame spread in 1939 after the Daughters of the American Revolution refused to let her sing at their Constitution Hall in Washington, D.C. because of her color. Instead she performed before 75,000 people, including Eleanor Roosevelt, at the Lincoln Memorial on Easter Sunday.

The popularity of jazz spread rapidly across the country in the 1920s because of new technologies such as live radio broadcasts and recordings. By 1933, Duke Ellington and his orchestra had popularized the swing form with "It Don't Mean a Thing If It Ain't Got That Swing." Singers such as Ella Fitzgerald, Sarah Vaughan,

Bessie Smith, and Billie Holliday added their voices to the expanding sounds of jazz. Beginning in the 1920s, record companies began marketing "race records," as they were called, aimed specifically at African American audiences. The companies aimed at this special population because they did not believe whites would buy recordings made by black artists. This belief proved wrong and by the time of the Great Depression, sales of "race records" soared and many of the buyers were white. Some performers got rich, others did not, as most of the money went to the record companies. Bessie Smith made only $25 to $50 every time she recorded, although sales of her records reached the thousands. Unemployment and despair brought about by the collapse of the economy quickly reduced sales of records in every category and race recordings suffered severely.

One of Billie Holliday's songs, however, stood out as an example of the power of music to inspire political and social reform. Her 1939 recording of "Strange Fruit" has been regarded by many critics as the first Civil Rights song. The words and music were the work of Lewis Allan but that was not the composer's real name. In an example of how racial and ethnic bias influenced popular culture in the United States, the author was a Brooklyn school teacher named Abel Meeropol. He knew that his Jewish name would make it very difficult to have his song produced. So he chose the much more American-sounding Lewis Allan and experienced no trouble selling the words and lyrics.

Meeropol had been disturbed by newspaper pictures of a lynching when he wrote his song. The "Strange Fruit" of the song are the bodies of young black men hanging from the trees. Billie Holliday, one of the most popular blues and jazz performers of the time, heard the song and insisted on recording it. It quickly became the anthem of the anti-lynching campaign. Holliday ended all of her performances with the song, crying all of the way through every time.[64]

Donald Bogle, a student of black images in the media, said of the 1930s: "no other period could boast of more black faces carrying mops and pails or lifting pots and pans than the Depression Years."[65] Hollywood, however, also signed a large number of black performers including the Hall Johnson Choir, Duke Ellington, Louis Armstrong, and Cab Calloway to appear in many films. Jazz stars appeared in musicals such as *I'll Be Glad When You're Dead* (1932), *Minnie the Moocher* (1932), *Rhapsody in Black and Blue* (1932), and *Jitterbug Party* (1935). The tap-dancing Nicholas Brothers amazed audiences with their movements in *Barbershop Blues* (1933) and *The Black Network* (1936). Black musicians and entertainers had an easier time being accepted by white movie audiences than did African American doctors, lawyers, soldiers, or scientists in films. These types of professionals did not appear often in Hollywood pictures. Perhaps they posed too great a threat to white visions of equality. Entertainers, on the other hand, filled a different role—they could be accepted because they were harmless, fun-loving, affectionate bringers of good times.

A few white directors placed blacks in more realistic, challenging roles. In *Hallelujah, I'm a Bum* (1933), Lewis Milestone included a black down-and-outer in his cast. In a movie called *Artists and Models* (1937), Louis Armstrong sang and danced with white actress Martha Raye, leading to the film being banned in several southern cities. Movies such as *I Am a Fugitive from a Chain Gang* (1932), *Cabin in the Cotton* (1932), and *Slave Ship, Jezebel* (1938) showed some of the difficulties of life for southern blacks. And in a few movies, *Arrowsmith* (1934), *Imitation of Life* (1934), *So Red the Rose* (1937), and *One Mile from Heaven* (1937), black actors appeared as intelligent doctors, rebels, and parents actually breaking through the stereotypes. Two movies, *Fury* (1936) and *They Won't Forget* (1937), dealt with lynching, although interestingly the victims were white (as were the lynchers).

Gone with the Wind (1939) brought the first academy award to an African American. Hattie McDaniel (1895–1952) won the Oscar for her portrayal of "Mammy," Scarlet O'Hara's loyal but very sharp-tongued substitute mother and maid. David O. Selznick, the movie's producer, wanted to have "the Negroes come out decidedly on the right side of the ledger," he explained to the screen-writers, so he hired two consultants (both white) to check for any errors in the film's portrait of race relations on slave plantations and the New South that emerged after the Civil War.[66] They told him not to have slaves break out in song while working in the cotton fields, for instance, and to make sure the slaves were not too subservient or overly happy.

Arriving at the ceremony with her black escort, McDaniel was first seated at the very back of the room, but Selznick quickly saw to it that the couple was moved closer to the stage. In McDaniel's brief speech, she thanked the members of the Academy for the honor and ended by saying "I sincerely hope I shall always be a credit to my race and to the motion picture industry." Her main rival for the category Best Supporting Actress, Olivia De Havilland—also for *Gone with the Wind*—told reporters, after first expressing grief, that "Hattie deserved it and she got it . . . I thought I'd much rather live in a world where a black actress who gave a marvelous performance got the award instead of me. I'd rather live in that kind of world."[67] In some ways Hollywood was ahead of the rest of white America.

Beginning in 1919 and continuing into the Great Depression, Hollywood produced numerous so-called race movies. Few African Americans worked as directors or producers in Hollywood except on these films produced for a specific market. One of the few black studio owners, Oscar Micheaux (1883–1951), not only produced and directed "race movies" but generally wrote the scripts. Born in Metropolis, Illinois, the fifth of 13 children, Micheaux worked as a Pullman porter for four years after leaving home, saving enough money to buy some land in Gregory, South Dakota. He married a preacher's daughter and they had a child who died shortly after birth. Although successful at farming, the young couple eventually divorced and Micheaux headed for Chicago. He published three novels based on his life in South Dakota and Chicago before turning to filmmaking. A black-owned movie company in Chicago—the Lincoln Motion Picture Company—took an interest in turning his third and most successful work of fiction, *The Homesteader* (1917), into a movie. Micheaux formed his own company—the Micheaux Film and Book Company—after the owners of Lincoln refused the let him supervise production of the film.

Filmmaker Oscar Micheaux. Courtesy of Photofest.

Besides writing the scripts, Micheaux acted in, edited, and marketed the films his company produced. Micheaux made 48 pictures (27 silent and the rest talking movies) between 1919 and 1948, although because of damage and deterioration, only 15 survive in full. He believed that his "race needed examples; they needed instances of successes."[68] Yet in his movies he tried to capture the difficult realities and darker side of life in African American communities. Micheaux's motion pictures depicted scenes of gambling, drinking, drugs, and criminal behavior. In his second film, *Within Our Gates* (1919), he dealt with a theme generally avoided by moviemakers, lynching and mob violence. Micheaux made his movies with little money and little artistry. White critics found them crude productions that featured actors forgetting their lines and stagehands crossing the cheaply made sets seemingly whenever they pleased. Several black critics thought Micheaux helped spread traditional negative stereotypes of black men and women. Many of his films depicted interracial love and featured multiracial casts. Black critics particularly disliked the rather disguised racism; the heroes generally had very light skins while the villains were usually very dark. One prominent black critic complained that Micheaux was "unwilling or unable to directly confront America's racism, Micheaux displaced his rage on his own people. In other words, part

Lobby card for "God's Step Children" showing a scene from Oscar Micheaux's 1938 movie. Courtesy of the Library of Congress, DLC/PP-2003:161.

of the price he paid for his Americanness was the internalization of American racial attitudes."[69]

Yet the race movies proved spectacularly successful in black communities, especially during the dreary days of the Great Depression. The so-called ghetto movie houses were filled with fans of movies starring Lorenzo Tucker, the "colored Valentino"; Bee Freeman, the "sepia Mae West"; and Slick Chester, "the colored Cagney." Famous actors like Paul Robeson and Robert Earl Jones (father of James Earl Jones) made their debuts in Micheaux movies. The movies Micheaux made were not very good cinematically, but the fact that he made them at all was significant and important for the African American community.

ASIAN AMERICANS

The novels and autobiographical writings of Younghill Kang (1903–1972) and Carlos Bulosan (1913–1956) figured prominently in Asian American literature in the 1930s. Kang left northern Korea in 1921 after taking part in anti-Japanese demonstrations. Japan had occupied the Korean peninsula beginning in 1894, and its occupying army treated the Korean people as racial inferiors. Tokyo refused all demands for independence and had imprisoned and tortured thousands of poetically active Korean students and nationalists. Kang entered the United States with $4 in his pocket to study at Boston University and then attended Harvard where he received a graduate degree in literature.

Kang began teaching in the English Department of Columbia University in New York City and in 1931 produced *The Grass Roof,* the first Korean American novel ever published. In this book, Kang relates the story of life in a small Korean village before and after the coming of the Japanese. At the novel's end, Kang's hero finds himself an exile without a country because of the brutal destruction of Korean society by the Japanese invaders. When he gets to the United States, he is, of course, ineligible for American citizenship because of the Asian exclusion laws and finds that he is an alien again. Kang never gained U.S. citizenship. In 1939, Congress refused to even debate a bill that would have declared him an "American."

Kang traveled to Europe in 1933 with a Guggenheim Fellowship where he wrote *East Goes West: The Making of an Oriental Yankee* a semi-autobiographical published in 1937. The Korean narrator of the story, a Shakespearian scholar called Chungpa Han, likens his position in the United States to that of African Americans. Both groups have faced a long history of discrimination and seemed trapped in a "dark and cryptlike cellar." They both came there to escape the wrath of a lynch mob that threatened to burn them to death.[70]

Like many Korean immigrants of the early 1920s, Han came from the wealthy land-owning class of Koreans. They had some education and lived privileged lives even under the hated Japanese. In America, however, the refugees could find jobs only as waiters, houseboys, farm workers, or miners. Their Korean background did not matter. Like blacks, Asians in the United States were still inferior to whites no matter how much they knew or how rich they were in the old country. They faced job discrimination and racism. Han eventually hitchhiked across America seeking a homeland but never found one. White Americans see him only as the Asian stereotype—he is either the opium-smoking evil genius, or the submissive, cowardly houseboy unfit to become a true American. Chungpa Han had become something like an American by the end of the novel, but as was true for African Americans, a citizen living on the margins of society. He refused to become white because he found their American culture brutal, shallow, ignorant, and cheap.

The Filipino American writer and political activist Carlos Bulason (1913– 1956) wrote an autobiographical memoir, *America Is in the Heart: A Personal History,* in the 1930s, but it was not published until 1946. During the depression he had jobs as a migrant worker, union organizer, and journalist. The book also describes his earlier life in a small rural village in the Philippines where his family lived in extreme poverty. After following his older brother to the United States in 1930, he witnessed the discrimination and abuse faced by his fellow islanders. From the lettuce fields of California to the fish canneries of Alaska, Filipinos were considered "brown-skinned little monkeys." In 1935, Bulason became a union organizer, but then ill health confined him to a Los Angeles hospital for two years. During this time he began reading classic works of literature and started contributing essays to labor newspapers. He summarized his experiences in America made him feel "like a criminal running away from a crime I did not commit. And the crime is that I am a Filipino in America."[71]

All immigrants arrested for illegally entering the United States in the 1930s were held in a detention camp on Angel Island in San Francisco Bay. They stayed indefinitely for anywhere from two weeks to two years. While in this virtual prison, they faced hours and hours of questioning by immigration agents before being returned to their dark, tiny cells. Even in prison, Asians received treatment different from Europeans. The Asians ate the worst food, took saltwater showers, were subjected to the most brutal treatment by guards, and got only a brief 15-minute period of recreation every day. On the walls of their cells, however, they left behind a record of their thoughts and mistreatment. They wrote, scratched, and carved poems on the walls that testified to their mistreatment and disillusionment with America. Immigration authorities painted over these poems several times trying to hide them from visitors. They disappeared until they were accidentally discovered in 1970, as the prison barracks were being torn down. One reads: "America has power, but not justice. / In prison we were victimized as if we were guilty. / Given no opportunity to explain, it was really brutal. / I bow my head in reflection but there is nothing I can do."[72]

Movie representations and images of Asian Americans were dominated by the Fu Manchu stereotype in the 1930s. Sax Rohmer's novels and short stories continued to bring him great wealth, fame, and recognition. He received honorary degrees from institutions such as Harvard University, which granted him a doctoral degree for his literary achievements. Hollywood films continued to present two opposite types of Asians—Charlie Chan versus Fu Manchu. But in early films of the decade a new stereotype appeared, the Asian servant. In a sequel to *King Kong* titled *Son of King* (1933), the model loyal servant from China makes an early appearance, waiting on his white boss with subservient glee. His master rewards "Charlie," as many movie houseboys from Asia were known, with frequent praise. "Good boy, Charlie," he says to an obviously adult human being. In *San Francisco* (1936), star Clark Gable has a Chinese servant who dresses Gable and works as his maid and cook. He wears "coolie" clothes and appears in many scenes in this portrayal of the great earthquake of 1906 but has only one spoken line (in Chinese pidgin-English), "How about going upstairs for some chop suey?"

China itself appears in *The Painted Veil* (1934), a love story starring Greta Garbo, but the country is a disease-ridden, rat-infested place of great ignorance and brutality. The same concept appears in *The Good Earth* based on Pearl S. Buck's famous novel about missionaries in China. The Chinese heroine is played by a white actress in "yellowface," as was true with most lead roles. "Yellowface" referred to the makeup and eye-shadowing necessary to make a Western performer look Asian. Asian actors usually played in only minor roles. Or they portrayed that stereotypical woman, the Asian dragon lady, the female equivalent of the sly, cruel, and evil Dr. Fu Manchu.

Warner Oland portrayed Charlie Chan in movies.
Courtesy of the Library of Congress, cph 3f05882.

Even in the fantastic world of *Flash Gordon*, a science fiction serial movie made in the mid-1930s, with a new episode shown every week in theaters across the country, the evil Asians, who want to destroy everything good and true, made an appearance. The leader of the diabolical forces of evil, Ming the Merciless, even looks like Fu Manchu, mustache and all. He lusts after Dale, Flash's beautiful partner, and in one episode drugs her so he can take advantage of her. Media-made stereotypes of mass hordes of evil-eyed, cruel, brutal, and inscrutable fanatics and "coolies" supplied inaccurate, grotesque portraits of Asians (few Westerners could differentiate between someone from Japan and someone from China) to the American public well before World War II.

EUROPEAN AMERICANS

James T. Farrell (1904–1979) and Michael Gold (1894–1967) wrote novels about the experience of immigrant groups in the United States during the Great Depression. Born to an Irish Catholic family in Chicago, Farrell attended the University of Chicago where he announced that he would write the truth about his community "regardless of the consequences." His *Studs Lonigan: A Trilogy* accomplished that goal with a realistic portrait of the racism and ignorance that infected Chicago's Southside Irish community. In *Young Lonigan* (1932), *The Young Manhood of Studs Lonigan* (1934), and *Judgment Day* (1935), he told the story of a young man, Studs Lonigan, from his boyhood to his violent and early death at the age of 30. Studs shared all the prejudices and misguided beliefs of his friends and neighbors. He was afflicted with the epidemic disease of his community—what Farrell called its "spiritual poverty."

Farrell had escaped this community by taking night classes at the University of Chicago and becoming a socialist. Most of the other residents of Irish Chicago never got away from the neighborhood and lived out their lives in ignorance and cultural poverty. Racism and hostility toward other groups, especially blacks and Jews, filled their daily lives. Studs's mother told him that blacks had "no souls." Studs's father listened faithfully to "Amos 'n' Andy," although he could barely stand the sight of a real-life African American walking down the street. Every Sunday afternoon he turned on his radio to hear the sermons of the Jewish-hating priest Father Charles Coughlin, broadcast from Royal Oak, Michigan.

In 1919, Studs and his friends joined the violent attacks against blacks during that summer's bloody race riot. Farrell described the intense hatred in the hearts of Studs and his friends. "They caught a ten year-old Negro boy. They took his clothes off and burned them. They burned his tail with lighted matches, made him step on lighted matches, urinated on him, and sent him running naked with a couple of slaps in the face." Studs and his friends often danced with black girls when they got drunk on weekends; however, "their faces went tight with hostility every time a white girl went by with a Negro." One of his friends talked about getting a machine gun and killing interracial couples he observed in the street. Instead of buying the gun, he took a taxi to an all-white neighborhood where he could walk to the corner without being offended.

Farrell's *Trilogy* described the influence (usually negative) of an individual's ethnicity and religion on a person's character. The Lonigan family, including Studs, attended church regularly, even as they harbored beliefs that created a world filled with violence and ignorance. No other people could be trusted. Even Italian and Polish Catholics were dangerous aliens in this Irish neighborhood. For Studs, his family, his neighbors, and his friends, racism established stark boundaries around their lives. Their culture imprisoned them and only the very brave escaped.[73]

Based on the author's own life, Michael Gold's *Jews without Money* (1930) describes life in a slum on New York's Lower East Side populated by eastern European Jewish immigrants. Born Itzok Issac Granich in 1893, Gold—who adopted that new name to avoid arrest for protesting American involvement in World War I—became a journalist and associate editor of the radical monthly *The Liberator*, where he met Claude McKay, the black poet, communist, and novelist. A lifelong communist, too, Gold helped found and became an editor of the *New Masses*, which he hoped would serve as "a magazine of workers' art and literature." He wrote two full-length plays in 1926 and 1927, both produced by a socialist theatrical group. He published his first novel, *120 Million* in 1929, followed by *Jews without Money* the next year and then his last work of fiction *Change the World* (1937). In 1933, Gold joined *The Daily Worker*, the American Communist Party's official newspaper, and wrote a column there for 33 years.

Jews without Money describes the life of a young man named Michael who drops out of school to go to work after his father, a house painter, falls from a ladder and becomes disabled. The family barely has enough to eat even after the mother gets a job in a restaurant. Gold describes in detail the rat-infested ghetto and the misery of penniless Jewish families. All they could do was try to survive in the squalor of New York City's immigrant neighborhoods. Jewish girls are forced into prostitution at age 14 because of their poverty, and many men turn to crime in order to survive. "Ku Klux Klan moralizers say the gangster system is not American," Gold writes, "they say it was brought by 'low class' European immigrants. What nonsense! There never were any Jewish gangsters in Europe. The Jews there were a timid bookish lot! The Jews have done no killing since Jerusalem fell. That's why the murder-loving Christians have called us the 'peculiar people.' But it is America that has taught the sons of tubercular Jewish tailors how to kill."[74]

Gold's American ghetto reeked of garbage, dead cats, live rats, and dying horses. "Many of the East Side women had this horrible custom. To save walking downstairs, they wrapped their garbage in newspapers and flung it in the street. In summer the East Side heavens rained with potato peelings, coffee grounds, herring heads, and dangerous soup bones. Bang, went a bundle, and the people in the street ducked as if a machine gun sounded."[75]

Farrell and Gold took realistic looks at immigrant groups in two major American cities. The United States was not the "promised land" people fleeing poverty and the anti-Jewish riots in Europe were seeking. The Irish had learned to hate blacks; they learned to live limited hated-filled lives in constrained communities and found release from their unhappy lives in alcohol, gambling, and meaningless, abusive sex. Jews in the New York ghetto found and learned little more. Coming to America had not opened any golden doors for either group. Ethnicity was a burden for them. It was not a way of connecting with the past or forming bonds of friendship with people with common traits and customs. To remain ethnic meant that a person would live a miserable life.

LATINOS

The two most prominent Latino American writers of the 1930s were women. Josephina Maria Niggli (1910–1983) was one of the first Mexican American women to publish literary works in the United States. Born in Mexico to a Swiss father, a cement plant manager, and a mother of Irish, French, and German descent, Josephina considered herself Mexican because she was born in Mexico. Her parents sent her to San Antonio, Texas when she was three years old to escape the violence and turmoil of the Mexican Revolution. She returned to Mexico seven years later but moved back to San Antonio in 1925 to complete high school. After graduation she entered the College of the Incarnate Word and decided to become a writer. One of her first stories won second prize in the *Ladies' Home Journal* College Short Story Contest. After receiving her bachelor's degree she attended graduate school at the University of North Carolina at Chapel Hill. She graduated with a master's degree in English in 1937.

Niggli published her first book, a collection of poems called *Mexican Silhouettes* in 1931, followed later by *The Red Velvet Goat* (1938), *Sunday Costs Five Pesos* (1939), both children's books, and several plays collected in her *Mexican Folk Plays* (1938). Josefina (the spelling she preferred because it sounded more Spanish to her) also worked in Hollywood as a "stable writer." The studios paid her to contribute scripts and dialogue to any movie then under production. She contributed much of the dialogue in the 1938 production of *The Mark of Zorro*. Her most well-known book, *Mexican Village,* a collection of 10 short stories, appeared in 1945. In all of her poems, short stories, plays, and other works of fiction, Niggli attempted to give white Americans a realistic view of Mexican culture. She hoped that her writing would help break them away from their stereotypes. After tiring of movie-writing, Niggli became a professor of literature at Western Carolina University. She finished her career with the novel *Miracle for Mexico* in 1964.

Adelina "Nina" Otero-Warren (1881–1965) published only one book, *Old Spain in Our Southwest* (1936), but it played a major role in educating Americans about Hispanic culture. She was born to a prosperous family in Las Lunas, New Mexico when it still was a U.S. territory and attended college in St. Louis, Missouri. Upon returning to her home, she worked briefly for her uncle Miguel Otero, the territorial governor. Nina, as she preferred to be called, became active in organizing the women's right to vote campaign in New Mexico when it became a state in 1910. Eight years later, she defeated a male candidate in an election for Santa Fe school superintendent. In 1919, Otero-Warren served as chair of the State Board of Health, a position she held for 10 years. While leading the board she became an outspoken crusader in a drive to improve the health and education of Native Americans. Otero-Warren became active in Republican Party politics in the 1930s and narrowly lost a race for the U.S. House of Representatives when she challenged a male opponent. In 1931, she edited a special edition of the magazine *Survey Graphic* called "Mexicans in Our Midst: Newest and Oldest Settlers of the Southwest."

In 1933, President Franklin Roosevelt appointed Otero-Warren to lead the Civilian Conservation Corps (CCC) in New Mexico. In this position she continued to expand her interests in education and healthcare. The CCC camps provided jobs and schooling for thousands of Mexican American, Native American, and Anglo teenagers in the state. Otero-Warren, surviving harsh criticism from traditionalists, defended bilingual education in public schools and CCC camps. In her view, knowing two languages would help keep families closer together. Spanish-speaking parents would not feel alienated from their English-speaking children, and their sons and daughters would learn that the language of their

Adelina Otero-Warren. Courtesy of the Library of
Congress, ggbain 36127.

parents bore no shame. Also, teenagers and young adults in CCC classrooms
would gain a better understanding of their lives by using the bilingual approach.

In the mid-1930s, Otero-Warren began writing her first and only book, actually a collection of essays, called *Old Spain in Our Southwest*. Her goal was to
educate Americans about Spanish culture and beliefs and promote respect for the
language and history of her people. The book sold widely and became the first
introduction for many American students to the Spanish contributions to their
history. She continued her life as an educator, writer, and advocate of Spanish
culture until her death in 1965.

Hot-blooded, tempestuous Latinos filled the silver screen in the 1930s. Latino
males in westerns were usually fat, vulgar, tobacco-chewing villains, or happy-
go-lucky, siesta-taking, usually pretty stupid sidekicks, such as Pancho, played by
Leo Carrillo (1881–1961), in *The Cisco Kid* series. Cisco provided a more positive image, the quick-thinking, good natured fairly debonair ladies' man (at least
with the seemingly always dancing, happy-go-lucky *senioritas* played by Delores
Del Rio or Lupe Lopez). Sometimes he even flirted with a white woman. The
same was true of Zorro, who was always played by a white actor, however. Cesar
Romero (1907–1991), a Cuban American, played Zorro several times before he

became even more popular as a Latin lover. Zorro was based on a real person, the famed nineteenth-century Mexican outlaw Joaquin Murieta, who robbed and harassed Anglo landowners in California during the 1848 gold rush, seeking revenge for their cruel treatment of Mexican farmers and laborers. The movies made one change; in the first Zorro film *Robin Hood of El Dorado* (1936) attacked Spanish landowners who had stolen land and property from their own people. Very few Anglo Americans even appeared in this picture.

Before becoming Pancho, Leo Carrillo played roles that left distinctly negative images of Spanish-speaking people. In the 1932 film, *Girl from Rio*, he appeared as a brutal Mexican bandit, or "greaser," as he was referred to in the script. "Greasers" were the typical movie-made Latino stereotype, although the humorous, good natured sidekick seemed to offer some balance to the cruelty of Mexican *banditos*.

NATIVE AMERICANS

In 1930, a book about Americans Indians received the Pulitzer Prize for Fiction, *Laughing Boy*, by the novelist and anthropologist Oliver Hazard Perry La Farge (1901–1963). A descendent of the famous War of 1812 admiral ("We have met the enemy and they are ours"), Oliver majored in anthropology at Harvard and spent one summer in Arizona exploring ancient Anasazi and Navajo ruins. He fell in love with the land and its native inhabitants. His fascination with Indian life and culture continued throughout his life. His prize-winning novel told the story of a young Indian, Laughing Boy, and his relationship with Slim Girl. She had returned to the reservation after working as a servant to a white missionary for several years. The couple soon married. Shortly after the ceremony, a jealous rival killed Slim Girl. Laughing Boy recovered from the tragedy but only after participating in the Navajo "Blessing Ceremony." As a result of this sacred ritual, he began to recognize the wisdom of the Navajo way of life. La Farge provided detailed descriptions of Indian ceremonies and dances and demonstrated a profound respect for Navajo culture in this work.

La Farge's second work of fiction, *Sparks Fly Upward* (1931), examined a conflict between Indian and Spanish culture in colonial Guatemala. In 1933, his *Long Pennant*, a historical novel about the War of 1812, appeared. That same year he moved from New York City to Santa Fe, New Mexico. His next book, *The Enemy Gods* (1937), portrayed life on the Navajo reservation during the Great Depression.

The novel portrayed the great social and economic changes threatening that traditional culture. It takes a critical look at Bureau of Indian Affairs' decisions made in Washington that made life more difficult on the reservation. La Farge also includes sensitive descriptions of the meaning of dancing, sand paintings, and the importance of traditional religion among the native peoples of the Southwest. La Farge contributed three more novels, an autobiography, and three collections of short stories, which had appeared in magazines such as *Dial* and *The*

New Yorker. He lived in the Southwest until his death in 1963. His preference for Native American culture over European culture remained true to the end.

The Native American writer (he was officially listed as one-eighth Osage on the tribal rolls) John Joseph Mathews (1894–1979) published two works in the 1930s, *Wahkon-tah: The Osage and the White Man's Road* (1932) followed three years later by *Sundown.* His first book presented a history of the Osage people and their encounters with whites. Mathews's based *Sundown* on his experiences in Oklahoma. The novel's main character, Challenge (his father named him that because he wanted him to challenge the new generation of Indians) "Chal" Windzer, does not want to remain on the reservation with the old generation of "blanket Indians." He believes they have sold their manhood for a few blankets and handouts from the white government. Chal, on the other hand, loves nothing better than to run through the hills of eastern Oklahoma dreaming of hunting bison, as real Indians did in the old days. All Indian traditions in him had not been rejected.

After his family started making money from oil found on the reservation, Chal's life changed. He enrolled in the University of Oklahoma where he fell in love with a white girl. He also faced a continuous stream of bigotry in the dormitories and classrooms. He volunteered for the army during World War I and served in the trenches of France. After the war he moved to California where he forgot his Indian heritage. He drank to excess, fathered two children, and gradually recognized the emptiness of white society. He finally concludes that his only salvation lies in going back to his Osage roots to help save the tribal culture. His revelation comes after hearing of two successful white businessmen who had escaped the "rat race" only through suicide. Mathews faced these problems in his own life, including the alcoholism and thoughts of suicide, before he returned to the Osage reservation. In 1938, he founded the Osage Tribal Museum, the first tribally owned museum in the nation. For the last years of his life, he lived in a little stone house on the reservation listening to his recordings of Osage songs, music, and dances. Visitors frequently told Mathews that he looked white not "Indian"; he responded, "Being Indian isn't in looks, in features or color, Indian is inside you."[76]

John Milton Oskison (1874–1947), born to an English father and Cherokee mother in Tahlequah, Indian Territory (later the state of Oklahoma), wrote essays, short stories, and novels and worked as a newspaper and magazine editor. He worked on his father's cattle ranch on a reservation before entering Stanford University where he received a bachelor of arts degree in 1898. Oskison attended graduate school at Harvard before becoming a reporter for the *New York Evening Post.* During his years on the *Post* he continued writing essays on Indian issues and Indian problems for various popular national magazines. He also became active in the Society of American Indians, a leading reform group. After service in World War I and spending some time in Paris, Oskison published his first novel, *Wild Harvest,* in 1925. It told the story of a young white woman struggling along with her father to survive on their farm in Indian Territory. They join with neighboring Indians to fight against cattle ranchers from Texas trying to take away their land.

Black Jack Davy appeared in 1926. In this novel a 19-year-old white boy, Davy, and his elderly parents fight against a corrupt rancher trying to drive an Indian family from their land. Indians and Davy's family join together to prevent any loss of land. In 1935, Oskison's most successful novel (in terms of sales), *Brothers Three*, appeared. In this story a white man is married to a part-Cherokee woman and they fight against devastation caused by the Great Depression. Based on the author's life and experiences, *Brothers Three* shows what happens to a family as they try to adjust to their desperate circumstances. Oskison also wrote fictionalized biographies of Sam Houston called *A Texas Titan* (1929) and *Tecumseh and His Times* (1939). Both books were well researched and critically acclaimed for their historical accuracy.

In 2007, the University of Oklahoma Press published *The Singing Bird: A Cherokee Novel*, an almost completed manuscript that Oskison left behind when he died. In this novel, he describes the impact of the Trail of Tears on the Cherokee. This infamous event in the 1830s led to the deaths of thousands of Native Americans, as the U.S. Army drove them from their traditional homeland in Georgia. The soldiers brutalized the Indians until they arrived at their reservation in Indian Territory. Oskison's account is told through the eyes of a Christian missionary. He describes his relationships with the Cherokee leader Sequoia and various U.S. military commanders, including Sam Houston.

D'Arcy William McNickle (1904–1977) published an important novel, *The Surrounded*, in 1936. His mother was a Cree Indian, his father an Irish-born rancher. Born on the Flathead reservation in Montana as William D'Arcy, he attended a mission school on the reservation before being sent, against his mother's wishes, to a Bureau of Indian Affairs boarding school in Oregon. The harsh methods of instruction at the school, including a ban on the use of Indian languages, disturbed him, but he learned to play the violin and graduated nevertheless. He then went to the University of Montana where he studied world literature and languages, including Greek and Latin. At the urging of one of his professors, McNickle left the reservation to study at Oxford University. Because of money problems (and difficulties transferring his credits), he left Oxford shortly after arriving and headed for Paris where he dreamed of becoming a writer or a concert violinist.

When McNickle returned to the United States, he became an editor for the *Encyclopedia Britannica* in New York City. At night he took classes at Columbia University and the New School for Social Research and continued to work on his novel. In the fall of 1935, he like many other writers of the 1930s got a job with the Federal Writers Project. Assigned to Washington, D.C., he worked on a series of books describing the history and culture of each of the states. He was told to make sure that each volume contained as much material on Native American history as possible. After meeting John Collier, McNickle became one of his administrative assistants at the Bureau of Indian Affairs, a job he held for 16 years.

The Surrounded was published in 1936, after seven years of revisions and publisher's rejection letters. Many of the events depicted in it were based on McNickle's life, including his possible involvement in the killing of a game warden. One major difference between the chief character (named Archilde) in *The Surrounded* and McNickle's own experience was that McNickle left the reservation for Paris while Archilde only dreamt of leaving. The novel includes vivid descriptions of Indian ceremonies and dances, as well as a consideration of Salish religion versus Christianity. Archilde admired the hard work and dedication of the reservation priests and missionaries but saw their labors as something ultimately to be pitied. Their task was difficult, but he felt that they were "spoiling good pagans to make bad Christians."[77]

By the conclusion of *The Surrounded,* the enormous difficulty of having to reject one's own culture and accept the beliefs of a totally alien one becomes starkly clear. Archilde's mother Elise hated the white man's world and especially its religion. She is dying and asks her son to take her on a last ritual journey into the mountains. Archilde's brother Leon accompanied them. The three become involved in the death of a game warden who had come to arrest Leon for a crime he had allegedly committed. Leon struggles and the warden shoots and kills him. Elise then grabs a gun and kills the warden. Archilde, however, is arrested for the crime and awaits his trial as the novel ends.

Probably the most prolific Native American author of the decade, Rollie Lynn Riggs (1899–1954) wrote 21 full-length plays, a dozen or more one-act plays, several Hollywood screenplays, hundreds of short stories, and two volumes of poetry. A Cherokee from Claremore, Oklahoma, Riggs had a white father who raised cattle just outside a reservation with his Indian mother. Riggs's most famous play, *Green Grown the Lilacs,* first produced on Broadway in 1929, provided the text for the more famous 1943 musical, Richard Rodgers and Oscar Hammerstein's *Oklahoma.* Riggs, who eventually dropped the "Rollie," graduated from Oklahoma Military Academy in 1917 and attended the University of Oklahoma where he taught freshman English for a year after receiving his bachelor's degree. After that he worked as a reporter for the Tulsa-based *Oil and Gas Journal,* although his real love remained the theater.

Riggs moved to New York in 1926 where two of his plays, *Big Lake* and *Sump'n Like Wings,* had shorts runs on Broadway. Both plays concerned Indians and whites living in desperate poverty around his hometown of Claremore. The main point of all his writing was to present a real-life image of the West. Most audiences found them shocking and depressing, preferring stories about the more idealized frontier featuring brave cowboys fighting against savage Indians and other evildoers. Riggs followed with another series of plays, *A Lantern to See By, The Lonesome West, Rancor,* and *Reckless,* that depicted the harsh lives faced by rural Oklahomans, as they eked out existences in obscurity and sadness. *Rancor,* first produced in 1928, concerned themes of suicide, unfaithfulness, jealousy, and parental abuse and neglect. Riggs's dark view of human relationships found critical success but failed to attract large audiences. With his comedies, however, it was a different story.

Roadside, his first comedy, appeared in 1930, by which time Riggs had moved to Hollywood and was busy with his first movie scripts. It ran briefly on Broadway and illuminated the wild and free lives of a beautiful Texas cowgirl and her handsome, straight-shooting cowboy friend named "Texas." Riggs followed with *Green Grow the Lilacs*, rated one of the 10 best plays of 1931 by the Theater Guild of New York. He had begun writing the play in Paris while on a Guggenheim Fellowship three years before. The musical included many traditional cowboy songs between acts (there were six in the original production). They were sung during the intermissions. Riggs's script told the story of a young girl, Laurie, who fell in love with a dashing cowboy, Curly. The evil hired hand Jeeter makes advances toward Laurie and is killed by Curly, who is arrested and charged with murder. The play ends happily, however, with pledges of everlasting love and prosperity in the future, at least for those who work hard. (When resurrected in 1943 as *Oklahoma*, with new songs and new music, the play ran for five years and nine months.)

Riggs's next effort, *The Cherokee Night* (1932), traced the life of a mixed-race Cherokee unable to fit into the white world. It chronicles the failure and impossibility of assimilation he faced and his ensuing loss of "Cherokee pride." In the closing scene an elderly Cherokee leader denounces the loss of Indian dignity and mourns "for a whole race gone down into darkness."[78] Riggs kept writing for the stage and for movies until his death and continued to tell as much as he could the truth about the hardships of life faced by early Oklahomans.

Ota K'Te (Plenty Kill), born on a Lakota reservation in Dakota Territory, changed his name to Luther Standing Bear (1868–1939) after being sent to the Carlisle Indian Industrial School in Pennsylvania. A white teacher who could not pronounce Indian names demanded that his students take European names as part of the assimilation process. (None of the teachers at the school could speak any Native American language.) Plenty Kill chose Luther from a list of names printed on the blackboard. Standing Bear was his father's Lakota name. Unlike the other Indian writers of the time, he was fully Indian. Standing Bear described his traditional upbringing in his autobiography, *My People the Sioux* (1928). He explained how he learned to hunt bison with his father, what games Indian children played, and how they were raised and educated by their parents.

Reservation life had changed everything. The buffalo disappeared so the Lakota had to raise cattle, or the "evil smelling spotted buffalo" as the Indians called them. Their whole way of life changed from what they ate, to how they were educated and to what they wore. Government agents handed out flour as part of the rations provided reservation families, but Lakota Indians had never made bread and did not know what to do with that white powder, so they threw it away. They did, however, use the sacks it came in to make shirts and clothing.

Luther hated the school he was sent to in Pennsylvania and its "civilizing process." Wearing white men's clothing turned into actual torture for the Indian students, especially the shoes and red flannel underwear that school rules demanded they wear. Standing Bear also discussed the difficulty of going back to the reservation after graduation. The returning children faced pressure from their parents and friends to abandon the English they spoke and the white men's ways they had adopted (forcibly) at Carlisle. Some graduates "returned to the blanket" and rejected all that they had learned and returned to their Lakota way of life. Others left the reservation to enter the white world.

Standing Bear did both initially, returning to the Pine Ridge Reservation, although he called it a "government prison." He opened a dry goods store. When that effort failed, he joined Buffalo Bill's Wild West Show where he performed on horseback with his wife. After 10 years of touring the United States and Europe, he returned to Pine Ridge and was chosen to lead the Oglala tribe. He left again a few years later, this time heading for Hollywood. He not only acted in many silent films but became an advisor to movie studios on how to portray Native Americans. Standing Bear first appeared in *White Oak* (1921) and ended his career with *Union Pacific* (1939).

Standing Bear's writing career began when he was 60 years old. He returned to the reservation in 1931, three years after publication of his first book, *My People the Sioux*. He followed this autobiographical work with *My Indian Boyhood* (1931), *Land of the Spotted Eagle* (1933), and *Stories of the Sioux* (1937). *My Indian Boyhood* was written for white children with the hope that "boys and girls who read these pages will be made kinder toward the little Indian boys and girls."[79] Although written for a younger audience, the book contains valuable insights into Lakota culture, religion, and philosophy. In *Stories of the Sioux*, also written for a younger audience, Standing Bear retells 20 traditional stories he had heard from elders of his tribe when he was a child.

In *Land of the Spotted Eagle*, Standing Bear asked a question raised by Indian writers of the time, "Who can say that the white man's way is better for the Indian? Where resides the human judgment with the competence to weigh and value Indian ideals and spiritual concepts and substitute for them other values?" In this book there are more details concerning Indian culture. It was written for an adult audience with the assistance of an anthropologist, Melvin Gilmore of the University of Michigan. The book is less autobiographical than his previous work and more critical of American policy toward Indians: "White men seem to have difficulty in realizing that people who live differently from themselves still might be traveling the upward and progressive road of life," he asserted. In his view the whole idea and history of assimilation was nothing but "a disaster."[80]

Had circumstances been reversed, Standing Bear wondered, how would whites have responded? Forcibly take away their language, their religion, their homes, and their land, what would have happened to them? "Had conditions been reversed and the white man suddenly forced to fit himself to the rigorous Indian mode of life he might now bear the stigma of 'lazy' if, indeed, he were able to survive at all," he answered.[81] Standing Bear recommended that Indians who had been "degraded by oppression and poverty into but a semblance of their former being" be allowed to take possession, once again, of their own lives. They needed to be educated as doctors, lawyers, teachers, and engineers, of course, because the

United States had an obligation to make up for the long history of neglect of its native people.[82] When John Collier took over the BIA, he adopted some of these suggestions, but as Standing Bear recognized, many problems still remained.

Native American writers of the 1930s agreed that white American culture had little to offer Indians. They unanimously ended up choosing the Indian way of life over that of whites, at least in their novels, plays, and stories. They found white Americans arrogant, vulgar, and excessively violent. As Luther Standing Bear, who, despite having found success in white American society, concluded in 1933, "If today I had a young mind to direct, to start on the journey of life, and I was faced with the duty of choosing between the natural way of my forefathers and that of the . . . present way of civilization, I would, for its welfare, unhesitatingly set the child's feet in the path of my forefathers. I would raise him to be an Indian!"[83]

Movie Indians remained savage and bloodthirsty in the hundreds of westerns Hollywood turned out in the 1930s. As Luther Standing Bear, who acted in dozens of these films, remarked, "I have seen probably all of the pictures which are supposed to depict Indian life, and not one of them is correctly made." He says he tried to correct directors and writers when they did not get it right but he always got the same response, "The public don't know the difference, and we should worry?" He also complained bitterly that most significant roles for Indians went to white actors. (In 1939, Standing Bear died while making a western [*Union Pacific*] during a flu epidemic in California.)[84]

INFLUENTIAL THEORIES AND VIEWS
OF RACE RELATIONS

In the 1930s, sociological and anthropological theories of race and race relations began to overshadow the biological and genetic ideas prominent in the previous decade. The influence of eugenicists declined in the United States, but their ideas became extremely influential in certain areas of Europe. Shortly after Adolf Hitler took office in 1933, the Nazis passed a law modeled after sterilization laws adopted by two dozen American states in the 1920s. Leading American eugenicists began traveling to Germany to study the impact of the Nazi laws and while there praised Hitler for taking such bold action to rid his nation of future generations of "defectives." Harry Laughlin, a director of the American Eugenics Society (AES) and architect of the Virginia sterilization law, received an honorary degree for his contributions to biology from the University of Heidelberg, a hotbed of Nazi science in 1936.

Lathrop Stoddard, another AES director, praised the Nazis for "weeding out the worst strains in the Germanic stock in a scientific and truly humanitarian way." Stoddard was also thrilled by Hitler's racial policies. He insisted that the "Jew problem" in Germany was "already settled in principle and soon to be settled in fact by the physical elimination of the Jews themselves from the Third Reich."[85] The Hitler years in Germany marked the darkest hour for the eugenics movement. After the Nazi experience the term *eugenics* evoked not a biological concept but a sense of death and horror in many people. It had become a perverted form of "science" favorable only to advocates of racism and mass murder. The science of race lost much of its popularity and many of its supporters in the aftermath of the Holocaust.

The theories of Franz Boas in anthropology and Robert Park in sociology, with their emphasis on culture and experience as the keys to understanding racial and ethnic identity, dominated the field of race relation in the 1930s. Race was no longer a matter of physical traits and genetic inheritance; instead it was an idea—a human invention—a matter of conscious thought. Hence, racism and prejudice could be eliminated; ideas could be changed more easily than genes. One more important point: all cultures were equal. Human cultures developed in response to specific environments. The results were different because physical environments differed widely, from the heat of the Amazon Basin to the extreme cold of the Arctic, but no culture was superior to any other. Social scientists believed that a successful culture enabled people to survive in whatever climate and geographical surroundings they lived in.

Franz Boas argued that a culture could be analyzed only in its full context. The science of anthropology (literally "the science of man") could not make judgments concerning "good" or "bad" practices a people adopted anymore than a geologist could declare two different rocks "good" or "bad." They might be different but not better than one another—they were rocks or cultures. This philosophy of cultural relativism influenced many anthropologists going into the field to study human societies in the decade of the 1930s, and most of them had studied under Boas at Columbia University.

Ruth Fulton Benedict (1887–1948) began graduate study under Boas in 1921 at the age of 34. Her dissertation completed in 1923 concerned religious experiences in North America, but her most important work began in 1924 when she lived with Zuni Indians in the Southwest. Here she began to study the differences in culture and attitudes between the Zuni and Indians of the Great Plains. In 1934, her book, *Patterns of Culture*, appeared. In it she analyzed three different cultures: the Pueblo Indians, the Dobu people living on a small island close to New Guinea, and the Kwakiutl Indians of the American Northwest. Each culture had a distinct personality type; the people of the Pueblos were "placid and harmonious," the Dobu—practitioners of witchcraft, headhunting, and cannibalism—exhibited traits of cruelty and paranoia, whereas the Kwakiutl, famed for their "potlatches" or parties during which the party-giver tried to give away as much of his own property as he could, were self-promoting and arrogant. These differing traits did not come from genes but from upbringing and education. Diverse cultures developed from the experience of adapting to specific geographical places and environments. A universal human nature did not exist; the world was too complex to allow for such uniformity.

In 1939, Benedict began a yearlong study of the Blackfoot Indians of Montana. This experience helped her produce *Race: Science and Politics* in 1940. In it she reemphasized the importance of culture, custom, and learning rather than genetics and nature in creating human differences. This book came in response to a plea from Franz Boas, now 80 years old, to write a book for the "common man" that would provide an anthropological explanation of race, diversity, and the right all peoples had to live by their own rules. Throughout the decade Boas had exhausted himself in tireless efforts to promote human rights for all people, particularly his fellow Jews of Germany. He put so much effort into finding housing and support for the refugees coming out of his Nazi-dominated homeland that his students feared for his health. They pleaded with him to cut back on the hours he spent working with refugees, "Why don't you limit your refugees to one day or something? I don't think it's age which tires you out so much, it is the everlasting hopelessness of all these people," one wrote. But Boas kept to this work almost to the day he died.[86]

Ruth Benedict agreed with her mentor on two key points. First, anthropologists should not remain silent on the key issues of the times. Social scientists had a responsibility to speak out against racism and discrimination. Second, they agreed that all human beings had the capacity to learn and to change, and that human possibilities were limited only by their own imagination and limited knowledge. Her book translated the academic writing of Boas into more popular language. Race, both anthropologists insisted, was a biological concept, but in popular and political usage it had become much more—an excuse for persecution, abuse, and mass murder. Racism was "merely another instance of the persecution of minorities for the advantage of those in power," she wrote.[87]

Boas and his students, not content with describing cultures and their values, offered some solutions to the problem of racism. "What ever reduces conflict, curtails irresponsible power, and allows people to obtain a decent livelihood will reduce race conflict," Benedict asserted. Such conflict-reducing actions included better housing and job opportunities for minorities, improved education for all, and material security for every family. She believed in people's ability to build a better world. She concluded *Race* by observing, "Our Founding Fathers believed that a nation could be administered without creating victims. It is for us to prove that they were not mistaken."[88] Benedict's views on race in American culture and history allowed for an optimistic view of the future. Change would not come easily, but with education and patience Americans could achieve their dream, equality for all. As she wrote, "All things fail save only dreams."[89]

Sociologist and psychoanalyst John Dollard provided a less hopeful analysis of the future of race relations. He looked at the influence of social class and economics on relations between whites and blacks and conducted extensive research on racial attitudes in a small city in the South in the 1930s. He reported his findings in *Caste and Class in a Southern Town* (1937). He found two castes, one white, one black; and members of these castes were just as distant from each other as they were in the rigid caste system found in Hindu India. In the Hindu tradition, caste dominated everything about a human being's life chances; individuals could not move out of the caste they were born into. An individual's occupation, cultural values, and standing or status in society was determined at birth. Dollard found similar rigidity in Southerntown, as he called the city he lived in and surveyed (actually it was Indianola a town in the Mississippi Delta, considered the most impoverished region in the United States). Blacks and whites lived in totally separated worlds that had been established strictly because of skin color. The white minority in the region had subjugated and dominated the African American population since the end of the Civil War. Many whites lived in huge homes and were extremely wealthy. The divide between white and black was so wide that Dollard likened it to the caste system in India where high caste Brahmins treated members of lower castes with hostility and contempt. Low caste people were hardly human in their eyes.

A class system existed within each of the Delta castes. There were a few wealthy African Americans, mainly the undertaker and local barber. Individuals could move up or down the social classes within their caste, but no African American, no matter how wealthy or successful, brilliant or wise, would ever be accepted into the dominant caste, the ruling white elite. Even the poorest white living in the most wretched conditions, on the other hand, might be reviled by wealthy whites for their ignorance and awkwardness, but they could temper their rage by realizing that they still belonged to the dominant caste and they were still considered superior to the most successful black.

Hortense Powdermaker, a white anthropologist, had lived in and studied Indianola earlier in the decade from 1932 to 1934. She lived in a black community during that time and reported her findings in *After Freedom: A Cultural Study in the Deep South* (1939). Powdermaker interviewed one moderately successful black who told her the secret of his achievement. It was "hard work" and "slow saving" but also "staying in my place, acting humble" to avoid white hostility.[90]

Both Dollard and Powdermaker came to similar conclusions. Whites enjoyed tremendous economic benefits from the caste system while blacks lived on the verge of starvation. One white woman boasted to Dollard that she could ring for her maid at any time, even three in the morning, and she would come with a glass of ice water. When the maid, whose salary was $2.50 a week, asked for a quarter a week raise, the woman, who claimed to "love" her servant, told her to "go to hell."[91]

Both social scientists saw little chance for progress or change. Caste distinctions would not disappear through education, economic growth, political action, or appeals to the brotherhood of humanity. The white caste dominated and exploited the black caste, and it would do that far into the future, if not forever. In Southerntown, railroad tracks divided the white area from the black area and the differences in living conditions on each side of town symbolized the disastrous state of American race relations. "On the white side of the town the houses are in general, commodious, well painted, shrubbed, and neat. . . . The streets are paved in the white area and telephone wires run through the trees." Walk across the tracks, however, Dollard reported, and you enter a different world. "Here the houses are small and cheap. . . . A well-cropped lawn is a rarity, as is a well-built house. . . . Only two paved streets traverse this area where fifteen hundred people live."[92] The bleakness of the buildings and their surroundings spoke volumes about the vast economic and social barriers that separated the races, the castes, the town, and America.

Black sociologist E. Franklin Frazier (1894–1962) made a major contribution to the study of race relations with the publication of *The Negro Family in the United States* in 1939, one of the first published works by a black social scientist. Frazier had studied at the University of Chicago. He described the history of blacks in America from slavery through the Great Depression and emphasized the role of the family in helping African Americans survive. Frazier traced the "natural history" of the family from slavery, through the sharecropping era, to the Great Migration, during which thousands of blacks left the South for the industrial cities of the North. Certain patterns emerged that greatly influenced black life. These patterns included single-parent households, a large number of illegitimate children, and higher incidents of divorce, poverty, crime, alcoholism, and drug addiction.

The realties could be traced back to the violent conditions associated with slave-life, the racial and social isolation suffered by blacks because of segregation and discrimination, and the difficulties of life in great cities for which the largely rural southern black population was unprepared. Finally, Frazier found white society responsible for establishing a culture of prejudice and hate that contributed directly to the disorder and hostility found among African Americans. The social, psychological, and economic conditions among blacks in the United States resulted from attitudes and prejudices that affected them and their ancestors over hundreds of years, not from defective genes. History, not biology, had determined their status in American society.

By the end of the decade, the American Anthropological Association (AAA) adopted a resolution that rejected any "scientific" definitions or explanations of race. "Race involves the physical variations by large groups of mankind, but its psychological and cultural connotations, if they exist, have not been ascertained by science." Franz Boas's long war against scientific racism had borne some fruit as the consequences of racial politics became more visible in Nazi Germany. "The terms 'Aryan' and 'Semitic' have no racial significance whatsoever. They simply denote linguistic families," the AAA asserted. "Anthropology provides no scientific basis for discrimination against any people on the ground of racial inferiority, religious affiliation, or linguistic heritage."[93] A social science based on culture— human-made things—and environment challenged the supremacy of biological determinism in the field of race relations by the end of the decade.

RESOURCE GUIDE

SUGGESTED READING

Bayor, Ronald H. *Neighbors in Conflict: The Irish, Germans, Jews, and Italians of New York City, 1929–1941*. Baltimore, MD: Johns Hopkins University Press, 1978.

Carter, Dan T. *Scottsboro: A Tragedy of the American South*. Rev. ed. Baton Rouge: Louisiana State University Press, 1979.

Katznelson, Ira. *When Affirmative Action Was White: An Untold History of Racial Inequality in Twentieth-Century America*. New York: W. W. Norton, 2005.

Kuhl, Stefan. *The Nazi Connection: Eugenics, American Racism, and German National Socialism*. New York: Oxford University Press, 1994.

Sitkoff, Harvard. *A New Deal for Blacks: The Emergence of Civil Rights as a National Issue*. New York: Oxford University Press, 1978.

Sullivan, Patricia. *Days of Hope: Race and Democracy in the New Deal Era*. Chapel Hill: University of North Carolina Press, 1996.

FILMS AND VIDEOS

Images of Indians: How Hollywood Stereotyped the Native American. (2003). O'Brien, Chris, director. A 25-minute documentary depicting Hollywood's portrayal of Indians from the silent era to the twenty-first century. Includes interviews with actors, directors, and Indian filmmakers. DVD and VHS.

Marian Anderson. (1991). Williams, Juan, director. A TV film biography. Includes interviews with Marian Anderson. Opera star Jessye Norman performs Anderson's songs accompanied by violinist Isaac Stern. VHS only.

Richard Wright—Black Boy. (1994). Lacy, Madison, director. An Emmy Award-winning film biography of the writer It traces his life from his Mississippi birth in 1908 to his death in New York City in 1960. Includes interviews with friends, critics, and fellow writers. DVD and VHS.

Scottsboro: An American Tragedy. (2000). Goodman, Barak, director. An award-winning documentary from the PBS *American Experience* series. DVD and VHS.

Studs Lonigan. (1979). Goldstone, James, director. A six-hour TV miniseries covering James T. Farrell's trilogy. Stays faithful to the book. It should be available on VHS or DVD but for some reason is not.

WEB SITES

Father Charles Coughlin. The Social Securing Administration, http://www.ssa.gov/history/cough.html. A collection of photos, speeches, and radio broadcasts.

Great Depression. Oakland, California Museum of History, http://www.museumca.org/picturethis/3_7.html. Includes pictures and other sources on Asian Americans during the Great Depression.

Indian Reorganization Act. The University of Oklahoma Law Center, http://thorpe.ou.edu/IRA.html. Includes a complete set of Indian Reorganization Act constitutions and charters.

Library of Congress, http://memory.loc.gov/ammem/fsowhome.html. Photos of blacks, Native Americans, Latinos, and Asian Americans made by the Farm Security Administration during the Great Depression.

State of Utah, http://historytogo.utah.gov/utah_chapters/american_indians/utahspaiutein diansduringthedepression.html. Includes a photographic exhibit from the Paiute Reservation during the Great Depression.

The Yale-New Haven Teachers Institute has images, interviews, and essays on minority groups in America, http://www.yale.edu/ynhti/curriculum/units/1998/4/98.04.04.html.

NOTES

1. Camille Guerin-Gonzales, *Mexican Workers and American Dreams: Immigration, Repatriation, and California Farm Labor, 1930–1939* (New Brunswick, NJ: Rutgers University Press, 1994), 79.

2. Camille Guerin-Gonzales, *Mexican Workers and American Dreams*, 84–85.

3. Mae M. Ngai, "The Strange Career of the Illegal Alien: Immigration Restriction and Deportation Policy in the United States, 1921–1965." *Law and History Review*, vol. 20 (Spring 2003), 48–49.

4. Mae Ngai, "The Strange Career of Illegal Aliens."

5. Mae Ngai, "The Strange Career of Illegal Aliens," 61–62.

6. Camille Guerin-Gonzales, *Mexican Workers and American Dreams*, 82.

7. Richard B. Meynell, "Little Brown Brothers, Little White Girls: The Anti-Filipino Hysteria of 1930 and the Watsonville Riots," *Passports*, Volume 22 (1998).

8. Carlos Bulosan, *America Is in the Heart: A Personal History*, (New York: Harcourt, Brace and Company, 1943; Seattle: University of Washington Press, 1973), 140–42.

9. *New York Times*, April 7, 1931.

10. Michael Maher, "The Case of the Scottsboro Boys (1931): 'Bigots whose mouths are slits in their faces,'" in Lloyd Chiassen Jr., ed., *The Press on Trial: Crimes and Trials as Media Events* (Westport, CT: Greenwood Press, 1997), 103–9.

11. James Goodman, *Stories of Scottsboro* (New York: Pantheon, 1974), 5–6.

12. James Goodman, *Stories of Scottsboro*, 6.

13. *New York Times*, April 8, 1933.

14. *New York Times*, April 10, 1933.

15. Haywood Patterson and Earl Conrad, *Scottsboro Boy* (New York: Doubleday, 1950), 256.

16. *New York Times*, January 23, 1936.

17. Haywood Patterson, *Scottsboro Boy*, 257–58.

18. Clarence Norris and Sybil Washington, *The Last of the Scottsboro Boys: An Autobiography* (New York: Putnam, 1978), 121–22.

19. Graham D. Taylor, *The New Deal and American Indian Tribalism: The Administration of the Indian Reorganization Act, 1934–45* (Lincoln: University of Nebraska Press, 1980), 34.

20. Graham D. Taylor, *The New Deal and American Indian Tribalism*, 22.

21. Roger Daniels, *Guarding the Golden Door: American Immigration Policy and Immigrants since 1882* (New York: Hill and Wang, 2004), 78.

22. David Wyman, *Paper Walls: America and the Refugee Crisis, 1938–1941* (Amherst: University of Massachusetts Press, 1968), 162–63.

23. Roger Daniels, *Guarding the Golden Door, 79.*

24. Rafael Medoff, *The Deafening Silence: American Jewish Leaders and the Holocaust* (Urbana: University of Illinois Press, 1987), 34.

25. "Voyage of the *St. Louis*," *Holocaust Encyclopedia* (Washington, D.C.: United States Holocaust Museum, 2006).

26. Statistics from *Report on Negro Housing* (Washington, D.C.: Brookings Institution, 1931), iv–v.

27. Kenneth W. Goings, *"The NAACP Comes of Age:" The Defeat of Judge John J. Parker* (Bloomington: Indiana University Press, 1990), 23.

28. Ira Katznelson, *When Affirmative Action Was White: An Untold History of Racial Inequality in Twentieth-Century America* (W. W. Norton & Company, 2005), 23.

29. Katznelson, *When Affirmative Action Was White*, 48.

30. All quotes from Oswald Garrison Villard, "Slumbering Fires in Harlem," *The Nation*, April 15, 1935.

31. For more information, see Jill Watts, *God, Harlem, U.S.A.: The Father Divine Story* (Los Angeles: University of California Press, 1992).

32. Charles M. Christian, *Black Saga: The African American Experience* (Boston: Houghton Mifflin Company, 1995), 358.

33. Charles M. Christian, *Black Saga*, 359.

34. Marian Anderson, *My Lord What a Morning* (Urbana: University of Illinois Press, reprint ed., 2002), 180.

35. Michael L. Mullen, "Ethnicity and Sport: The Wapato Nippon's and Pre-World War II Japanese American Baseball," *The Journal of Sport History* 26, No. 1 (Spring 1999), 82–114.

36. Federal Writer's Project, *A Documentary History of Migratory Farm Labor in California* (Berkeley: University of California, 1938), 12–13.

37. *Time*, October 3, 1938, 7.

38. *Time*, October 3, 1938, 8.

39. Chicago *Abendpost*, May 22, 1934.

40. *The Walther League Messenger*, April 1933, 461.

41. Leslie V. Tischauser, *The Burden of Ethnicity: The German Question in Chicago, 1914–1941* (New York: Garland Publishing, 1990), 191.

42. Leslie V. Tischauser, *The Burden of Ethnicity*, 198.

43. Sander Diamond, *The Nazi Movement in the United States, 1924–1941* (Ithaca, New York: Cornell University Press, 1976), 221.

44. Roger Daniels, *Guarding the Golden Door*, 78–79.

45. Manuel G. Gonzales, *Mexicanos: A History of Mexicans in the United States* (Bloomington: Indiana University Press, 1999), 147.

46. Daniel Montejano, *Anglos and Mexicanos in the Making of Texas, 1836–1986* (Austin: University of Texas Press, 1987).

47. Daniel Montejano, *Anglos and Mexicanos*, 253.

48. Alfonso San Miguel, *Let Them All Take Heed: Mexican-Americans and the Campaign for Educational Equality in Texas, 1910–1981* (Austin: University of Texas Press, 1987), 72.

49. *Independent School District v. Salvatierra*, 33 S.W. 2d, 790.

50. Robert R. Alvarez, Jr., "The Lemon Grove Incident: The Nation's First Successful Desegregation Court Case," *The Journal of San Diego History*, Spring 1986 (Volume 32, Number 2), 1–16.

51. Graham D. Taylor, *The New Deal and American Indian Tribalism: The Administration of the Indian Reorganization Act, 1934–45* (Lincoln: University of Nebraska Press, 1980), 121.

52. Graham D. Taylor, *The New Deal and American Indian Tribalism*, 129.

53. Alden Stephens, "Whither the American Indian?" *Survey Graphic*, December 1939.

54. Alden Stephens, "Whither the American Indian?"

55. Marilyn Kern-Foxworth, *Aunt Jemima, Uncle Ben, and Rastus: Blacks in Advertising, Yesterday, Today and Tomorrow* (Westport, CT: Praeger, 1994), 45–46.

56. Richard A. Oehling, "The Yellow Menace: Asian Images in American Film," in *The Kaleidoscopic Lens: How Hollywood Views Ethnic Groups*, edited by Randall M. Miller (Teaneck, NJ: Jerome S. Ozer, 1988), 187.

57. Mary Ann Weston, *Native Americans in the News: Images of Indians in the Twentieth Century Press* (Westport, CT: Greenwood Press, 1996), 61–65.

58. *Brown v. Mississippi*, 297 U.S. 278 (1936).

59. *Missouri ex rel. Gaines v. Canada*, 305 U.S. 337 (1938).

60. *Nixon v. Condon*, 286 U.S. 73 (1932).

61. Robert Zangrando, *The NAACP and the Case Against Lynching, 1909–1950* (Philadelphia: Temple University Press, 1980), 133.

62. Roger Daniels, *Guarding the Golden Door: American Immigration Policy and Immigrants since 1882* (New York: Hill & Wang, 2004), 76.

63. Arna Bontemps, *Black Thunder* (Boston: Beacon Press, 1988), Introduction.

64. David Margolick, *Strange Fruit: The Biography of a Song* (New York: Ecco Press, 2001).

65. Donald Bogle, *Toms, Coons, Mulattoes, Mammies, and Bucks: An Interpretive History of Blacks in American Films* (New York: Continuum, 2001), 33.

66. Jill Watts, *Hattie: The Life of Hattie McDaniel* (Lanham, MD: Madison Books, 1990), 52.

67. Jill Watts, *Hattie: The Life of Hattie McDaniel*, 53.

68. Patrick McGilligan, *Oscar Micheaux: The Great and Only* (New York: HarperCollins, 2007), 99.

69. Henry T. Sampson, *Blacks in Black and White: A Source Book on Black Films* (Metuchen, NJ: Scarecrow Press, 1977), 42–55.

70. Younghill Kang, *East Goes West: The Making of an Oriental Yankee* (New York: Charles Scribner's' Sons, 1937), 400.

71. E. San Juan, Jr., *On Becoming Filipino: Selected Writings of Carlos Bulosan* (Philadelphia: Temple University Press, 1995), 171.

72. Philip Zonkel, "Walls of Broken Dreams: 1930s Chinese Poetry Reflects Disillusion in American Dream," *San Francisco Press-Telegram*, May 31, 2006.

73. James T. Farrell, *The Young Manhood of Studs Lonigan* (New York: Vanguard Books, 1932), 217–18.

74. Michael Gold, *Jews without Money* (New York: Carroll & Graf, 1930), 131.

75. Gold, *Jews without Money*, 56–57.

76. Virginia Mathews, Introduction to *Sundown* by John Joseph Mathews (Norman: University of Oklahoma Press, 1988), xiv.

77. Dorothy R. Parker, *Singing an Indian Song: A Biography of D'Arcy McNickle* (Lincoln: University of Nebraska Press, 1992), 57.

78. Phyllis Cole Braunlich, *Haunted by Home: The Life and Letters of Lynn Riggs* (Norman: University of Oklahoma Press, 1988), 137.

79. Luther Standing Bear, *My Indian Boyhood* (Lincoln: University of Nebraska Press, 1988), preface.

80. Luther Standing Bear, *Land of the Spotted Eagle* (Lincoln: University of Nebraska Press, 1978), preface.

81. Standing Bear, *Land of the Spotted Eagle*, 168.

82. Luther Standing Bear, "The Tragedy of the Sioux," *American Mercury* 24, no 95 (November 1931), 273–78.

83. Luther Standing Bear, *Land of the Spotted Eagle*, 271.

84. Luther Standing Bear, *My People the Sioux* (Lincoln: University of Nebraska Press, 1975), 285.

85. Stefan Kuhl, *The Nazi Connection: Eugenics, American Racism, and German National Socialism* (New York: Oxford University Press, 1994), 5, 61–62.

86. Judith Schacter Modell, *Ruth Benedict, Patterns of Life* (Philadelphia: University of Pennsylvania Press, 1983), 248.

87. Judith Schacter Modell, *Ruth Benedict*, 251.

88. Judith Schacter Modell, *Ruth Benedict*, 253.

89. Judith Schacter Modell, *Ruth Benedict*, 256.

90. James Cobb, *The Most Southern Place on Earth: The Mississippi Delta and the Roots of Regional Identity* (New York: Oxford University Press, 1994), 156.

91. John Dollard, *Caste and Class in a Southern Town* (New Haven, CT: Yale University Press, 1937), 46–47.

92. John Dollard, *Caste and Class in a Southern Town*, 2–5.

93. *American Anthropologist*, 41 (1939), 303.

Selected Bibliography

Archdeacon, Thomas J. *Becoming American: An Ethnic History*. New York: Free Press, 1983.

Avrich, Paul. *Sacco and Vanzetti: The Anarchist Background*. Princeton, NJ: Princeton University Press, 1991.

Baldwin, Neil. *Henry Ford and the Jews: The Mass Production of Hate*. New York: Public Affairs Press, 2001.

Bayor, Ronald H. *Neighbors in Conflict: the Irish, Germans, Jews, and Italians of New York City, 1929–1941*. Baltimore, MD: Johns Hopkins University Press, 1978.

Black, Edwin, *War Against the Weak: Eugenics and America's Campaign to Create a Master Race*. New York: Four Walls and Eight Windows Press, 2003.

Bogle, Donald. *Toms, Coons, Mulattoes, Mammies & Bucks: An Interpretive History of Blacks in American Films*. New York: Continuum, 2001.

Boyle, Kevin. *Arc of Justice: A Saga of Race, Civil Rights, and Murder in the Jazz Age*. New York: Henry Holt, 2004.

Carter, Dan T. *Scottsboro: A Tragedy of the American South*. Rev. ed. Baton Rouge: Louisiana State University Press, 1979.

Chang, Iris. *The Chinese in America: A Narrative History*. New York: Penguin Books, 2000.

Choy, Bong-youn. *Koreans in America*. Chicago: Nelson-Hall, 1979.

Daniels, Roger. *Coming to America: A History of Race and Ethnicity in American Life*. New York: HarperCollins, 2002.

Daniels, Roger. *Guarding the Golden Door: American Immigration Policy and Immigrants Since 1882*. New York: Hill and Wang, 2004.

Dray, Philip. *At the Hands of Persons Unknown: The Lynching of Black America*. New York: The Modern Library, 2003.

Egerton, John. *Speak Now Against the Day: The Generation Before the Civil Rights Movement in the South*. New York: Alfred A. Knopf, 1994.

Gerstle, Gary. *American Crucible: Race and Nation in the Twentieth Century*. Princeton, NJ: Princeton University Press, 2001.

Gonzales, Manuel. *Mexicanos: A History of Mexicans in the United States*. Bloomington: Indiana University Press, 1999.

Hirsch, James S. *Riot and Remembrance: America's Worst Race Riot and Its Legacy*. Boston: Houghton Mifflin, 2002.

Katznelson, Ira. *When Affirmative Action Was White: An Untold History of Racial Inequality in Twentieth-Century America.* New York: W. W. Norton, 2005.

Kuhl, Stefan. *The Nazi Connection: Eugenics, American Racism, and German National Socialism.* New York: Oxford University Press, 1994.

Lewis, David Levering. *When Harlem Was in Vogue.* New York: Penguin Books, 1997.

Nabokov, Peter. *Native American Testimony: A Chronicle of Indian-White Relations from Prophecy to the Present, 1492–2000.* New York: Penguin Books, 1999.

Prucha, Frances Paul. *The Great Father: The United States Government and the American Indians.* Lincoln: University of Nebraska Press, 1984.

Reisler, Marc. *By the Sweat of Their Brow: Mexican Immigrant Labor in the United States, 1900–1940.* Westport, CT: Greenwood Press, 1976.

Sitkoff, Harvard. *A New Deal for Blacks: The Emergence of Civil Rights as a National Issue.* New York: Oxford University Press, 1978.

Smedley, Audrey. *Race in North America: Origin and Evolution of a Worldview.* Boulder, CO: Westview Press, 1999.

Sullivan, Patricia. *Days of Hope: Race and Democracy in the New Deal Era.* Chapel Hill: University of North Carolina Press, 1996.

Takaki, Ronald T. *A Different Mirror: A History of Multicultural America.* Boston: Little, Brown, 1993.

Takaki, Ronald T. *Strangers from a Different Shore: A History of Asian Americans* Boston: Little, Brown, 1998.

Thernstrom, Stephan, ed. *The Harvard Encyclopedia of American Ethnic Groups.* Cambridge, MA: Harvard University Press, 1980.

Tolney, Stewart and E. M. Back. *A Festival of Violence: An Analysis of Southern Lynchings, 1882–1930.* Urbana: University of Illinois Press, 1995.

Wu, William T. *The Chinese in American Fiction, 1850–1940.* Hamden, CT: Archon Press, 1981.

Index

About the Author

LESLIE V. TISCHAUSER is Professor of History at Prairie State College, Chicago Heights, Illinois.